THE ASIAN ROAD

HOW A WANDERING VAGABOND DISCOVERED HIMSELF

The Asian Road
How a Wandaring Vagabond Discovered Himself

Additional copies may be ordered from the publisher for educational, business, promotional or premium use. For information, contact ALIVE Book Publishing at: alivebookpublishing.com, or call (925) 837-7303.

Book Interior and Cover Design by Alex P. Johnson

ISBN 13
978-1-63132-140-5

Library of Congress Control Number: 2021910068

Library of Congress Cataloging-in-Publication Data
is available upon request.

First Edition

Published in the United States of America by ALIVE Book Publishing
an imprints of Advanced Publishing LLC
3200 A Danville Blvd., Suite 204, Alamo, California 94507
alivebookpublishing.com

PRINTED IN THE UNITED STATES OF AMERICA

10 9 8 7 6 5 4 3 2 1

THE ASIAN ROAD

HOW A WANDERING VAGABOND DISCOVERED HIMSELF

MIK HAMILTON

Author's note:

This story feels nearly unbelievable to me—even though it's the story of my life. Some parts are easy to tell because they are just adventures, but some parts are so personal and get so close to my center that they are difficult to verbalize. For a time, my psyche was totally unstable, and my core value system was ruptured, culminating in an event that I consider the only real thing that has ever happened to me. That event became the focal point in my life in the sense that eventually it caused me to realize that everything that had ever happened before that event led up to it, and everything that happened after that event proceeded from it. I've tried my hardest to put it all on the page for anyone who's interested.

Chapter One

Humble Beginnings and Wondering What's Next

Looking back, I was always looking for *something*: I left the U.S. when I was eighteen years old for the army. After being discharged, I lived on the streets of New York City before returning to Germany, marrying, and leaving on my first journey to India. My wife and I returned from our around-the-world trip in 1966 and lived for six months in Santa Barbara before leaving again for our second trip to India. I returned to the States in 1968, now twenty-five years old. All that seeking at such an early age. But what had I found?

Let me backtrack a little: I was raised in an American Christian Protestant family, and we went to church on Easter and a few times in between. But we had good Christian values, following the Ten Commandments and the Golden Rule. For a time, my parents made me go to Sunday school and there I heard about the life of Jesus. As I reflect back on those stories, though I didn't disbelieve them at the time, they sounded too good to be true. How could there have been such a person? I remember feeling a dichotomy between the message that I should fear God and the message that Jesus loved me. The preacher and his claim that we had only one chance, that God saw all, and that burning hell was just nearby: This was what faith meant to me.

In high school I fell in love with a Roman Catholic girl. I also had an older, married Catholic cousin I looked up to, and so I decided to learn about Catholicism. Simultaneously, I had begun investigating western philosophy, existentialism, Sartre, Camus, and then later Nietzsche, Kant, Hegel, Heidegger and Goethe.

About the time I started reading comparative religion and scripture from Eastern religions, I read *On the Road* and got lost in the Beat Generation writers. Anyway, I went to my local Catholic church with the support of my parents and took the catechism from a Catholic priest. I was lost as to what I was really looking for, but for some reason the ritual of the mass seemed better to me than a lecture from some guy who had prepared a speech the night before, and I converted, was baptized, confirmed, made confession and took the sacrament of holy communion. I was a Catholic. My parents were happy and so was my girlfriend.

I grew bored with the mass and realized that the priests were all-too-human. I read more Beat poetry, confusing that type of freedom with the freedom I was really looking for. I graduated from high school and had no idea what to do with my life. I was never encouraged to go on to higher education, either by my parents or by my high school teachers. My biological father, whom I did not know very well since he and my mother divorced when I was four (I was raised by a loving stepfather), and had had contact with only once or twice a year since then, offered me a job in his factory where he manufactured fractional horsepower electric motors. After a summer of grooming show horses, I took him up on his offer and moved back to Racine, Wisconsin (my birthplace) and started my job. After a short time, I realized that this was not for me, but not wanting to disappoint my father or hurt his feelings, I had to find a way out that seemed plausible. About that time the Berlin Wall went up and John F. Kennedy was president and asking for recruits. I saw my way out and told my father that I felt I needed to serve and joined the U.S. Army.

On my first day at boot camp I realized that I had made a huge mistake. I tried to say, "Hey, time out guys, this is not really the place for me," but that didn't work. I went through basic training and advanced individual training and was sent to

Germany, where I worked in the Intelligence Division of a headquarters company of an Engineering Brigade, stationed at Rhein Main Air Force base, outside Frankfurt/Main, West Germany. I oversaw classified documents relating to espionage reports from Estonia, Latvia and Lithuania.

I discovered that I had a knack for languages, and in three months was speaking fluent German. I met some Spaniards in Frankfurt from whom I scored pot. For some time, I was the only person I knew in the military using dope. Eventually, I met a few other "heads" and enthusiastically introduced many other fellow soldiers to weed.

Unlike most other soldiers stationed in Germany, who spent most of their time with other Americans and never learned a word of German, I spent a lot of time in the city of Frankfurt. I loved jazz and eventually found some kindred souls in the "gammler." The gammler were the vagabonds, the beats, the bohemians of Europe. They all used dope and listened to jazz. The common trek for the gammler was Tangiers to Berlin with stops in Madrid, Paris, Munich, and Frankfurt with side trips to the Cote Azur, Costa Brava and Costa del Sol. I could write a whole book about these characters alone.

One day I was hanging in a Schnellimbis (a small sausage stall) in Frankfurt with some gammler, and there appeared a beautiful young girl named Uschi. We were both immediately smitten with each other and were together at every possible opportunity after that.

I came under suspicion by the U.S. Army CID for buying, smuggling, and selling marijuana because some German nationals had been busted with dope and made statements to the effect that they had bought it from me, which was untrue; I had given it to them. Fortunately, I received some advanced warning and cleaned up my territory so that by the time I was busted, my space was spotless. They even dusted my pocket linings for residue, but I had thought of that and had even disposed of some things that couldn't be adequately cleaned. For days I was interrogated (and believe me, in the military, that is *not* like mere questioning) while being incarcerated and was eventually almost court-martialed. After a thorough investigation, the article 32 officer determined that there was not enough evidence to convict me, but I was discharged from the military after being sent by troop ship to New York. I served two years and ten months.

I left for New York City after my discharge. Uschi was waiting for me to come back to Germany, where we planned to marry.

Throughout all these years, I couldn't stop thinking, "What is next?" And besides that, just below the surface of my consciousness were questions: What lies beyond what I can see from the road? What is that mysterious secret that is beyond what is visible to me? I am just seeing a swath that is in my line of sight, but what is "over there" past what I can see?

I now know that ultimately it was a sojourn of the soul in a quest to know itself; to answer the original question: Who am I? It was my fate, my destiny, my karma.

Chapter Two

A Pale and Wan Poet

A bird cannot appreciate its freedom unless it has been caged. I had just spent the two most "caged" years of my life in service to my country in the United States Army.

I was standing on a subway going from Queens to Manhattan with two paper bags containing all my worldly possessions in my arms, thirty-two dollars in cash, a bus ticket from Port Authority to Chicago, and my Army discharge in my pocket. I had never felt such a feeling of freedom in my life. I hadn't made a very dedicated soldier and had longed for this day like a man stranded in the desert longs for water.

I arrived at the West 87th Street pad of Ken Weaver, a former Army buddy with whom I had been stationed in Germany for the past two years and who had been discharged a few months before I was. I was most anxious to see if the suitcase with the false bottom I had sent there had arrived. I met his roommate Bobby Brown and felt as if I had known him all my life. He was one of those people you meet rarely, where you barely have to speak to communicate; it's like telepathy. Together we ripped the suitcase open and pulled out the kilo of Moroccan kif I had shipped through the A.P.O. and smoked a few bowls. I was so happy I thought my chest would explode.

Bobby turned on the stereo and asked me if I had ever heard of the Beatles. He played the first Beatles album, which had been released a couple of weeks before, and sat there looking at me, grinning from ear to ear, waiting for my reaction like he had just turned somebody on to the greatest news of the century. He had a gleeful, devilish gleam in his eye, which I was to see hundreds of times over the next few months that I lived with him. Bobby had a zest for life like I had never seen before and he was also the first openly homosexual man I got to know really well. He was fairly promiscuous but never once even hinted at anything romantic with me, even though we had an instant deep friendship.

I ran out of money quite quickly and had no motivation to work. My buddy Ken was a good writer and hung around with some of the early Village poets. I suddenly found myself needing a new identity. I was no longer an American soldier in Germany, but a free soul living in New York City. I decided I was a poet, stopped shaving and cutting my hair, and tried to find my way into the Beat world that was so alive in the Village and Lower East Side at that time. I lived on the streets and crashed with Bobby, who had a job and had moved to a forty-five-dollar-a-month one-room apartment with the bathtub in the kitchen on Elisabeth Street in Little Italy.

During this time of my first poetry writing since high school, I lived on the streets of Greenwich Village and the Lower East Side, hanging out a lot in Washington Square Park. I met a lot of the early Beat poets, some of whom later would become well-known and some who disappeared into obscurity. I panhandled for food and money. I had very poor nutrition and lost a lot of weight. My gums bled and I became very pale. Once, by chance, a *New York Times* reporter who was doing a story on the Village street scene happened upon this disheveled, long-haired, bearded "beatnik" hanging around the The Circle in the Square of Washington Square Park: me! He interviewed me and I gave him my best impression of a beat poet. He later described me in the *New York Times* as a "pale and wan poet."

I met a lot of strange and interesting people at the "Circle in the Square," from the tiny cute nymphomaniac runaway who followed me home, screwed my brains out for three hours and then stole my boots, to a Jamaican cocaine addict who introduced me to his friend, the author Leroi Jones. I met a mad poet from Minnesota named Ezra. He had Coke-bottle eyeglasses that magnified his speed-freak eyes so he looked like a maniac. He always had a pencil stub behind his ear and a note pad in his hand. We would do speed and walk the streets of the Village all night long together. On one of our walks near Sheridan Square, we ran into Moondog and later ran into him all the time and would spend nights roaming with him. Ezra introduced me to his friend Bob Dylan, who he knew from their hometown. I met a guy who introduced himself as "Bill Beckman, Texas' most obscure abstract expressionist." He followed his introduction by stating that if anyone ever recognized his name, he intended to drop the "most obscure" part of his title. He took me to his loft on the Bowery where he had a tank of pure nitrous oxide, which we inhaled through a baggie and then hallucinated the night away. He was one of the most intelligent creative people I ever met. (Or maybe it was just the nitrous.) He showed me his collection of handmade books with quotes from Blake and other mystics. Bill later did a lot of the investigative work for Mark Lane's book *Rush to Judgment,* the critique of the Warren Commission's study of the Kennedy assassination. I could write a book on just the people I met in that park in the summer of '64.

Chapter Three

Back to Europe

Perhaps it was a sign of my lifelong wanderlust that when I was a year and a half old, a man knocked on the front door holding a child under his arm asking my mom if this was her kid. She said no, her child was sleeping… but on second glance, it did look like me. She went to my room to check and sure enough, I was not there. He had discovered me on my first solo jaunt a few blocks down the boulevard at 6:30 am. I had climbed out of my crib and gone out the front door for a little adventure.

Fast forward to one hot summer day in Washington Square when I was sitting by the fountain (the Circle in the Square) thinking about what a great life it was to be free as a bird, write poetry, smoke pot and be hip. Suddenly my thoughts turned to how I was going to get back to Europe and the German fiancé I had left there several months before with a promise to return. I stopped writing, looked up from my notepad and saw a tall blond walking toward me. He looked like a combination of Viking and surfer. I couldn't take me eyes off him. He had an incredibly striking appearance. He walked by me and turned around, walking backwards away from me, so as not to lose eye contact. He walked about ten feet and stopped with a huge smile on his face. He had long blond hair past his shoulders and a long blond beard to the middle of his chest; one of those beards that grows all the way to the lips and high up the cheeks to the eyes. His eyes were electric blue and they shined with enthusiasm. Turns out he was a surfer. In fact, he was Sam Buell of the famous Buell brothers from Seal Beach, some of the earliest

Southern California surfers. I stood up and walked toward him; we beamed at each other and threw our arms around one another in warm and familiar embrace. "Hello Brother," I said. "Hello Brother," was his response.

We sat down on the fountain rim and he told me how he was on his way to Europe. I said that was a coincidence because I was also. He had no money and asked if I had any. I told him I had a subway token, twelve dollars, and a nickel bag. We smoked a joint and hatched up a plan to stow away to Europe on a freighter. I dug a paper out of the trashcan and studied the shipping schedule. I noticed that in two days' time there was a Yugoslavian freighter leaving Brooklyn for Tangier. What could be more perfect?! I had heard about this Yugoslavian line before. It sailed under Panamanian registry and was the cheapest way to get to Tangier. They took about twelve passengers per trip and of course, in my mind, who would be going to Tangier on a $112 freighter ticket but a bunch of potheads, right? We decided we only needed enough supplies to get past U.S. territorial waters because once we were in international waters, if we were discovered there would be very little that the authorities could do. They certainly weren't going to turn back to port and besides that, they wouldn't want the publicity to get out that it is possible to stow away on their ship for fear of encouraging others. We figured we'd hide out for a day or so and then just jump out and say, "Hey...where are the roast beef sandwiches?" First thing's first. We went to Harlem and scored another nickel bag, then bought a loaf of rye bread and a bottle of water. We each had a small backpack containing all of our belongings when we headed for the Red Hook district of Brooklyn by subway about midnight.

I can't believe we actually had the balls to try this or that we got as far as we did. We stood outside an eight-foot chain link fence looking at the freighter lit up like it was daylight, with our packs on our backs and not a doubt in our minds. We looked at each other and without saying a word, simultaneously scaled the fence and headed for the wharf. With great stealth we walked through the warehouse, past an inattentive guard, crept along a one-foot-wide wharf extension and marched up the gangway. We walked over to a lifeboat, set our back packs down on the deck, pulled out our sleeping bags, unlaced the lifeboat cover, spread our sleeping bags out in the lifeboat, climbed in, and replaced the cover behind us. All right! We were stowing away! Next stop Tangier!

The ship was due to sail at 12:30 p.m. July 23, 1964. By the time noon arrived the next day it was stifling hot inside that lifeboat and we had eaten all the bread and drank all the water. Suddenly I heard someone speaking an Eastern European language outside the lifeboat. I raised my finger to my lips to signal "quiet." We held our breath. I breathed a sigh of relief when the voice stopped and I heard the guy walk away. Relief didn't last long because within a few minutes there were a bunch of voices outside the lifeboat and the cover was being unlaced. We were busted. There, standing on the deck, was a bunch of Yugoslavian merchant seamen pointing their fingers at us and laughing. We jumped down to the deck and they laughed all the harder pointing to something in one guy's hand. I looked and saw that one of them was holding Sam's toiletry bag. While we were getting out our sleeping bags the night before, he had left his toiletry bag sitting on the deck! We were taken to the Captain's quarters where we met the ship's Captain. We explained to him that we absolutely had to get to Europe as soon as possible and didn't have any money and pleaded with him to let us sail with him. He was quite a nice man and explained apologetically that there was just no way he could allow that. We even told him we would send him the money later but to no avail.

So much for plan A. We were undaunted, however, and the next day scouted another ship leaving from Manhattan ten days later, a Dutch liner, *The Grote Baer*. This time we went to the ship in the daylight on a recon mission to case it out. While walking around as if we knew somebody, we were stopped by the purser who asked us what we were doing. We told him we had come to book passage to Rotterdam. He took us to the booking office and we booked the last two berths available and told them we would be back to pay them in one week. Sam called his sister, who sent him the money for the ticket, and I called my fiancé, Uschi, in Germany from a pay phone using a phony I.D. to ask her to wire me the money.

We got the money at the last minute and paid for the tickets. My Army buddy from Germany, Chris West, came to the dock to see us off. After we were on board waving to him I noticed that he had a small paper bag in his hand. He grinned from ear to ear and put it on the conveyor belt that was sending luggage up to the deck in full view of everyone. I picked it up off the belt and looked inside to see a bag full of dried peyote buttons. Well, this would be a very interesting voyage. Very soon we realized that we were the only freaks on the ship. It was filled with 1,200 college students on their way to Europe for the summer. We were the center of attention and everyone wanted to talk to us to find out what the hell two weird-looking dudes like us were doing on this ship. This was good for a lot of free meals and drinks. The chicks were on us like they had just met Tarzan or something. The two nickel bags didn't last the trip so we had to start on the peyote. Stoned out of our minds on the open deck in the North Atlantic, the stars looked like peering into a Maharaja's bag of diamonds.

At this point in my life I had no conscious question about who I was. I was a free spirit, a freak, a roadman. I had no responsibility to anyone. My only goal was to get to Frankfurt, marry my fiancé, Uschi, and put together enough money to bring a couple of kilos of kif from Tangier to keep us in dope and money while we traveled the roads between Tangier and Berlin. I just wanted to experience the Beat/gammler/vagabond scene I had left several months before for who knows how long.

When we arrived in Rotterdam we were stopped at customs and asked how much money we had. I told them I had none and Sam said he had $250. I was told that I could not enter the country without enough money for a return trip to the U.S. I explained that I would be out of Holland within hours; I was only passing through on my way to Germany where I had family waiting for me. That was not good enough for them and I was told that I would be placed in custody until I could be sent back to the U.S. I told Sam to go to Germany, give Uschi the money he had and let her come back here and bail me out. I was put in jail and charged with "vagabondage," vagrancy. In my jail cell I was served open-faced chocolate sandwiches for my meals with cake sprinkles. At least I got a good laugh at mealtime. The customs authorities interviewed me again and this time I had a plan. My fiancé's family had rented a room in their flat to a Russian Baron for many years so I wrote down his name, "Herr Baron Rheinholdt Staehl von Holstein," and told them to contact this man in Germany and he would vouch for me. I was counting on the fact that they would be impressed by his title and sure enough it worked. They called him and he told them he was sending my fiancé with money to bail me out on the next train. They took me from the jail and put me up in a hotel room until she arrived the next day. Once she showed them enough money for my return ticket they released me and we were reunited for a relaxing train trip to Frankfurt.

My fiancé, Uschi Reinhart, lived in her family's flat in the Westend of Frankfurt. I had lived there with her before I was sent to the U.S. for my discharge. Sam decided he would wander a bit in Germany and France and said he would be back in a few months. I spent the summer hanging out in the parks of Frankfurt with my gammler buddies getting high. I met a guy named Ulli, who had just returned from India and had some wicked Nepali hash. We spent days and weeks together sitting in parks along the Main River smoking hash and telling stories. He told me about his trip to the East and how cheaply one could live and how available and damn-near-free the drugs were. At this point in my life I felt like I was living my own "On the Road." My main object was to avoid responsibility and stay as stoned as possible. I was a "head" and was convinced that anyone who didn't turn on was deprived and ignorant. Ulli got me really stoked to go to India.

In September of 1964 Uschi and I were married in a civil ceremony at the Rathaus in Frankfurt. We were so stoned during the ceremony we could barely keep from laughing all the way through it.

In the meantime I had met a Persian rug dealer named Abraham. He owned a big fancy rug store on the main shopping street of downtown Frankfurt, the Zeil. He told me that he bought Mercedes Benzes in Germany, drove them to Teheran where he sold them, bought rugs with the money and shipped them to Frankfurt to sell in his shop. He said that he was going to buy three Mercedes and needed two drivers for the other two cars and would pay $250 each. According to Ulli, one could live on a dollar a day in India so that sounded great to me; I was on my way to India. Sam returned to Frankfurt and I told him about the plan and he agreed to drive the other car.

There were two young (sixteen and eighteen years old) sisters hanging around the scene and they said they wanted to come with us. I told them they could come on one condition: They had to tell all their friends that they were running away from home and going to Tangier. They agreed. When the time came to leave I told Abraham that they were on school holidays and were going to ride along with us to Teheran. Abraham's German was very broken and he was quite an innocent and gullible guy so he didn't think anything about it, not even to question their ages. The two girls, Rennate and Inge, were a sight to behold. They were two extremely beautiful and innocent

German teenagers. Rennate had flaming red hair and could stop traffic with her looks.

When the day arrived for us to leave, we all met at Abraham's and Sam and I were assigned a car to drive. We rolled out of town in a caravan of three Mercedes Benzes filled to the top with such German goods as car radios, leather coats, silk suits, dress shirts, silk scarves, etc. presumably to be sold in Teheran. I remember thinking, "how in the hell are we going to cross borders with this stuff?" It didn't take long for me to find out. At each border Abraham would embrace each official like a long-lost brother, liberally spreading around leather coats, silk suits, watches and dress shirts. Our passports and triptych would be dutifully stamped and we would proceed without delay.

Chapter Four

Turkey and Iran, Abraham and his family

When we crossed the Bospurus heading for Istanbul, Abraham pulled over to the side of the road and motioned for Sam and me to get out of the car for instructions. "Hier ist Asien, immer huppen." "This is Asia, just keep honking." He explained how the Turks would see a Mercedes and throw a child out to be injured so that they could collect money from the driver and sometimes there were known to be lynchings, so if we hit someone, don't stop until we get to a town that has a consulate.

In Istanbul we stayed in a small cheap hotel near the Aga Sofia. The hotel's luggage boy liked to practice his English so we would be sitting there in our room and would hear a knock on the door. When I opened it I would see the luggage boy standing there, English phrase book in hand, unfortunately opened to the "visit to the barber" page. He would say, "Excuse me, Sir but you have placed the brush in my mouth," or "pardon me, Sir, but you have cut my visage." Sam and I decided we would try to score some hash so we asked the luggage boy. He didn't speak anything but Turkish. I can still see Sam trying to tell this kid he wanted to buy hashish. He would pantomime smoking by holding two fingers to his mouth and going "Tffffff," sucking air in backwards through his teeth then wave his fingers wildly above his head indicating a head rush and repeat over and over, "hashish, hashish?" At last he understood and disappeared only to return with cigarettes. He thought Sam wanted cigarettes for free. (Bakshish, the word for begging, rhymes with hashish).

We didn't know yet that once you get past the Bosporus hashish is called charas.

When Abraham heard of this, he nearly had a seizure. He told us that there is the death penalty on drugs in Turkey and that at least we could go to jail forever. We told him that we absolutely had to have charas or we could proceed no further. Finally he said O.K. but he would get it for us. After spending a day wandering around in the incredible bazaar of Istanbul, we cruised on out across the Turkish countryside headed east.

By afternoon we were past Ankara and came to a village where Abraham pulled over to the side of the road. He walked back to my car and handed me a wad of bills that would choke a horse and said to hold this and wait here while he went to get the hash. Abraham's mother was Turkish, so he spoke Turkish like a native. After a half-hour or so, I heard a horn honking in the distance getting louder by the second. I looked in the rear view mirror and saw Abraham speeding down the main street of town, whizzing by us waiving his arm wildly out the window that we should follow. We raced out of town and stopped after a few miles. Abraham told us the story of how he scored the hash. Everything was going fine until they got suspicious and asked him to smoke some. Unfortunately he had never smoked anything before and his lungs went into a coughing spasm. They immediately thought he was the police and tried to capture him. He ran, got in his car and sped out of town, escaping by the skin of his teeth. The good part was that we had the long-awaited fresh, genuine, Turkish charas! We got stoned and celebrated by dancing up and down on the roadside.

As we got into Eastern Turkey it was like going back in time. It was very stark and mountainous. Every man in every village had these huge dark brown eyes staring at us from above a huge mustache. It was the first time I had seen the so-called "third world." There was extreme simplicity but did not seem to be abject poverty. When we would stop for food, Abraham would take us straight to the kitchen and explained that it was the custom in Turkey to go to the kitchen and lift the lid on each pot to see the food, and then make your selection. Another custom that was immediately adapted was the concept of Chai. Chai (tea) is taken frequently, leisurely, and copiously throughout Western and South Asia. It is like the lifeblood. After a short time in Asia, one cannot live without Chai and any circumstance becomes an excuse to "take" chai. In Turkey it is drunk without milk but with sugar, from a small narrow-waisted glass.

Ezerum is the last major town before reaching the Iranian border. It was a mountain town with no modern amenities. Very few women were seen in the streets, just more brown-eyed mustached men. The bazaar was open air and we picked up some oranges and nuts. Outside of Ezerum, on the way to the Turkish border, the treacherous mountain road nears the border of Armenia and just across that border is Mount Ararat. It is one of the most incredible sights I have ever seen. We could see it for a day in advance. It stuck out from the surrounding landscape like a majestic snow-capped monolith with a power and majesty that I have never seen equaled. Legend, and some research, says that this is the place where Noah landed his Ark.

At the Turkey/Iran border one of the Mercedes gave out and would not start. Abraham seemed to be having trouble getting all of our caravan and us across the border, even after liberally distributing gifts to everyone in sight. Eventually, after long negotiation, we ended up having to leave the broken-down Mercedes with the main border official in exchange for allowing everything else to be smuggled into the country.

After we crossed the Persian border, I saw my first camels. I said, "Abraham, look, camels!" Abraham replied, "Ja, Ja, in Persien ist eine ganz andere *Qualität.*" "Oh Yes, in Persian is a completely other quality!" I could tell he was proud of his homeland. I didn't want to bring him down so I didn't mention anything about the quality of the roads! Persian roads were nothing more than dirt washboard, on which the bigger boulders have been pushed out of the roadway.

We stopped in a small village between the Turkey/Iran border and Tabriz and went to the home of one of Abraham's relatives. There, we sat on the floor on a pile of Persian rugs and had tea and snacks. The host served the tea from a samovar, a beautiful brass water reservoir heated by coals. On top of the samovar was a small tea pot which contained a concentrated tea from which he filled the small glasses about a third of the way up, then filled it the rest of the way with water from the spigot on the samovar. The samovar sat on a brass tray and there was a small brass bowl under the spigot to catch any drippings of water. Next to the samovar was a large brass pitcher that contained additional water with which he re-supplied the samovar. Next to the samovar set was a small bowl containing small hard sugar cubes. The proper Persian way to drink tea, we were told, was to hold a piece of the hard sugar at the front of the mouth and pour the tea over the sugar. It was a hospitality ritual of which the host seemed proud and honored to perform for his guests. Sort of like the Persian version of the Japanese tea ceremony. Biscuits, dried fruits and pistachios, were served with tea.

After tea we drove to Tabriz, Abraham's mother's childhood hometown. Tabriz, Abraham bragged, has the world's largest covered bazaar. It is worth a trip to Tabriz just to see the bazaar; it is unequaled, even by Istanbul's.

The trip to Teheran was uneventful. Before I left Germany, I thought that past Teheran there was nothing but jungles full of tigers. So far, I was pretty much in the custody of my own eyes. Everything was completely different than anything I had ever seen in my life; it was as if there was a 360-degree movie surrounding me.

Teheran was a big city with all that goes with big cities. The bazaar was huge and both beautiful and ugly at the same time. The bazaars of Asia are so arranged that all the shops of similar trade be grouped together. In one area will be the rug bazaar with hundreds of rug dealers. In another area are all the brass dealers; sweaty tinkers, naked from the waist up with the stain of metal ground into their bodies, pounding brass into various shapes and sizes. You could hear the approach to the metal bazaars for quite a distance as small to large hammers rang against brass, bronze, iron and steel. One thing we discovered immediately about the Teheran bazaar was that a huge percentage of men had the hobby (more like a job) of grabbing women's asses as they passed by. I took delight in walking several steps behind Uschi and sticking my foot out, tripping them on their faces each time they grabbed her ass. It was sort of a sport. Also for the first time, we saw women observing purdah. The Teheran (and most of the rest of Iran) version of purdah was a large scarf worn over the head and pulled across the face, leaving only the eyes exposed. Quite different from the veils I had seen worn by Moroccan women. They also wore long, cotton, mostly black colored robes over their clothing. In the Muslim world, women are not seen very much outside the home, except in the larger cities.

Abraham took us to his "cousin/brother" in the Teheran bazaar where they had a rug shop. His name was Hassan. He greeted us in the Persian way; hand over heart saying "Salaam." I felt an affinity with him and pelted him with questions about the Persian way of doing things. He taught me to squat, crouched on my haunches to pee like most Asian men do and how to use the water jug next to the squatter-toilet that I had seen at Abraham's mother's house.

Abraham paid us the 250 bucks each and Sam and the girls checked into a hotel. Uschi and I stayed with Abraham at his mother's home and enjoyed her home cooking. She cooked all of Abraham's favorite dishes and it was our first taste of the real variety of Persian cuisine. Up to this time, on the road it was mostly chello-kabab, rice and ground meat kabobs. We were out of hash by this time and had to score, which was very risky in

Teheran. First of all, even though there was lots of it around, it was a serious crime, and secondly, everyone was seriously paranoid about the Savak, the Shah's secret police. I had never experienced an entire population in fear of its own government. I found out that brother did not even trust brother when it came to anything illegal or making any statement whatsoever that even vaguely criticized the Shah or government. The Savak was huge and we were told that every other man was an informant. We did manage to score, however, and the hash was good quality.

We enjoyed the warm nights of Teheran, taking the cheap taxis to various sights, driving along the wide boulevards, communicating with the people with a few words of Farsi, using gestures and a lot of arm waving. Everything was different. It was a whole new experience and there was a world of education every day. "Abraham, why are there so many Persian rugs lying in the middle of the streets at night?"

"They clean them by having the cars drive over them, driving the dust out," he replied. How strange, I thought, cleaning rugs by letting cars drive over them! "Abraham, what is that guy over there selling?"

"He's selling beets prepared the Persian way."

"Abraham, how do you say 'brother' in Farsi? And 'honey' and 'yogurt'?" I had a thousand questions every day.

I bought forty watches in the Teheran bazaar for about two dollars each. Ulli had told me to take watches to Pakistan and India because they had a ban on imports and they could be sold for about twenty dollars each. I was becoming a smuggler.

We told Abraham that we were leaving Teheran by road through the Great Salt desert to Pakistan. He told us that we would need an exit visa to leave the country. We went to the American Embassy/Consulate on Takhat-e-Jamsid Ave in central Teheran to check our mail and were told by a worker in the consulate that we had better get the hell out of there because we were wanted by Interpol for kidnapping minors. I was in total shock. I quickly reviewed in my mind the seriousness of this crime. "Let's see, its murder, rape, and then kidnapping minors," I thought.

I went to the hotel were Sam and the girls were staying and ask them if they had told anyone where they were going and didn't use the "running away from home to Tangier" story we had made up. They confessed that they had told their best friend. Upon further questioning I found out that their father was a German cop! I reasoned that, even though he knew they had run away from home, he, being a cop, also knew that you couldn't get Interpol involved unless there is an international crime. Running away from home is not a crime, but kidnapping minors is, so he probably told Interpol that we had kidnapped his daughters. In retrospect, it was a pretty stupid thing to do, taking two gorgeous teenagers to Teheran with us, but only one of many other stupid things we did that indicated that we were not really thinking as if there were consequences to our actions.

In any event, we told the girls that the jig was up and that they would have to turn themselves in to the German Embassy and be repatriated. They agreed and we waited in the lobby while they got their things together. After a long wait we realized that Sam and the girls had skipped out the back door and left us high and dry. That meant that we could not get an exit visa because as soon as we showed up at the government office to get the visa, we would be arrested. I had heard that Persian jails are so bad that they have to pump air in to you. That was the last time I ever saw Rennate and Inge.

There was only one thing to do: "Abraham, you are not going to believe this, but those girls told us they were on school holiday, but really they were running away from home. Their father has reported to Interpol that we kidnapped them and now we can't get an exit visa." Abraham didn't show the slightest bit of emotion. He just stood up, went in his bedroom and came back out with a roll of bills he could hardly get his hand around.

We got a taxi, went to the government office where the exit visas are issued and he told us to sit on a bench in the hall outside the room. After fifteen minutes he came out of the room with the bulge in his pocket visibly shrunken and asked for our passports. Five minutes later he walked back out with our passports stamped with an exit visa. We thanked him profusely and not another word was spoken about the matter. We said goodbye to Abraham and his family and that is the last I time I ever saw him.

Chapter Five

Toward Pakistan

Now we were really on the road; no more Mercedes Benz for a home. "Hip" was no longer a state of mind, it was a fact of life. All my worldly possessions consisted of the clothes I was wearing and what was contained in a five-kilo backpack. We hitchhiked our way southeast toward Pakistan, riding in trucks and jeeps. On the first evening we stopped in the middle of the desert at a small roadside restaurant for dinner. The "restaurant" was nothing more than a small wooden shack with a dirt floor. You only have two decisions to make in a place like this: Do you want chello-kabob or not and do you want tea or not. It was full of truck drivers and their travelers. Each truck driver had a helper whose job was to watch the truck's load; we called him "the traveler." As we were eating I noticed that the Farsi din was getting louder. I looked up and everyone was looking at me and shouting at my driver. It got louder and more animated but, of course, I could not understand a word of what was being said. I just knew it was serious and that they were talking about me.

I looked at my driver and he turned his eyes toward the truck and gestured with his head to go. I told Uschi, in German, that I thought we had better get the hell out there. We both stood up and started walking toward the truck with the driver and traveler following us. About fifteen other truck drivers got up and started following us. We sped up and they did too. The driver shouted "Burro" which I had learned means "get the hell out of here." We ran and jumped into the truck and started driving away with all the other drivers chasing us some hanging from the truck, shouting, "Chor, Chor."

I had learned this word too; it means thief. I kicked the last truck driver free from the truck and we had made a safe escape. Suddenly, I looked down and saw a jacket on the seat, which had not been there before. I figured out that the traveler had stolen someone's jacket and put it in the truck. They thought I had stolen it. It was nearly a lynching. I had heard that the penalty for theft in the Muslim world was chopping off the hands. It was our first dangerous close call, if you don't count the little incident that had the possibility of going to jail forever for kidnapping minors.

Next stop: Isfahan. The Persians have a saying: "Isfahan is half the world." We made a quick tour of the city accidentally visiting the famous early17th century Royal Mosque with the inlaid turquoise walls and filigree panels. I say accidentally because we would never have intentionally visited a tourist location. It just wasn't hip. We were not tourists. We were travelers! We slept the night in Isfahan at a truck stop and early the next morning we got a ride in an ugly truck with bad shocks.

We rode all day passing through Yazd. Late that night the driver stopped and gestured that we had to get out because he was turning off here. We were fairly amazed because we were in the middle of the desert and there could not possibly have been a road that went anywhere except straight ahead. Anyway he insisted we get out and after we did, he just drove off into the middle of the desert. It was a moonless night and as I stood there in the middle of nowhere I looked up and saw a star-filled sky like no other I had ever seen. The Milky Way looked like a solid river of light. We thought it better to just stay there for the night and try to figure out where we were in the daylight.

We pushed the big rocks out of the way to make a smooth place to roll out our sleeping bags and climbed in for the night. About an hour later I awoke and saw someone squatting next to Uschi's backpack with his hand inside. I reached under my rolled up towel/make-shift-pillow for the Italian stiletto switch-blade knife I slept with and slowly and quietly pulled it out. I raised my hand in the air and pushed the button. "Klatsch" it opened with an ominous sound that, combined with the starlight reflecting off its shiny blade, scared the crap out of our visitor. I could see his eyes widen in the starlight and he went running off across the desert. I went back to sleep, thinking, "sleeping out on the desert floor is not a good idea and should be avoided as much as possible in the future."

When we awoke in the morning, we were surrounded by Persian soldiers. They were just jabbering away probably discussing the weird sight: two European people sleeping on the ground in the middle of the desert. We quickly got up, rolled up our sleeping bags and stuffed them in our backpacks. They spoke no English and the only thing that identified them as soldiers was their disheveled uniform. They were unshaven and looked very poor. The wall I had spotted turned out to be one side of a square compound and was made of clay bricks, in a bad state of repair. The soldiers seemed very friendly. One of them had stripes on his uniform and seemed to be in charge. He motioned that we should follow him. We walked toward the road and I could see that there were actually two identical compounds, one on each side of the dirt road.

The Sergeant led us through an opening in the wall facing the road and when we entered, I felt like we had just stepped back about five hundred years. Inside the compound, the walls were lined with small rooms, all dirt floored with openings but no doors. This is where the soldiers' families lived. Their wives were cooking on open fires and wore what looked more like rags than clothes. Their faces were not covered, and they didn't seem to mind that I saw their faces. The sergeant led us to his hovel, where a small child slept in a hammock. He gestured that we should sit on the dirt floor and then handed us a bowl of the most disgusting rancid gruel that I had ever seen. I had learned by this time that it is considered extremely rude and thought that it may even have been dangerous to refuse it. I was also hungry. We ate the gruel, managing not to throw up, and then he pulled out an opium pipe. He went through the ritual of burning the opium in an open flame to burn off the impurities and rolled the remaining opium into a ball over the opening at the pipe's end. We smoked opium together and got really stoned.

After a few hours we heard a vehicle approaching. He jumped up and ran out of the compound and stood in the middle of the road so that the approaching Land Rover had to stop. He told the driver that he should give us a ride to the next town, Rafsanjan. Before leaving, I wanted to give him a present in exchange for his warm hospitality. In my backpack I had about fifteen cigarette lighters I had brought with me from Germany to sell in India. I pulled one out, took off the gas cap of the Land Rover and showed him how to fill the lighter from the gas tank.

This whole episode occurred with barely a word being spoken. We gave each other hugs and Salaams and parted with us driving off in a cloud of dust toward Rafsanjan, the pistachio capital of the world. Rafsanjan is a small town and really a beautiful oasis town and the "pistachio capital of the world" moniker is no exaggeration. I have never seen so many pistachio trees in my life. At the time, I had never even seen one pistachio tree. We just passed through and continued on to Kerman.

In Kerman we stopped at a real restaurant for lunch. The waiter was a young boy who spoke a little English. He asked where we were going and when we told him we were on our way to Zahedan, then on to Pakistan. He told us that when we get to the next town of Bam we must look up his brother and stay the night with him. He told us that his brother's name was Abbas Jehuni and that he was the English teacher of this small town. He said to just ask anyone in town and they would direct us to his brother's house. When we arrived in Bam, a small oasis town in the Great Salt Desert, we asked the first person we saw for Abbas Jehuni. He gestured that we should follow him. It was just approaching sundown as we followed him through the small dirt streets and lanes to a walled compound where he knocked on the door. A handsome Persian man in his twenties opened the door, took one look at us and said, "Welcome home." He led us into his humble abode. It was a typical Persian village home with a courtyard that had a water cistern/pool. We had dinner with him and told him our life story and he told us his. I'll never forget the name "Abbas Jehuni" because of the warm hospitality he showed us.

The next morning we went to the edge of town where the main road leads to Zahedan. The main road, of course, means a one-lane dirt, washboard road. There was a small abandoned mud hut at the crossroad, which we decided to take a look at. It had a dirt floor and no coverings to the windows. When we got inside we were amazed to see that the walls were covered with writing. It seems that this small crossroad's hut was a place that a lot of road bums like us had stopped before us and had written messages on the walls. We had been on the lookout for an English friend named Roger that had left Germany heading east a week or two before us. We had asked all the other travelers we had seen in Istanbul if they had seen him but no one had. There are certain bottlenecks on the road virtually everyone has to pass through and these are places where you can check up on friends and acquaintances you had lost track of by asking others if they had seen them and where they were. We searched the walls to see if Roger had left a message but saw that there was no sign that he had been there. We were sure we would meet up with Roger somewhere on the road and were a little worried about him because he liked to smoke dope but every time he did, he would have hallucinations. We waited several hours before a truck went by that gave us a ride. When you hitchhike in places like this, it is not a matter of someone passing you by without giving you a ride, it's a matter of WHEN someone will drive by. They are all so curious about who you are and what the hell you could possibly be doing out there hitchhiking in the middle of the desert, that you always got a ride with the first thing that went by. Sometimes you had to wait a long time before anything with wheels and a motor came along. We had no place we had to be and nowhere we had to go. Time was not a consideration for us. We just smoked hash until the next event unfolded.

Zahedan was the last small town before the Pakistani border. Virtually nothing but the train crosses this border. It is one of those bottlenecks I spoke of where every road bum passes through to go on to India unless they go the northern route through Afghanistan. We stayed the night in a small hotel, which cost us about one dollar. On the main street of Zahedan the next morning we saw a tourist information office. God only knows why a tourist would end up in Zahedan. The tourist office people told us that the train to Quetta, Pakistan had left the day before which meant that we had to hang out in Zahedan for a week. We walked the main street of Zahedan and saw the sights. A policeman with the world's largest mustache who later, when we talked to others who had passed through town, related that he was about the only thing they remembered about Zahedan. He was famous among the Asian road bums. There was a man who stood in rags on the main street and begged while beating himself on the chest over the heart with chains, singing "Allah Hu Akbar" ("God is great"). His chest was stained black from the corrosion of the chains.

We had gotten to really like the Persian breakfast of tea, flat bread, goat's cheese, yogurt and honey, so we went to the bazaar and enjoyed our breakfast every morning. That night we went back to the tourist office and asked them if we could sleep on the floor of the office, explaining that we did not have money for a hotel. They not only consented to let us stay there for the night but said we could stay in the quarantine bungalow on the outskirts of town until the train left for Quetta. The quarantine bungalow was a beautiful spot just on the edge of town surrounded by palms. It was clean and even had beds. We had the whole place to ourselves, as apparently no one had come across the border that required quarantine. It was great; we would go to town for breakfast, return, and stay high and talk all day.

November 16 the train left Zahedan for Quetta. This was a very interesting train. It went from Zahedan to Quetta, passing through Mirjaweh, the Persian border, then eighty-six miles of no-man's-land, after which came Taftan, the Pakistan border through southwestern Baluchistan to the mountain town of Quetta. Each border station was just a single building in the desert. The passengers were of two classes. There were Kashmiris wearing expensive woolen shawls, smoking small water pipes and what appeared to be villagers dressed in dust stained long blousy shirts, loose fitting pajamas and very bulky looking sandals.

There was also one young stuck-up Pakistani Sindhi returning from London. He announced with pride and superiority that he was a "British subject." The Kashmiris asked, "What happened, did you fall in the Black Sea on the way back here?" He and they were immediately suspicious of each other. A few hundred meters before we came to Mirjaweh the train slowed and the "villagers" put huge bundles wrapped in cloth on their heads, jumped off the train and ran out into the desert. I watched in amazement as they ran out around the border station while the customs agents threw rocks at them. The officials would catch one or two, take some of their smuggled goods and let them go. As the train passed through, they would run and catch up and jump back on the train. These people were traveling without tickets and without passports, smuggling stuff from Iran to Pakistan. They were citizens of no country. They lived in no-man's-land. As they ran to catch up with the train, the Kashmiris would shout, "Chello, chello." In Iran I learned that "chello" is Farsi for "rice." In Urdu (the language of Pakistan) it means "to go." We passed through the eighty-six miles of no-man's-land and the same scene repeated itself at Taftan, the Pakistan border station. But this time there was huge celebration because we had now crossed into Pakistan. Then my mind was really blown because the villagers started giving the goods to the Kashmiris, who paid them their fee and jumped back off the train. They were just runners for the Kashmiris, who were the actual smugglers!

After all the business was taken care of, the Kashmiris whipped out huge chunks of hash for all to smoke. This was the first time I saw hash smokes prepared the Pakistani way. They took a cigarette and twisting it between the thumb and forefinger of one hand, emptied the contents into the palm of the other hand except for the last two centimeters, which they left in the paper. They picked up tobacco from their palm and blew away the tobacco dust, removed the very large pieces, then placed the piece of hash between two match heads, holding the other end of the matches between the thumb and forefinger of the same hand, above the tobacco. With the other hand they lit another match and ignited the matches holding the hash. After it burned for a few seconds it became soft.

They loosened the hold of the matches and dropped the piece of hash into the tobacco, tossing the matches aside. With the thumb of the other hand they mixed the hash and tobacco together in the palm of their hand and refilled the cigarette. It was mostly hash, with a small amount of tobacco to improve the taste, keep it burning and, so they said, "drive the charas" into the lungs.

I explain this in detail for a couple of reasons. First, I spent the next two years doing this several times a day and secondly, to explain what a delicate feat of manual dexterity is required. One must eliminate just the right amount of dust and large pieces and add just the right amount of charas so as to make the entire "batch" refill the emptied cigarette exactly. It must be done with grace, casually, and come out perfect each time. I mastered this batch making process in no time and found it the absolute best way to smoke hash, with the possible exception of the chillum, smoked in India, the ritual for which I will explain later. I asked the Kashmiris why they smoked charas with tobacco because I had always smoked it pure and they explained that the tobacco "opens the lungs" and made the charas have a more powerful effect.

The train stopped in a small Baluchi village called Dalbundin and we were able to get down for about two hours. The first thing we saw was a group of about seven Baluchi men standing in a circle wearing baggy pajama bottoms, long loose shirts with their huge bulky sandals laying on the ground outside the circle. They were all laughing and jumping up and down, having a great time so we looked closer. One of the men was shaking a can open on one end and then threw a few really mad scorpions out of the can into the middle of the circle. They all hopped around laughing to avoid being stung. If one got stung, he would be the fool, we were told.

An old man with hair twisted into two horns just above his forehead came up to us and said he was "The Joker." He asked us to please give him ten rupees so he could buy charas. I admired his honesty but for ten rupees you could by about a pound of charas in this part of the world. Also, unlike Iran, charas was plentiful and cheap in Pakistan. Virtually every uneducated male smoked charas.

When we re-boarded the train we started up a conversation with a man named Hafiz Ullah. He told us he lived in Quetta and invited us to stay at his home while we were in Quetta. We accepted his invitation and he was to become a good friend whom we would see again later in Lahore, along with some of his family who lived there. Hafiz was a botanist and had a really nice home in Quetta. He knew the Koran by heart, thus the name

Hafiz. Hafiz is a name given to a man who has memorized the Islamic holy book.

Urdu seemed much easier to learn than Farsi and I was picking it up really quickly. Besides that, the Pakistanis seemed much more curious and eager to communicate, so with a little English, a little Urdu and a lot of gestures, it was easy to make oneself understood. After a short time in Pakistan, I was communicating in Urdu. Also, the Pakistanis were extremely hospitable. Wherever we went, the Pakistanis offered food, tea, and a place to stay or just about anything else they could think of that they thought we might like. I have never been to a more hospitable place than Pakistan. Women were not seen on the streets very much and when they were, they were in full purdah, covered with a pleated sheet like garment, called burka, from head to toe. There was a crisscross stitching over the eye holes so that they could see out, but no one could see in. The only thing uncovered was their hands and feet. One would occasionally get a glimpse of an ankle, which was comparable to seeing a woman in a short skirt by our standards.

During the night when everyone was sleeping, the "British Subject" began shouting, "Shoe, Shoe." Everyone in the bogie jumped up and lit the lights and started totally freaking out. Apparently British Subject woke up and couldn't find his shoe and thought someone had stolen it. Unfortunately in Urdu (or Baluchi, I'm not sure) "shoe" means snake. Everyone else in our bogie thought there was a snake loose somewhere. There was a lot of shouting and commotion, and finally laughing, before British Subject found his shoe and everyone resumed their sleep.

This train ride was also the first time I saw what, all over the Indian Subcontinent, is referred to as bedding. Everyone has to have his bedding with him whenever he travels. Bedding is a roll of blankets wrapped in a piece of canvas with leather straps. These bedding rolls were about one meter wide and when rolled, about half a meter in diameter. They had to be carried by coolies on and off the train, of course. One could not carry his bedding himself.

Quetta was a beautiful town surrounded by mountains at about 1,500 meters elevation, near the Afghan border south of Kandahar. The bazaar was beautiful, full of shops with winter fruits, dry fruits, good restaurants and friendly people. Hafiz Ullah had invited us to stay in his home. On our first day we wandered into the center of Quetta to an area marked by signs, which read, "Out of Bounds." We found out that the out-of-bounds area is created as a tribal area in the middle of town. Tribal area means, no police, no army, just the law of the Koran and the chief. We were astounded and found it quite civilized, not to mention incredibly cool, when we found a shop with a big sign over the door, which read, "Ganja and Opium Shop." I thought I must have gone to heaven! It was a shop openly selling marijuana and opium. We went into the shop and tried to score charas. We were told that charas could not be sold there because it was a concentrated form and they were only allowed to sell marijuana, opium and opium poppy pods for those who want to cook their own. But since they were so hospitable they sent someone to get some charas for us and insisted that we have chai while we waited.

Chai is the Pakistani/Indian national drink and pastime. In Iran we had learned to like tea but here it was cooked together with milk and sugar making a rich, life-sustaining liquid that, to this day, I must "take" on a regular basis. When the shop helper returned with the charas we were told that this type was from Kandahar. It was still in the powdered, un-pressed form which we nicknamed "Kandahar Crush." He gave us a huge pile, probably about a pound, and insisted that there was no charge as we were guests in his country and it was his duty to show us his hospitality.

We smoked openly and profusely on the streets without the slightest fear of being seen or questioned. Around lunchtime we were sitting in a park when an American named Joe approached us. He explained that he was a flagpole painter and that he made such good money at his job that he would work for three months out of the year in the U.S. and then travel for nine months around the world. He was attempting to visit every country in the world; he was a country collector. He was completely straight but we invited him to take chai with us at a local "hotel." (In Pakistan and India restaurants are called "hotels.")

We went to a local hotel. In Pakistan the hotels all have tables partitioned with hanging cloths so that the women could remove their veils to eat without being seen. We went into one of the partitions to have chai and after it was served I mixed up a batch and filled an emptied cigarette with Kandahar Crush. Uschi and I smoked and passed it on to Joe. He said he had never turned-on before but he wanted to try it.

Within a few minutes he turned red, green, and then white after which he fell off his chair on the floor, pissing and shitting his pants. We got the hotel owner who, of course, knew what had happened because the whole place was filled with the smell of charas. The owner, instead of being pissed about the mess that was made, picked Joe up and physically carried him to his hotel, down the street. Talk about hospitality; he wouldn't even allow us to pay for the chai!

When we returned to Hafiz's house he told us that he had heard a story today about two foreign men who had come to the Ganja and Opium Shop and bought charas. We realized then that they thought Uschi was a man. It was easier for them to imagine a man with long hair than a woman, dressed in man's clothing, smoking charas. We had a great dinner with Hafiz prepared by his wife. The next day Hafiz took us to the train station in a tonga, a two-wheeled cart pulled by a single horse and bought us two train tickets to Jacobabad.

This ride would be a descent from the high mountainous region of Quetta to the Indus Valley below. We passed through the

Brahui Hills with its tribal people of mysterious origin and the Bolan Pass. We came to Sibi, the town Kipling called "hell on earth" because it is so HOT. Even on a winter's day like today it was near 100 degrees F! We had tea in the station, and soon after leaving Sibi I noticed for the first time since leaving Istanbul two months ago some moisture in the air and some greenery in the overall landscape starting to appear. By the time we reached Jacobabad the change was dramatic. We had gone from barren, desert, and mountainous terrain to full-fledged jungle in a matter of hours.

The Indus Valley! The name alone gave me shivers. It just seemed so ancient, like I was in another time. The landscape was lush green with humidity closing in on me. My eyes were not used to the temperature of the colors saturating my brain's sense of vision. Hafiz had only purchased tickets to Jacobabad so this was the end of the train ride for us. We went immediately to the edge of town and hitched a ride to Sukkur on the banks of the Indus.

This was the first time I saw what I would consider "teeming masses." Oh, I had seen crowded, overpopulated places like the Istanbul or Teheran bazaar but this was a whole other magnitude. I found myself in the middle of town renting a hotel room that was nothing more than a ten by ten-foot square room on the second floor with nothing in it but two charpois. (A wooden framed string bed with four wooden legs for which it is named "charpoi," four legs). Each bed had a mosquito net over it. I put my backpack inside the room, closed the handmade brass bolt on the door and locked it with a typical huge, handmade brass padlock.

Looking over the balcony to the street, I saw the most amazing conglomeration of people, animals and modes of transportation and cacophony of sound that I had ever witnessed. This was to become the norm in most Pakistani and Indian towns and cities. It was too much to watch for long so we went to the hotel restaurant and ordered the vegetable and bread. As it was placed before me I could see the heat waves coming off it like the pavement before you on a hot desert day.

As the aroma reached my nose, my instincts nearly stopped my breathing and by the time it hit my eyes they began to water. I looked at the bowl and it was nothing but curried chili peppers. I decided to taste it anyway because I was really hungry. I tore a piece of chapatti (flatbread) and scooped some of the subji ("vegetables") with it and placed it in my mouth. As soon as I started to chew I realized I had made a big mistake! This was my first introduction to really hot foods. I thought my mouth was on fire. I couldn't eat it so went to the kitchen and supervised the cook while he fried me some eggs to have with my chapatti.

After eating and having chai we went for a walk to the Sukkur Barrage, a bridge/dam complex over the Indus. We were sitting at the edge of the river, which was extremely wide at that point, smoking a charas joint when a middle-aged bright-eyed Pakistani man approached me and began a conversation in Urdu.

I had learned a few words by this time so after referring to each other as "brother" a few times I got the drift that he wanted us to come to visit his home. I agreed and we walked to where we could get a tonga and he ordered the driver to take us to the bazaar. In the bazaar he bought fruit to take home and enjoy when we arrived there. He inspected each orange meticulously and, when it met his satisfaction, held it up for my approval and ask, "Catching? Catching?" I would waggle my head side to side in the Pakistani/Indian gesture of approval and say "Ji Haan, catching." We proceeded to his house where, as far as I could figure, he taught young men to repair radios.

The several boys who were his students held him in utmost esteem. He ordered them to bring him a knife and for the first time I learned the proper way to peel an orange and have used this method ever since. First the top and bottom of the skin is removed with the knife. Next, the skin is scored from top to bottom six times and finally, using the knife-edge, the skin is removed from top to bottom in six sections. After having peeled the orange he set it on a plate and ordered one of the boys to bring him a spoon and a lit candle. He put a large piece of charas in the spoon and, after heating it over the flame, made a hash joint in the usual Pakistani manner, emptying a cigarette, mixing the hash and tobacco and refilling it. We smoked, got stoned, ate oranges and exchanged our few common words of Urdu over and over again, mostly a lot of "Tikke, aacha, bhaisahib," etc. ("O.K., good, brother.")

It was a great time and proved once again the Pakistani hospitality and eagerness to communicate. I had been told that it is a doctrine of the Islamic faith to show hospitality to travelers and now I was seeing it in action. There are strict rules regarding hospitality and protection of guests among Muslims and one must be very sensitive to these types of customs. Big trouble could ensue if some taboo is committed. People have been known to have been fed to death, not knowing how to stop more food from being placed on their plates or, worse, shot on the spot for certain infringements, like looking at someone's wife in the tribal areas of Pakistan. If you are a guest in their house, they must feed you before they feed their own sons but, if you go out, they can shoot you in the back.

After a night in the illustrious hotel without sleep due to the cacophony outside, the next morning we hit the road south for Karachi. Standing on the road in the lush green of the Indus Valley, looking over the Indus river, I felt like I was in another world. Everything was different: the foliage, the wildlife, and the people. The roads were "metaled" or made with broken stones, then covered with tar. It was the closest thing to a paved road I had seen for a long time. Most of the traffic consisted of trucks, almost all Bedford lorries. The lorries all had a huge wooden bed with wooden sides and an open wooden box over the cab to carry bedding and misc. items like tools. The outsides of the lorries were painted in bright colors depicting flowers, scenic views and the Arabic names of God, written in Urdu and Arabic. On the back of the trucks there was always written a sign for others to see which said, "Horn OK Please."

The Pakistanis seemed to use their horn in place of brakes. Inside the cabs were ornate decorations usually made from plastic. There were plastic flowers, baubles, beads, all in bright garish colors, on every surface and hanging from every possible place. A driver and a chokidar manned all the trucks. The "Chokidar" was the watchman/servant/traveler. It was his job to do everything except drive. He had to check the load, check the tires, and generally be the servant of the driver. A truck stopped and I told the driver we needed a ride to Karachi. He indicated that we should get in and he would give us a ride.

It was fairly crowded for four people but since he lit up a hash joint and was passing it around, I didn't say anything. After getting really loaded, I realized that this truck had no shocks. It was a really rough ride. We were traveling at about 50 km per hour but it felt like about 100! It was then that I noticed that all the other drivers, coming from the opposite direction were passing hash joints back and forth between themselves and their chokidars. Virtually every truck driver in Pakistan that I saw smoked hash. This was fine by me because I was always ready for a smoke but what I also realized was that the roads were not wide enough for two trucks to pass each other from opposite directions without one or both putting two wheels onto the shoulder.

The problem was that the shoulder was full of huge potholes and the drivers didn't want to pull over until the last minute so this resulted in a game of "chicken." They would drive at full speed, stoned out of their minds on charas, bearing down on each other to see who would pull off onto the shoulder first.

Finally, at the last moment they would jerk the steering wheel and put two wheels onto the shoulder, hitting these huge potholes, in fully loaded trucks with no shocks. The effect was a huge bouncing and jolting which resulted in everyone being thrown around in the cab while all the baubles and beads hanging from everywhere flailed in every direction. At some point at a chai stop, I suggested that we ride in the box on top of the cab, which was agreed to.

Now, this was a real experience. The box was nothing more than a wood framed box over the cab with sides about half a meter tall. It was an incredibly exhilarating experience to ride along the Indus, the wind in your hair, watching a totally alien world go by. It was like being in a 3D movie. I was later to view thousands of miles of Pakistan and India from this vantage-point. We slept that night at the side of the road in the truck in Hyderabad, Sind.

I knew nothing about Karachi in advance so my only thought was that I really needed to see the ocean. I longed to see water. We went immediately to the Bazaar (Saddar Bazaar) to have breakfast and score some hash. We scored a few ounces of hash from a young cobbler with long black ringlets and a beautiful brown, statuesque, chiseled face with black eyes. He was squatting in a small dirt byway with open sewers and a few charpoys scattered about. He was so startlingly handsome that we sat on the charpoy, smoked a few joints and chatted with him while he went about repairing sandals that looked like they should have been thrown in the trash two generations ago. Then we found a "hotel" to have breakfast.

While were having chai, omelets and toast, a gentleman approached us and introduced himself. He was Dr. Manzoor. After some small talk he asked if he could help us in any way. I replied that he could take us to the beach. He said he would be more than happy to take us in his car; however, he would be most honored if we would accompany him to his house, meet his family, have dinner and stay the night and then, the next morning, he would take us to the beach.

We stayed at Dr. Manzoor's home that night and after breakfast the next morning he drove us to Hawkes Bay. Hawkes Bay had a beautiful beach which was completely deserted. We arrived there on November 25th so it was the off-season. The natural vegetation was very sparse; seaweed rising in tangles, and mangroves on some of the shores. It was mostly coarse grass, cactus, and castor plants on some of the hills. Date and coconut palms grew in the river valleys. The common wild animals were wolves, chinkaras (a type of gazelle), hog deer, jackals, wild cats, wild dogs, and hares. There were lots of domesticated animals around including sheep, goats, horses and cows. Local birds included geese, ducks, snipe, cranes, flamingos and ibis.

When we thanked Dr. Manzoor for the ride and he was shocked when we said we would not be going back with him. He took his leave and that was the last we ever saw of Dr. Manzoor.

We were sitting on the beach taking in the splendid view of the Arabian Sea and spreading out our sleeping bags when two policemen walked up to us. They asked what we were doing and we communicated that we were planning to spend a few nights on the beach. They said that was not possible, as it was very dangerous because of wild animals and bandits (dacoits). We attempted to assure them that it would be no problem but they would not hear of it. "You are guests in our country and we must accommodate you," they said.

They took us with them to the police station, which was a small adobe building about four meters by five meters and showed us the charpoys where we could sleep. We were very thankful to them and offered them to smoke some hash with us. The older sergeant, who was obviously the headman, smoked with us and told us that the next night he would arrange for us to stay in the hotel down the road for free. We asked him where we could buy some more charas and he said he would get it for us. Later that day, he commandeered a passing vehicle for a ride to Karachi City and went to the charas walla and confiscated several ounces of top-quality hash and brought it back for us. The next day he took us to the hotel down the road (the only other man-made structure anywhere in sight) and informed the hotel staff that we would be staying there for a few days and that they should feed us and give us anything we want without charge. We were the only guests in the hotel so the staff waited on us hand and foot.

That day, the Sergeant took us to a small fishing village a few miles down the road. As we approached the village, we passed Paradise Point. At Paradise point I witnessed one of the most incredible natural geological formations that I have ever seen. There is a natural stone breakwater twenty meters tall that juts out into the Arabian Sea. At the end of the wall is a huge hole worn through by water and wind which is a perfect circle approximately fifteen meters in diameter. I stood there in awe for a good half-hour looking at it. The fishing village consisted of stick huts and about 80 to 100 inhabitants. Almost every person I saw was a victim of hydrocephalus due to incest. Men, women, and children with enlarged heads, bulging foreheads and a strange downward gaze going about the daily chores of cleaning fish, winnowing grains, washing clothes. I had heard of this before but never witnessed it. I was shocked. It was eerie, to say the least. It left me stunned and I can never forget it.

Back at the Hawkes Bay police station there was a young policeman who had taken a liking to me and who spoke fair English. As each day went by he became more and more infatuated so that by the end of our stay, he was so emotional that he could hardly even speak Urdu when he saw me. One night we were walking along the beach in the full moon when I noticed some ruts in the sand about one meter wide, going from the ocean to the beach. I followed one of the ruts to the end and saw a huge sea turtle laying eggs in the sand. There were dozens of them that had used all four flippers to dig a hole the size of their entire bodies. Then they used their back flippers to dig another hole at the back of the first hole, and laid about thirty soft-shelled eggs into each hole. After laying the eggs, they covered the hole and crawled back into the ocean, leaving their babies to their fate. Their fate was that wild dogs ate most of the eggs but the ones that survived emerged later from the sand and crawled to the sea. On that night the young Pakistani policeman took my hand as we strolled along the beach and said, "Oh Brother Mik, swear to me under the moonlight, that we are brothers eternally." I swore to it.

The next day we were sitting at the beach looking at the ocean when I heard the sound of a motorcycle. I turned around and looked behind me to the road and saw the passenger get off the bike and start to walk toward me. He was a long way off and just looked like a small dot at first but as he got closer his walk looked familiar. The closer he got, the more I strained to see who it was and the more he craned his neck toward me to see who I was. Finally, he got close enough and we both recognized each other at the same time.

He was so astounded that he fell backwards onto his butt into the sand. It was Wiener Wolf! Vienna is Wien in German and Wolf was from Vienna, hence, the nickname Wiener Wolf. The last time I saw him was on Pont Neuf in Paris a few weeks before we left on our journey to the East. We hugged and laughed and smoked, and then he told us that we had to go with him to Karachi because he had a job for us. We would be tour guides for three busloads of Bavarian tourists who were arriving in town the next day. He had been hired by a travel agent, but they needed two other German-speaking guides for the other two busloads. They were paying really good money, so we agreed and went back to Karachi with Wolf after tearful good-byes at the police station and relieved "Allah is praised" from the hotel staff. The police sergeant commanded a truck driver coming from the village of mongoloids to give us a ride into town. We had stayed five days at Hawkes Bay.

After being dropped from our fish truck we took a taxi to the travel office with which Wiener Wolf had made the arrangement to be tour guides. We received instructions to return in the afternoon and were given a list of the sights to be visited. When we returned in the afternoon we found that the German tourists were Bavarian ministers and their wives, three busloads of totally straight and mostly grossly overweight Bavarians. They spoke Bavarian amongst themselves, which was difficult for all of us to understand, but they attempted to speak High German with us so communication was no problem.

They nearly freaked when they saw us. I don't think they had ever seen a longhaired male before except in pictures of Jesus. So off we went with absolutely no knowledge of Karachi except for the list we had been given. The German wives spent so long hoisting themselves onto camels at the beach for camel rides that we got behind in the allotted time for the tour. Without mentioning anything to the "tour guides" the travel agent decided to leave out a couple of things on the list and just sort of whiz by other sites without stopping.

The tourists were taking pictures of everything in sight and writing down in their note pads what the site was we had just passed after consulting with their guide. Since none of us knew what the sites were and we were totally out of sync with the list, one of us would tell our busload that they had just seen the tomb of Mohammed Ali Jinna, the father of Pakistan, another told their busload that it was the Frere Hall Post Office and the third, the library. You should have seen the chaos when they compared notes at the next stop. In any event, the tour finally came to an end and the worst possible thing happened. The travel agent thanked everyone and then said, "Please don't tip the guides." We were planning on cleaning up on the tips. Oh well, at least we made the rupees the travel agent had promised us.

We got a room at the Bukhara Hotel near Saddar Bazaar and hatched a plan with Wiener Wolf to double our money by selling five hundred dollars' worth of traveler's checks on the black market. This was all the money we had in the world besides rupees we had just earned that day. We had bought the traveler's checks in Teheran from the money Abrahim had paid us to drive the cars. After selling them we would report them lost and have them reissued and presto, double your money. We planned to meet Wiener Wolf the next day to carry out the plan and went to the hotel for dinner.

The food was so spicy hot that I was having a hard time getting my taste buds accustomed to it so I was living on bread and eggs. Eventually I did adapt to the spiciness of the foods and to this day savor heat. When I finally did realize one day that I was eating really hot food without breaking out in a full sweat, I was quite proud of myself!

While eating eggs and "slices" (toast), a Pakistani approached us and introduced himself as Lateef. He was a very nice middle aged man with a short trim beard and dark eyes. Anyone over thirty was middle aged to me at that time. I don't know how old Lateef was but his beard was just beginning to show shades of gray. He asked all the usual questions but he was obviously a very educated man who spoke perfect English. He invited us to stay at his house, which was nearby, for as long as we wanted to stay. We of course took him up on the offer and arranged to meet him the next morning at the eggs and slices hotel.

The next morning we met Lateef and he took us to his house and we dropped off our backpacks and went back into town to meet Wiener Wolf for the traveler's check scam. Wolf sold the checks to a black market agent then we went to the bank and reported them lost and were issued new checks.

We spent two weeks in Karachi hanging out with the cobbler,

sitting on his charpoy smoking copious amounts of nearly free hash. I ate so many eggs, I developed a rash all over my body and realized that sooner or later I was going to have to learn to adapt to the local food. I bought Wiener Wolf a gold stud earring and a parrot for helping with the scam.

We decided to head north and thought it would be cool to go by train. I don't remember how I got the idea but I decided to go to the train station and ask the stationmaster if we could ride the goods (freight) train to Lahore about 900 miles to the north up the Indus Valley in the state of Punjab. I had learned that Pakistanis can never say "no" to a request from a foreigner, especially if it had to do with any form of hospitality. Besides the Muslim laws of hospitality, they just didn't seem to be able to say "no," even if they had no intention of fulfilling the request. The stationmaster was quite cordial and told us to return the next evening at 11:00 p.m.

When we returned the next evening, we were shown to our accommodations. The stationmaster had arranged for a special passenger bogie to be attached to the goods train for our ride north. While waiting in the station, I was approached by a man who was there with a large family. He struck up a conversation with the usual Pakistani curiosity and enthusiasm and the conversation ended with the usual request for our address. Ulli had told me to always give a phony address to these kinds of requests but for some reason I gave him our real address in Germany. This guy showed up months later at my sister-in-law's flat in Frankfurt with a V.W. busload of family members and told her that I said they could all stay there till they got their feet on the ground. Needless to say, she was shocked. I'm not sure exactly what she told them and have no idea what ever happened to them.

By the time the sun rose the next morning we had passed through the barren Sind and were slowly chugging along through lush green tropical forests of green filled with millions of grass-green rose-ringed parakeets, red munias, golden orioles, and fawn-colored hoopoes. At one point during the day, we pulled over on a side shunting for a few hours to let a train coming from the North pass by. The engineer, brakeman and three or four other trainmen made chai by the side of the tracks on a primus stove and we all had tea, smoked charas, talked about how to properly make chai, the names of the flora and fauna surrounding us and enjoyed the timeless moment with nothing to do but wait. It was a short time of being totally in the moment without any thought of yesterday or tomorrow. That evening as it got dark we pulled over on another side shunt and noticed that, in a small clearing in the nearby tiny village, someone was setting up to show a movie to the villagers from the back of his truck.

We wandered over and watched the movie, leaving the entire goods train in the hands of the chokidar. The movie was a documentary of a safari in Rajastan. In the movie, the hunter, a Rajastani raja, had had his men dig a huge pit about three meters deep and four meters square. They were hunting tigers and had heard that an Indian lion had been spotted in the region recently but had not much hope of trapping one because there were so rare. When they returned to the pit they had trapped not only a tiger but the lion as well.

The next forty-five minutes of the movie was a fight to the finish between the tiger and the lion. It was brutal, and guess who won? The king of the jungle! It was his mane that gave him superiority in battle. After he had finally killed the tiger he turned to swagger away, but suddenly turned around and pounced on the dead tiger and killed him again just to make sure.

The next day we continued traveling northeast, leaving the Indus to travel along the Chenab River to Multan, entering the Punjab. The Punjab (five rivers) is known as the "breadbasket" of India. In 1947, during the partition of India at the time of independence, it was divided. It was the first time I had seen so much land under cultivation since leaving Europe.

We arrived in Lahore late at night. It was extremely foggy. We walked out of the train station into the foggy night observing how the street lamps sent their light rays penetrating into the fog creating huge glowing balls in the fog. There was not a person in sight. It was eerie. I saw horses asleep in harness at their tongas. I had this weird feeling as if something was very wrong. Suddenly I heard a voice from behind. "Saab, Saab." (Sahib) I turned to see a small raggedy old man emerge from the fog. He said, "Saab, guess what happened today." I thought, "Oh my God, the entire city has died of the plague or something." "What happened?" "Alan Ladd died!" I wanted to laugh hysterically, but the scene was so weird I was just dumbstruck. It was a total disconnect in the sense that it was the absolute last thing I could have expected to hear. How had this guy in the middle of the foggy night in Pakistan ever *heard* of Alan Ladd—and then approached me to tell me about it? It was the most incongruous thing I had ever heard. Finally, remembering my youth, the only reply I could think of was to say, "Come back Shane, Shane come back. We need you Shane," remembering the final lines of my favorite Alan Ladd movie. The little man walked away, disappearing into the fog as eerily as he had appeared a few minutes before.

I woke up a tonga driver asleep in his tonga and he drove us into town to the Anarkali Bazaar where we got a room in the Anarkali Hotel and had a night's sleep.

The next morning we set off to find Hafeez's relatives. He had given us the address when we left him in Quetta. Very commonly Pakistanis and Indians will introduce someone as their brother. When you press them they will say that actually, "He is my cousin-brother." I found out that cousins are quite frequently like brothers. Sometimes, people don't really know how they are related. They have a lot of cousins and the confusion is made worse by the fact that they frequently marry their first or second cousins. They also commonly don't know exactly how old they are or when their birthday is.

When we went to the address that was given by Hafeez we found a storefront with a sign above the door, which read "Chaudrey Scientific Store." We entered to introduce ourselves and whom should we see but Hafeez himself. The store was chock full of weird scientific equipment and medical models of plaster-of-Paris painted in bright colors. There were brains, intestines, arms, legs, etc. They took us to a house and gave us a room in which to sleep. It was hard to sleep because the room was also full of the medical models of human parts.

We stayed three days in Lahore. Lahore is a beautiful city of the upper Indus plain on the Ravi River, full of history, especially since the Muslim period all the way back to the time of Babur. The old walled city was ancient and full of tiny lanes with hovels in which teeming masses of humanity lived in total squalor amid open sewers. In contrast the mall was a huge boulevard with nice coffeehouses, eating hotels and shops. On the mall was the YMCA, which had a great restaurant. We ate there frequently. Once I was having a meal there and wanted some onions to eat with my meal. I asked the waiter, a Punjabi, in Urdu, to bring some onions. The Urdu (and Punjabi) word for onions is "Pias." I asked him three times in perfect Urdu, which he repeated but still said he didn't understand. I asked the gentleman seated at the next table to tell the waiter to bring some onions. He told the waiter, using the exact same words I had used, and the waiter immediately went off to fetch the onions. The waiter expected me to speak English to him and when I spoke Urdu his mind was not prepared for it. A German boy once told me "Ich bin ein boy scout." I didn't know the German word "boyscout" so didn't understand him.

We walked out on the mall after eating that day and saw a dead body lying in the middle of the street. A car had hit him.

The police had put rocks around his body and seemed to be investigating. A scene like this always draws a crowd of people and long discussions ensue. The body was still there the next day.

Speaking of crowds, they were an everyday occurrence. It was very difficult to stay in one place in public at that time. The people, out of curiosity, would just stop and stand and stare at you. Even if you ask them to leave they would not. Quite often it got frustrating. I saw many foreigners totally freak out because they got so frustrated at constantly being stared at. Once I told a crowd in Urdu to go away and one of the men replied in English, "No Saab, we shall remain." They would often ask the same questions over and over again. "Saab, what is your mission?," "Saab, what is your native country?," "Are you traveling at the expense of your government?"

Once we were sitting with Spider, an English guy we met in Lahore. He was a scruffy, dirty-looking freak, which the English travelers frequently were. He was stone-broke, had no shoes, and was living on the streets. A Pakistani asked him, "Saab, what is your condition?" He didn't really mean what he asked. All these questions mean the same thing. Where are you from, what are you doing here, and how do you support yourself? Spider looked up at him, peering through his filthy matted bangs and replied, "I reckon I'd have to say it's fairly desperate."

Between the Old City and the mall lies Anarkali. This is one of the finest bazaar areas I have ever seen. It's hard to say what it is about certain unique places that steal a place in your heart. Just the sound of the word "anarkali" (pomegranate) brings a feeling of home to me. I'd estimate that it is about twenty blocks square of small shops of every kind, some no bigger than four square meters. The smells, the colors, the people all combine to give a sensual feeling that you don't want to leave. It makes you want to stay and wander from place to place, stopping to chat with everyone you meet.

Lahore is the second largest city in Pakistan. It is not high on the list of places to visit for tourists. The old city, Anarkali, Bad Shahi Mosque (one of the most beautiful in the world) and the Shalimar Gardens of Lahore combined with the friendliness and hospitality of the people make it a place not to miss.

It was December 17th, 1964 and for some reason we decided to go to Kabul, Afghanistan before entering India. I can't remember the reasoning behind the decision but in retrospect it didn't seem to make too much sense because of the climate; we had no cold weather clothes. In any event we hitchhiked out of Lahore and spent the first night in Jhelum, which is named for the river on which it lies, one of the five great rivers of the Punjab. We spent the night with two engineers we met on the street and who invited us to stay with them.

Since Lahore we had been riding on the Grand Trunk Road which extends from the Khyber Pass to Calcutta. It is the most incredible road in the world. We arrived in Rawalpindi, then the capital of West Pakistan, around lunchtime. We had lunch and wandered some shops full of antiques. There were ancient coins and statues from the time of Alexander the Great's time from the nearby area of Gandhara.

This is a historic region in what is now northwestern Pakistan. It was a meeting place of Indian and Mediterranean influences in times past. It was subject to Persia in the 6th and 5th centuries BC and was conquered by Alexander in the 4th century BC. The Mauryas, Indo-Greeks, Sakas, and Parthians later ruled it. From the 1st to about the 7th centuries AD, Gandhara was the home of a distinctive Buddhist art style called "Gandhara Art" and this is what was for sale in these shops. These pieces should have been national treasures but in strictly Muslim Pakistan where idols are religiously forbidden, they held little value or respect.

There are museums where Gandhara art is present and is most magnificent but hardly anyone goes to see it. Once I noticed a pile of small sculptures in the corner of a museum room stacked up like rubble so I picked up a small head of Buddha carved in schist and slipped it into my bag and later mailed it to the States. I don't know what got into my mind and can't really remember if it was I or Uschi who put it into her bag. It was a mindless and thoughtless moment. (When I retrieved it after returning to the States, I felt so guilty for having stolen it that I packed it up and mailed it back to the museum in Pakistan even though I knew that they never missed it and would probably just throw it into another pile of rubble.) Other shops sold something which I had not seen for a while: cold weather clothing. Hmm, was this a bad sign? I didn't want to be any place cold. That would mean wearing a jacket and putting on shoes. No, that would never do. There were many shops selling sheepskin coats, the fur inside and the hide on the outside covered with brightly colored embroidery.

Back on the road in the afternoon for another spectacular stoned-out ride on the top of an elaborately decorated lorry to the incredible unique city of Peshawar. Peshawar is the capital city of the district, division and province of The Northwest Territory. It lies just west of the Bara River, a tributary of the Kabul River, near the Khyber Pass. Nearby Peshawar are the ruins of the largest Buddhist stupa in the subcontinent (2nd century AD), which indicate the cities' long association with the Buddha and Buddhism. It was the capital of Gandhara. The city has been known by various names throughout history but the name Peshawar (pesh awar: "frontier town") was supposedly given by Akbar, the Moghul emperor of India in the mid to late 16th century. It has always been a great historic center of caravan trade with Afghanistan and Central Asia.

By the time we arrived it was dark. The truck that we were riding in dropped us off in the middle of town on the G.T. Road. I saw a sign that read "Hotel Star first floor." We started up the stairs and had gone half way up when I heard a voice from below, "Saab, Saab, where are you going. Do not go there. Come down here." I stopped and turned to see a young, well-groomed Pathan gentleman, dressed in suit and tie. I told him we were travelers and were going to check into this hotel. "Oh no, Saab, I cannot allow you to stay in a hotel. You are guests in my country and I will see to your accommodations. Please do me the honor of staying at my humble home." Well, I thought, what the hell, why not save a buck? I was beginning to see that they were highly serious about the Muslim laws of hospitality here.

We arrived at his home just in time to bid farewell to his chokidar/cook that was leaving on holiday for the month of Ramadan which began at midnight, in just a couple of hours. This was the first time I had heard of Ramadan, or as they say in Peshawar, "Ramzan." He explained that it is a Muslim month of complete fast during daylight hours and that they were very strict about it in Peshawar. He explained that people had their main meals after sunset prayers and that there was an exemption for travelers who were allowed to have one meal during the day. Some food hotels would accommodate travelers.

Nevertheless, a few years ago some travelers had been pulled from hotels while eating and put on donkeys backwards, their faces blackened, and paraded through town for the townspeople to jeer at and throw stones. Thus, he reasoned, it would be best if he brought food from the hotel and we could close all the curtains so no one could see inside and we could eat our meals at his house in safety. He left and returned with lunch. He spread it out on the table and I have never seen so many dishes served at one time in my life. There were at least twenty different dishes to choose from. He was extremely cautious, with good reason, as he covered all the windows securely so that there was no possibility that anyone could see in. Then we feasted.

Of course there was no way that we could have possibly consumed all that food at one sitting. I was praying that he wasn't going to insist that we do because I had read stories about the

Pathans feeding people to death as part of their hospitality. Fortunately he did not, and the leftovers were packed for later consumption. Another interesting thing about this gentleman was that he wanted my body. He made no bones about being homosexual and would, at every opportunity, hold my hand, feel my bottom caress my penis or rub himself against me as if there were nothing out of the ordinary about it whatsoever. He never became aggressive or asked if I was interested, he was just very sexually affectionate.

The next morning, the first morning of Ramzan, we walked to the Kissa-Khwani-Bazaar, (Street of Story Tellers) It is a meeting place for foreign merchants who deal in dried fruits, woolen products, rugs, carpets, sheepskin coats, lambskin (karakul) caps and long Chitrali cloaks. It is an ancient bazaar from the Silk Route days where storytellers would gather to weave their tales of adventure. One of the first things I noticed was that most of the men were armed. The majority were Pathan tribesmen who wore a rifle or shotgun slung over their shoulders, a pistol in their belts and a bandoleer of ammunition across their chests. This was normal. No one even gave it the slightest notice. They would sit down for tea, take off their rifle or shotgun, stand it in the corner as if it were a walking stick and have their tea. These were just like the guys we saw in the "Out of Bounds" area of Quetta.

Ancient buildings surrounded the main square of Kissa-Khwani-Bazaar with tiny shops selling grains, spices and everyday things. These goods would all be piled high on brass plates for all to see. The spice shops were especially colorful. Then there were the tea stalls. They were just big enough for a man to squat and build a fire to boil tea. In Peshawar, for the first time since Iran, I encountered tea without milk. And green tea at that. It was served in a small ceramic teapot, which held two or three cups. The pots had invariably been damaged over the years by heat (they were placed directly over flames) or dropping or whatever. In any case, these were valuable commodities not to be thrown out merely because they were damaged.

Every teapot that I saw had been repaired dozens of times by soldering some pieces together or filling in cracks by soldiering them with metal. You would have to sit on a bench on the street and drink your tea. There were also indoor coffeehouses. These are very popular in Peshawar and are called "Qahwah Khanahs."

Once, while taking tea at a Qahwah Khanah, a young Pathan man sitting next to me drinking coffee, nonchalantly pulled out his works, and set it on the table along with some pure pharmaceutical German morphine. He pulled some up into his syringe, put his foot up on the bench and skin-popped it into his thigh through his cotton pajamas, took a sip of tea, looked at me and said, "You see Saab, I am addicted, hopelessly addicted, what to do?" No one even gave the slightest notice to the fact that he had just shot up in a public restaurant. Why should they? He is hopelessly addicted isn't he? What to do?

Leading off from the main square of Kissa-Khwani-Bazaar are tiny cobblestone lanes perhaps two meters wide with an open sewer on each side. The three- or four-story buildings on each side are so ancient and decrepit that they lean in toward each other and many times nearly touch at the top. As you look up to see the beautiful intricately carved ancient wooden facades of the buildings, it can't help but cross your mind that it is just a matter of time until they fall. Everything is patched like the teapots.

If there is any part of the population in Peshawar that is not Muslim it is too small to calculate. Nearly every adult male had a full beard; some were spectacular specimens, especially the older men with long white beards. Many men color their hair and or beards with henna in remembrance of the prophet. For all one knew the women could have had beards too because there was no way you were going to see any woman's face.

Women were hardly seen but when they did go out of the house they observed complete purdah, which in this part of the world meant wearing an over-garment called a burkha. This consisted of either a white or black coverall from head to ankle with two openings for the eyes which were woven across so that the inhabitant could see out but outsiders could not see her eyes. They looked like walking shuttlecocks.

It truly did amaze me how, after a while of this atmosphere of purdah, that even a glimpse of a female hand, wrist or ankle could become almost as an erotic vision as seeing a beautiful woman nearly naked in the West. After some time you began to pick up the subtle gestures that they were watching you or deliberately showing you an ankle or wrist. You could feel their smile and subtle flirtatious eye gestures. The excitement of this was heightened by the fact that if you were caught deliberately looking at a woman's face, you could be shot on the spot without consequence to the shooter.

After a good breakfast of tea and slices we bid our friend farewell, saying that we were going to Kabul for Christmas and would return in a week or so. He invited us to return and stay with him on our return.

Eventually we made our way toward the G.T. Road and headed for the Khyber Pass. The town at the entry to the Khyber Pass is called Landi Kotal, the home of the four-dollar kilo of hash! Landi Kotal is a small village completely made up of smugglers and traders. They trade everything from drugs (hash, opium, morphine, and heroin), to weapons, then bolt action rifles, now, stinger missiles. Money and goods flew through that place like a wildfire. I was tempted to buy a kilo of charas but I didn't want to carry an extra kilo and it was more fun to score every day or two or three. It was part of the ritual. Also, then I would have been stuck smoking the same kind of hash for a long time, denying myself the pleasures of the local dope. Also, not to be forgotten, you have to cross borders with it, a foolish thing to do when not necessary. Hey, I was going to Afghanistan, home of some of the best hash in the world.

It was also part of the identity of being a traveler. You just didn't carry anything extra and you lived from day to day. This is a very hard thing for most people to grasp but it is an incredible feeling of freedom. There were no commitments, no entanglements, no obligations, and no responsibilities. There was no place we had to go and no place we had to be. We traveled until we got somewhere we wanted to be and stayed there until we wanted to move on.

If you could ignore the sight of the appliances that were being sold and traded and the trucks used to transport goods, being in Landi Kotal was like going back a few hundred years. Armed men sat around fires smoking and drinking tea. Pack camels snorted steam into the morning cold. Nearby stood a group of men gathered in a circle making bets on two fighting birds they had thrown into the ring. These birds were their pride and joy and they carried them around in little cages or with a tether on their leg and a hood over their head. They would get them all hot and bothered by stroking them over the head then removing their hood and tossing them into a ring, shouting bets back and forth at each other until one of the birds drew blood. Once blood was drawn, the fight was over, the birds were collected, and money traded hands. Then everyone would sit down at the fire drink more tea and smoke more cigarettes or charas.

Chapter Six

The Power of Afghanistan

Eventually we arranged a ride to Jallalabad, the first major town in Afghanistan past the Khyber Pass. Oh, the Khyber Pass! Just hearing or saying the name brings back emotional feelings. There are some things that are just beyond the ability to describe; they have a power beyond description. The Khyber is one of those things. The first thing I noticed is that the road was excellent, comparable to any I had seen anywhere in the world. I found out that the main road crossing Afghanistan from Herat in the west to Khyber in the East was built in three parts respectively by Germans, American and Russians. The road through the Khyber Pass is a masterpiece of engineering as it snakes through the Hindu Kush Mountains along the Kabul River. Looking down below you can see the ancient animal tracks next to the river, still in use today. We stopped for smokes at a point along the road where there was a giant waterfall. There were hundreds of flying fish attempting to climb the fall.

It was dark by the time we reached Jallalabad and the end of the line for our trucker so he let us out at the local police station. The altitude was higher and it was cold. Our sleeping bags were strictly tropical. The police said we would sleep on the floor of the police station, for which we were grateful. Sleep was difficult because hundreds of mice were scampering over our bodies all night long.

With the excellent roads we made good time and were in Kabul by noon the next day. Kabul itself sits on a high plateau valley (1,800 meters) overlooked by the Asmai and Sherawaza Mountains. From a distance it is quite beautiful and has an ancient history. Kabul has existed for over 3,000 years. It is mentioned in the Rigveda (Indian scriptures: circa 1,500 BC) It owes its longevity almost purely to its strategic location. Genghis Khan inflicted considerable damage to Kabul in the 13th century. It was the capital (1504-26) of the Mughal Empire under Babur and remained under Mughal rule until 1738 when Nadir Shah of Iran captured it. Kabul has been the capital of Afghanistan since 1776.

We checked into the Maiwan Hotel for a dollar a day and went to the bazaar to change money and get some warm clothes. The money changers were all Russian. There was one lambskin coat dealer after another along the same road. After getting some warm clothes we found a decent-looking hotel in the center of town right next to the Kabul River. We went into the restaurant and found out that this was where the rest of the western travelers hung out. What a bunch of characters we met here. A few of them deserve description.

First we met Max and Michael. These two were a unique pair. They had been travelling together for years and were several years older than us. The two of them had spent many years on Crete. They spoke English, German, Greek, Turkish, French, Italian, and Spanish. The macaronic result was a mixture of these languages that resulted in their own language that they called "Tibotanian." They planned to start their own country, Tibotania. Max waxed romantically how easy it would be; "You only need three people: One to print the money, one to print postage and one to stamp passports!" They were a traveling print shop. Their specialty was forgery. They could produce, in their own hotel room, a near perfect passport, driver's license, student I.D. or just about anything else you needed, for a decent price.

Then there was Jean Sullivan. His mother was French, his father Irish and he had Paraguayan citizenship. He'd decided at an early age that he wanted to be a smuggler. One of the keys to success for smuggler he said in his thick French accent was to "always have a cover." He decided he would become a chemist as a cover. He got a job in Pakistan as a chemist and flew several times a year to Paris, Hong Kong, Beirut, or wherever the gold price was good, and bought gold, which he smuggled to Pakistan. He had a special vest made that could hold 25 kilos of gold. He would walk around Paris for two days, even attending the opera, wearing his vest so that his body could get used to the weight, before flying into Karachi with the gold.

Eventually, someone informed on him and he was arrested at the Karachi airport, the gold was confiscated and he was put in jail. Using some knowledge of his chemistry background he faked that he had a bleeding ulcer and produced a bloody handkerchief. He was transferred to the hospital where he had arranged an escape and safe crossing of the Afghani border. Here he was in Kabul starting over. On Christmas day the three of us decided we would cook an omelet on our Primus kerosene stove in our hotel for Christmas dinner. I remember going to the bazaar to buy eggs with Jean. He had a really heavy French accent and would pick up each egg and inquire, "cheep cheep?" Then he would hold the egg next to his ear and shake it listening for a baby chicken inside. If he was satisfied that there was no embryo he would then pronounce, "cheep cheep no" and place the egg in our basket. Back at the Maiwan Hotel we had Christmas dinner, the omelet cooked on the Primus, together with Jean Sullivan, a man I will never forget because of our fast friendship and how warmly we all felt for each other, but that was the last I ever saw of him or heard about him. I'll never forget that primitive Christmas dinner we shared and have often wondered what ever happened to Jean Sullivan.

The Maiwan Hotel was quite a place. Our room was barely bigger than the bed. The toilet was down the hall. The toilet was a room about two meters square with a hole in the middle of the floor. If you needed to urinate or defecate, you straddled this hole and let it drop down to the ground floor. It had already filled up half way so it didn't have to drop all three stories. Next to the hole was a box full of dirt clods. That was the Afghani idea of toilet paper. I never wiped my butt on a dirt clod. If you used toilet paper, you had to fold it up and throw it away later because if you dropped it down the hole the freezing updraft was so strong that it just blew it right back at you. There was an opening in the wall (if it had had a covering I would have called it a window) at the back of the room. I looked out in the mornings and saw that the poor were gathered to get their daily dole of grain down below. Then I noticed that the shit-shaft had a door or opening of some kind that allowed the excrement from the half full shaft to ooze out into the alley about three meters, just a meter or so away from where these poor folks were getting their grain distribution.

The hash in Afghanistan is excellent and comes in the shape of a disc usually about 10 cm round, about 2 cm thick in the middle, tapering thinner to the edges. I wondered why they came in this shape. In Pakistan for instance, the hash came is uniformly pressed blocks about 20x8x2 cm. So whatever amount you bought it was always 2 cm by something else, depending on how much you paid. A char anna piece weighed one tola (11.7 grams, the weight of a silver rupee.) Now that is what I call perfection. One tola of hash—-char anna.

One day we needed to score and were led to a small den in a small lane. We entered a small smoke filled room-full of men sitting on benches against the wall. There was a huge hookah in the middle of the room that had several hoses which could be puffed from. The bowl was big enough to put a complete hash disc on, topped by a large glowing charcoal. While we smoked some of the men picked up their instruments and began playing music. A piece of plastic was laid on the floor and a pile of hash powder, much like the Kandahar Crush I described at the Government Ganja shop in Quetta, was placed on top of the plastic. Another piece of plastic was placed over the "crush," then a young boy stood on it and began to dance to the rhythm of the music being played. When the disc in the hookah was finished, the newly created disc from below the dancer's feet was placed in the hookah and the whole thing repeated again. That is how I saw the famous hash discs of Afghanistan being made. I doubt that every disc was made that way but it is a memory I can never forget. I got totally wrecked, heard some good music, saw some good dancing and scored a disc of the finest Afghani hash.

The morning of our planned departure from Kabul, there was a huge earthquake and the Maiwan shook at dawn. Our bed was rattling against the floor and walls, literally bouncing up and down on the floor. I ran out into the hallway to see that fifteen Muslims were kneeling on the floor in prayer, some of them covered in soot from a stovepipe that had been knocked down in the quake.

Chapter Seven

Back to Pakistan

We made one last stop at the U.S. Consulate to check for mail and hitched a ride back to Peshawar, arriving by early evening, December 29th, 1964. Our old friend the gay Patan greeted us with open arms. It was still Ramzan so we had to be very careful about eating, drinking or smoking.

After a good night's sleep the first thing I wanted to do was go the Kissa Khwani Bazaar and hang out. It was less fun in the daytime because of Ramzan. You couldn't even swallow your own spit! At the approach of sunset I noticed everyone start filling their hands with their favorite things. You would think the first thing they would want would be a glass of water, but no, it was cigarettes and sugar cane. At the first sound of the Mullah's call for evening prayer, the cigarettes were lit and after a few long puffs the other hand shoved in the sugar cane. They were like gluttons who had been deprived for months. This was not a fast taken on for spiritual reasons. It was a forced ritual and every day at sunset, the same thing would occur.

We were told that it was a month of fast, but now I realized that they just shifted the hours of everything and gorged themselves at night! The smoking fast was probably the most difficult for the men. A huge percentage of Pakistani men smoke cigarettes and a not-too-small-minority also smoked charas. We smoked charas openly at this point whenever or wherever we wanted. (With the exception, naturally, of during the daylight hours of Ramzan; I didn't want to ride a donkey naked, backwards with my face blackened.)

The food was a lot different here from that which I had experienced in Baluchistan, Karachi or Lahore. It was not as hot, different spices were used and there were a lot of meat dishes. It was a relief on the palate and since it was considerably cooler here, the meat dishes were welcome also.

I don't remember how it was arranged but one day the local radio station offered to pay Rs. 500 for a one-hour interview with us. We agreed and showed up at the appropriate time. Unfortunately for the radio interviewer, we were both stoned out of our minds and were not the type of tourist interview that he had had in mind. I answered every question with complete honesty but the answers blew his mind. "What do I like about Pakistan?" "The cheap hash." "What do you do for a living?" "I'm a smuggler." "What are your plans for the future?" "I have none." He was totally relieved when the interview was over and fortunately I had asked for and gotten payment in advance.

One day we decided that we would like to visit a tribal area outside of Peshawar. Just to remind you, "tribal area" means that there is no army and no police, just the law of the Koran and the chief of the village. Every adult male is armed and if there is one who doesn't smoke cigarettes and charras, I never met him. Justice is simple and swift. If I look at your wife, you shoot me. The chief comes and asks what happened. You say, "He looked at my wife." The chief says, "Bury him." End of story.

We chose the village of Dara Adam Khel about an hour's drive directly south of Peshawar. The main street through town was lined with gun shops. Armed men would enter the shop, choose a weapon, take it out in the middle of the street and shoot it into the air to test it. It was much like kicking the tires of a car to us.

I was amazed at the quality of guns they made. There in the shops were perfect replicas of all the best guns in the world, including rifles, shotguns and handguns. Also popular was the walking stick gun. It looked just like a walking stick but was a single action rifle. We were introduced to the chief of the village and he invited us to his gun manufacturing place for a tour. There we saw guns being made on primitive lathes and other old-fashioned tools. We passed a man squatting over a huge bowl of pink stuff that he was kneading like pastry dough. "Oh Saab, no smoking please—gunpowder," he said, gesturing with his head toward the pink stuff with a huge smile on his face. Even in the tribal areas of Pakistan more people spoke English than in the major cites that we had visited, like Teheran or Istanbul due to the fact that India including what is now Pakistan was ruled by the British for two hundred years.

If you ever get to go to Peshawar, visit the museum to see the museum full of Gandharan art, and the Mahabat Khan Mosque (1630) a monument of Mughal architecture in pure white. Peshawar is well known for their industries of small arms, knives, wax and embroidery work, leatherwork, copper utensils, glazed pottery, ivory work, chappals (sandals) and lungis (men's loincloth-like wrap around skirts).

I remember thinking often during my travels in Pakistan and India how incredible it must have been before the partition of India into Pakistan and India in 1947. It must have been less crowded, even simpler and more bucolic. It was now 1964, seventeen years after partition and at the time partition seemed like a long, long time ago. Now, nearly 75 years after partition, I think, "Wow, that was only seventeen years after partition." Then, when there were 400 million people in India, I thought how incredibly overpopulated it was. Now, with the population over one billion three hundred million those days seem like heaven; comparatively, no overcrowding, pollution, or inflation.

I met tourists who would ask me how I could stand the fact that everything was so dirty. Well, it's true that it was hot and dusty and sanitation was not good. But at least the dirt was organic. Yes, you did see piles of human waste where the sweepers had dumped it after collecting it from the toilets in buckets, but you did not see bottles, papers, metals and the like. Those things were too valuable then and were collected and resold or reused the moment they were discarded. Also, even though a cup of tea was only char annas (25 Naya Paise, about 2.5 cents American), I heard stories about how you could buy a charpoi (string bed) for that price before partition. From this, probably in a charras haze, I developed the theory that all the world's problems could be solved if every item in the world cost char anna.

The gay Patan host was starting to get on my nerves. First of all, he started hauling out stale food. Secondly every time he got near me he wanted to touch me, rub me, fondle me, stand close to me with his erection touching me or try to sneak into bed naked with me. I told him I wasn't interested in being his "Johnny-walla," as he put it, but he didn't care. "Oh yes, yes, I understand, never mind," he would say. Then, ten minutes later, he was rubbing my dick under the table. He told me that the Patans have a saying: "A woman for duty, a man for fun, and a goat by choice." In all of our travels there were very few instances like this that occurred and I don't remember any incident similar happening to Uschi. I told him that I had seen some really nice-looking goats on the road that morning and bade him farewell after a week's stay, which included celebrating the beginning of 1965 in Peshawar.

We got a ride with a truck that was going straight through to Lahore so we made it there in one day, stopping in "Pindi" for lunch on the way. In Lahore we had been invited to stay at the home of Zia Chaudrey, another cousin-brother of Hafeez. He had a large, beautiful home with a compound. His wives and daughters would hang out all day in the central courtyard and jabber. He had two wives and four daughters, all teenagers. Zia was an insurance agent and quite affluent. The bathroom was across the courtyard from our room so if I wanted to go to the toilet, I had to be announced so that they could leave or cover themselves from being seen by me. We stayed a week with Zia and his family.

I sewed twenty watches into a plastic band to put around my waist and put another twenty or so in another bag at the bottom of a shopping bag that we filled with foodstuff bought in Anarkali before leaving for the Indian border at Wagah.

The Wagah border is the border created in 1947 during Indian independence and partition. There were a few small buildings and a few immigration and custom officials. Leaving Pakistan was nothing more than a stamp in the passport. Entering India required an interview, probably because the official was bored and wanted to see if he could get a bribe. The first thing he asked was, "how much money do you have?" "I have no money," I replied. "Welcome to India. India is the Motherland, she must accept her children rich or poor," was his response. "Sit, sit, let us take chai," he gestured toward the two chairs before his desk. A servant brought hot chai. I saw the official notice the watch Uschi was wearing. "How many watches do you have?" "One," I replied. "What is this?" he asked, gesturing with his head toward Uschi's open purse on the desk. There was clearly another watch in plain sight. "That is another watch, we have one EACH." "Achha" (in the "I see" sense of the word.) He obviously wanted one of them. He stood up and started walking toward the bag with the twenty watches in the bottom and asked, "What is in this bag?" Just as he was reaching for the bag with the foodstuff on top and the watches on the bottom, I blurted out, "Oh that's just some smoked *beef* we bought in Lahore." He instantly rebounded backwards like he had just hit an imaginary rubber wall. He was clearly repulsed at the idea of the holy cow being cut up in pieces and put in a bag. He quickly stamped our passports and wished us a happy journey.

Chapter Eight

Finally in India: Sikhism and Amritsar

We walked a few meters down the road and it hit me. I was in India. I stopped dead in my tracks, slid my backpack off my shoulder onto the ground and spontaneously fully prostrated myself on the ground and kissed the earth. "I'm home," I heard a voice inside my head say. I had no idea why I felt this way. It was a spontaneous emotion from within. It seemed like sacred ground. I was reeling from the emotion of the experience so I sat on the ground and leaned up against a mile marker and lit up a smoke, letting my mind wander and my eyes absorb the beauty before me of the empty road ahead, like a seemingly endless path towards God only knew what.

I was enjoying a cigarette when I heard faintly in the distance the "clop, clop, clop" sound of an approaching tonga. I looked up to see two tongas headed my direction. I might mention here that Indian and Pakistan had no diplomatic relations at the time, so there was no one else crossing this border and no one else using this road. This was the Grand Trunk road and it was deserted except for the two approaching tongas and us. Eventually the tongas stopped before us. Tongas can comfortably hold three or four people. Each of these had nine or ten. "May we offer you a lift, sir?" "I don't think there is room." "Nonsense, there is plenty of room. Come, come, and get in." We climbed aboard and the tongas turned around and headed back in the direction from which they had come.

This was my first encounter with Sikhs. Sikhism began as protest to the caste system of Hinduism by the Perfect Master Guru Nanak in the 15th century. "Sikh" is the Punjabi for the Sanskrit Shishya, which means learner or disciple. The Sikhs as a community are the followers of the ten Gurus, Nanak to Gobind Singh, who created out of the disunited and emasculated fabric of society in Northern India a well-knit homogeneous body of people devoted in a bold and selfless spirit to the service of their countrymen. Most Sikhs are from the Punjab and speak Punjabi. Their main temple is the Golden Temple in Amritsar, Punjab but their temples are all over the world.

Baptized Sikhs are enjoined by their tenth Guru, Guru Govind Singh to wear the same five signs all beginning with the letter K. Kesh (uncut hair), Kangha (a comb), Kachha (a pair of shorts), Kara (an iron bracelet), and Kirpan (a sword). Because the men wear uncut hair they are seen wearing brightly colored turbans. The women also wear a distinctive dress called Shalwar-Chemise. It is a loose fitting pair of pants covered by a long tunic like dress. On dress-up occasions though, they wear sari. This is usually accompanied by a Dobatta or Dupatta which means "two ends," a long narrow strip of companion fabric worn either over one shoulder or across the neck with both ends flowing toward the back.

This particular family was the descendent relatives of a very famous Sikh General, Sadar Sham Singh, Atari Walla. They told us that he had fought the last battle with the British, the Battle of Subhraon in 1846. They explained that they were in the third day of a wedding celebration and would be most honored if we would join them in their home in the nearby village of Atari. We agreed and before long were pulling into a 13th century castle where the great general's descendants lived. We were taken to separate rooms and I was dressed in the grooms clothing and Uschi in the bride's sari and jewelry. Photos were taken and dozens of different foods, snacks, sweets and drinks were served. I realized that we were just an excuse to continue to party! In any event, it was a most special welcome to India and an event I will never forget.

By evening we were in Amritsar gazing upon the mysterious, glorious, magical Golden Temple. The Sikh temples are places where mixed congregations (Sangat, one of the main principles of Sikhism) meet in the evenings and sing the hymns of the Gurus. Ulli, in Germany, had told me that the Sikh temples always have what is called a "Gurudwara" attached to them where travelers can stay for free. (Hindu temples have an equivalent called a "Dharamsala.") Along with a free place to sleep the temples have established free community kitchens, "Guru ka langar" or just "langar" for short, where all sit and eat together in the same row on the floor (Pangat), regardless of distinctions of caste, creed or status in life. Through the two principles of Sangat and Pangat, Guru Nanak brought Hindus and Muslims, Brahmins and Sudras (menials) to a common social level. These two principles persist today in absolute purity.

The city of Amritsar was founded in 1577 by Ram Das, the fourth guru of the Sikhs, around a sacred tank orcpool called "Amrita Saras," from which the city's name is derived. A temple stands on an island in the tank's center and is reached by walking over a causeway in the tank. After its copper dome was covered with gold foil, it was named the Golden Temple.

After locking our bags in a cabinet in the Gurudwara, we were walking toward the temple where non-stop singing of hymns could be heard throughout the temple grounds. I looked to my right as I was walking, into a vacant lot between two buildings, and saw one of the strangest men I had ever seen.

I stopped dead in my tracks as we looked intently into each other's eyes. He wore pants and shirt that looked like they had been woven from coarsely spun dark-colored hair. His hair was long and matted. His reddish-brown skin looked like he had just survived years of prolonged exposure. He wore an earring in one ear which was a piece of string through a hole in the lobe with a chunk of turquoise tied to one end and a chunk of coral tied to the other end. His huge smile made his almond eyes nearly close. I smiled back to him and he gestured toward his tent which had been erected on the vacant lot.

His tent had been pitched on the temple grounds and as we` entered it, I felt like I was time traveling back about five hundred years. This was the tent of a Tibetan nomad and his family, refugees in India from their occupied homeland. The tent itself was quite large, perhaps four meters in diameter, and made of dark woven yak hair. In the center of the tent was a small fire with a teapot in it. We sat around the fire and drank tea, smiled and exchanged gifts, just small tokens really. I have no idea why he beckoned us into his tent or why I felt so safe to follow him or what really happened there. Yet it was a timeless moment, my first encounter with Tibetans, which was one of the most raw experiences I had ever had. We had not a word in common but somehow, we touched each other's hearts with something beyond words.

After leaving the Tibetan tent we walked over to the Harimandir (Golden Temple) itself and observed what everyone else did before entering. Shoes were removed, ritual ablutions performed, and the head covered, even if only with a kerchief, before walking across the walkway over the water tank to enter the temple. Inside we sat on the floor, backs against the wall and listened to the hypnotic, entrancing sounds of harmonium, tabla and sacred hymns being played and sung. I was completely transported and reflected that on that very morning I had been in Muslim Lahore, at noon kissing the soil at the Indian border, in the afternoon in an ancient fort celebrating a wedding, by evening in a Tibetan nomad's five-hundred-year-old tent and now this! This had to be a dream. I was exalted with the magic of India. I felt so at home.

After a few hours of hymns, I really needed to smoke so we

went outside the temple grounds. (Smoking is forbidden by the Sikh religion) Once on the streets of Amritsar, I realized that not all Punjabis are Sikh but a majority is. I hung out having tea and meeting people, asking a million questions about India, Sikhism, customs, etc., all of which, everyone I met were more than happy to discuss. I discovered that Indians are very friendly and eager to communicate even if you have no language in common. A few words of English, a few words of Hindi/Punjabi/Urdu, a lot of gestures and you had a conversation going. Wherever I went, I first tried to learn the numbers, how to say brother (always helps get someone to listen if you call him Brother), and a bunch of nouns and verbs. Throw them all together with some arm waving and gesticulations and you could usually make yourself understood, especially in India where most people are aggressively curious.

We decided to take the train from Amritsar to Delhi. Ulli had told me that most people travel on third-class trains without tickets in India, so I decided to try it. Most of the trains at this time were coal-fired steam locomotives. A third-class train ride in India is not for the fainthearted. First, nobody in their right mind would travel by third-class train unless they had to.

I found out why they travel without tickets; they don't have any money. Also, the British during their rule built the train system in India and since their departure the Indians feel that it is now their train. They have liberated it; why should they have to pay? Today, third-class trains don't even exist in India. A third-class bogie has no compartments; it's just a series of wooden benches with luggage racks above and an aisle. The toilet is a one square meter room with a galvanized metal floor that has a hole in the center. Whatever waste comes out of your body goes through the hole onto the train tracks below. The stench is horrible. Just to get into the third-class bogie requires stealth, dexterity and aggressiveness.

Everyone tries to board at once to make sure that they get on and have a seat. There are no reservations, of course. The entrance is crammed with teeming masses of humanity with bedding rolls balanced on their heads trying to push their way onto the train. There is no order or line or courtesy when it comes to boarding a third-class train in India. It's every man for himself. Even the windows are means of access. I have seen people throw their bedding out the window of one train into the window of another then follow it by crawling across from train to train through the windows. Once inside it is no more pleasant. You may be lucky and get the edge of a bench to put one cheek on but most likely not. I have slept in luggage racks, under the benches and even squatted on one leg for hours on end, pressed in by the crowds of people around me. Generally, everyone keeps a fairly good attitude and it's all considered part of the sport. Every once in a while, someone will grumble or snap at a fellow traveler but I have never seen a physical confrontation.

The train ride from Amritsar to Delhi was quite nice. It was crowded but I could still enjoy the scenery and talk to some of the people on the train. As we passed through the Punjab, I saw that it was mostly farmland. The Punjab is a level plain drained by the great Punjab rivers mainly the Ravi and Beas. The word "Punjab" comes from the Persian Punj (five) and Ab (water). There are five great rivers in Punjab. Because of the dry climate the area's agriculture depends on irrigation from extensive canal systems. Wheat, cotton, pulses and corn (maize) are the biggest crops. The Punjab is known as the "granary of India."

Chapter Nine

Finally Arriving Somewhere: Delhi

Arriving in Delhi (popularly known as Old Delhi) was a new phase. It was like I had actually arrived somewhere instead of being on the way to somewhere, even though I had never thought of Delhi as a "destination." Delhi was kind of like the hub of a giant wheel known as the planet earth. We walked from the Delhi train station a few blocks to Chandni Chowk, the packed ancient bazaar of Old Delhi that sits in the shadows of the Mogul masterpieces of architecture, the Red Fort and Jamma Masjid, this all centered in Shahjahanabad - the mid-17th century walled city built by Shah Jahan as his capital when he moved from Agra. Now I was actually in India, not just the Punjab. The Punjab is in India, but it is like this little island within India called "Sikhastan." (Or as they would like to call it, "Kalisthan") Not that there aren't Hindu's in Punjab; there are. But the Sikhs predominate. They own and run everything.

Just as Pakistan was almost entirely Muslim, Punjab was overwhelmingly a Sikh experience for me. Delhi, however, was really the whole mix: Hindu, Muslim, Jain, Christian, and people from all parts of India. Walking through Chandni Chowk is an experience everyone should have. First, there are teeming masses of people of all kinds. Off the main street there are tiny lanes barely wide enough for two to pass each other, lined with small shops of various types.

There was no system for getting around. The streets and sidewalks (where they existed) were a free-for-all, everything and everyone vying for a space. At first it seemed chaotic, then you realized how naturally and smoothly things work out. Everyone just sort of automatically gravitates toward any empty space, like filling a vacuum, whether they be busses, trucks, cars, bullock carts, camel carts, scooter rickshaws, motorcycle rickshaws, taxis, cows, human beings; each just pushes a little bit toward the open space.

Of course, the bigger you are the better chance you have of arriving in that space first. And if you happen to have a horn it is sounded constantly. Vendor carts fill the streets with everything from bananas to shirts; some with glorious piles of various brightly colored powders of dye or spice. And the smell! The smell was a complex of the sweet perfume of burning incense, spice, sweet smelling jasmine, tuberose, frangipani, human waste running in the open sewers, diesel exhaust, body odor and burning dung. There is nothing quite like it. Hawkers line the street shouting their wares, from ballpoint pens and teryline shirts to water and shoes. "BALL POINT, BALL POINT, BALL POINT" superimposed by a man standing two feet away shouting, "TERYLINE, TERYLINE, TERYLINE" and next to him the waterman shouting, "PANI, PANI, PANI", all at the top of their lungs.

Meanwhile Hindi film music blares at top decibel from every other shop. Women examine fabrics off carts exhaustively with children straddling their hips, sari end in their mouth. A madman leans against a wall staring or mumbling into his shirt or shouting at passersby. Suddenly a small child tugs on my sleeve gesturing with her other hand toward her mouth as if putting imaginary food in it. She is probably seven or eight years old with a one-year-old astride her hip. "Saahb, no mama, no papa, no chappati, bakshish. Bakshish, Saahb." A group of young men stare at me for no reason except that I am different, and they have nothing else to do. One of them has that all familiar look in his eye: A slight glimmering of mind which just barely serves to render internal darkness visible. Just stand and gaze!

The Gurudwara Sisganj was in Chandni Chowk. When I inquired about sleeping there, I was told that it was full to capacity and was instructed to go to New Delhi to the three hundred-year-old Gurudwara Rakabganj for accommodations.

We passed through Ajmeri Gate from the old city into New Delhi in a motorcycle rickshaw and I felt like I had just gone from one world to another. New Delhi was a planned city built by the British and has been the capital of India since 1912. (Delhi has been the capital city of a succession of empires and kingdoms and had occupied various sites in the Delhi triangle.) The population density varies from about a half to a fifth of that of Old Delhi and in contrast to Old Delhi's convoluted street plan, New Delhi has an orderly diagonal pattern. The streets are wide boulevards with lots of roundabouts. It exudes a feeling of openness and quiet.

Arriving at the Gurudwara Rakabganj we entered a huge compound to see a few small single-story buildings adjacent to a large temple structure under renovation with bamboo scaffolding surrounding it from top to bottom. Just behind the temple sits the Cathedral Church of the Redemption. The compound is opposite Parliament House, the Central Secretariat and Rashtrapati Bhavan (President's Estate), all of which are huge beautiful structures which occupy the Central Vista Park. Central Vista Park is the dominant non-architectural feature of New Delhi, the main east-west axis, along which are located all the governmental buildings, museums, and research centers. It divides the city in two, with the major shopping center, Connaught to the north and residential districts to the south.

After locking our backpacks into a small closet, I needed a smoke, so we walked outside the compound and around the corner to the Chai Walla. The Chai Walla is of major importance in India. Time is marked from one cup of tea to the next. He is the source of caffeine and the place to hang out while talking and smoking. Tea, tobacco and hash, are major pastimes. I spent quite a bit of time at this particular Chai Walla over the next two weeks. His shop was nothing more than a cart on wheels in the dirt between the road and the compound wall with a few stools around it.

All of New Delhi was in the midst of preparation for Republic Day, the celebration marking the anniversary of the formation of the first Independent Indian Government. It is celebrated with a huge parade in New Delhi. There is a military display, marching bands, and people from every province of India in their native dress marching down the Rajpath in the middle of the Central Vista Park from the National Stadium, past India gate and all the houses of government to the President's Estate. It is the most magnificent and colorful parade I have ever witnessed.

Delhi is a very dry climate and quite cold in the winter. One night after chai and smokes, all bundled up in a tan-colored plain woven Kashmiri shawl, we walked down the road a bit and noticed a huge park marked Talkatora Gardens. Inside the park we saw a lot of tents with small fires before them. As we walked into the gardens, I realized that these were the campsites of the visitors from provinces afar, come to participate in the Republic Day parade. It was like walking over a map of India. Each tent had a family from a different place in India. Assam, Nagaland, Kerala, Sikkim, Gujurat, U.P., H.P., Bengal, Rajasthan, Punjab, Orrisa, Bihar, Adhra Pradesh, Tamil Nadu, every state of India was represented. They were all in their native dress and spoke their native tongue. We were welcomed to each campfire we went to with open arms and great curiosity. Everyone, to a person, gave us a smile and welcome and attempted to communicate even though we had not more than a few words in common. These were not the educated people of their districts. These were the villagers, mostly, if not all, illiterate but full of innocence and love. It was another one of those magical times, walking from tent to tent, from campfire to campfire, and meeting people that were as strange to each other as they were to us; tent after tent, fire after fire, smoke-filled air, primitive warmth and hospitality stretched as far as the eye could see.

One afternoon we were sitting at the Chai Walla, having tea, smoking and watching a couple of nearby monkeys pick lice off each other in between fucking, and another westerner walked up and sat down next to us. We started talking about who was in town. One of the main topics that freaks on the road talk about when together is who is where. It's like a network grapevine that stretches around the world. He told us that there was a couple of freaks who were sick and in the nearby Lady Hardinge Hospital. One of them was named Surfer Sam. Aha! It was Sam Buell, the "friend" who ditched-out on us in Teheran with the two German girls, leaving us hanging with an Interpol kidnapping-minors rap over our heads. I hope the son-of-a-bitch dies! In fact, let's go watch him die!

We walked into the hospital room and there was Sam lying in bed looking weak under a bright red wool blanket. The minute I saw him I was no longer angry with him. He was a freak; a road brother; how could I stay mad at him?

There was Sam, all thin and suffering with something, I can't remember what now, malaria or hepatitis. I gave him a hug and he said he was sorry for betraying me like that in Teheran. I found out that they all went to the Persian Gulf for a week or two. Then he realized that he couldn't get out of Iran either. Unfortunately for him, he didn't have Ebrahim to bribe the officials for the exit visa, so the girls turned themselves in at the German Embassy and were repatriated. Sam got his exit visa and made it this far before succumbing to one of the bugs that all Indians are resistant to but to which foreigners frequently fall victim.

Unfortunately, if you have hepatitis, they could easily treat you for malaria and usually come close to killing you. In the next bed was an old man with no teeth and a two-week beard under a similar red blanket dying and with every exhalation he made a raspy sound from somewhere between his throat and his lungs that sounded like "WHHHHY?, WHHHHY?, WHHHHY?" Stoned out of my mind as I was, I thought it was cosmic. We visited once a day for a few days before leaving Delhi and that was the last time I ever saw Sam. I heard later that he went to the Philippines, got married, had kids, worked in Hong Kong and eventually died in the Philippines of some strange disease.

New Delhi was cool. It was not the least bit crowded with wide boulevards and empty streets. We would spend our days at Connaught Place and its inner ring Connaught Circus, comprised of 2-storyed arcaded buildings, ranged radially with long colonnaded verandahs. There were three circular roads with a huge wide-open park in the middle and eight radial roads leading in all directions from the center. They are architecturally very distinctive and very un-Indian; the opposite of Chandni Chowk. The shops in the circular roads were under huge colonnades and were the expensive places like airlines, American Express, Wenger's restaurant, etc. in the inner circle and then progressively less expensive as you go to the outer ring. The radial roads had the smaller shops like Kwality ice cream, musical instruments and smaller shoe stores and restaurants. We would spend our days sitting in the park smoking dope, watching people, getting every bone in my body cracked by the massage guy who wandered the park, eating peanuts from the monpalli walla (a big handful of roasted peanuts for char anna…25 Naya Paisa), wandering the fabric and handicraft shops of the Jan Path or sipping coffee under the tent of the Price Rise Resistance Coffee Shop at Inner Circle and Jan Path. Connaught Place had expensive shops and therefore one would encounter more educated and affluent people there also.

English was still the official language and widely spoken but a form of Edwardian English that is unique to India. For example, you would not be asked, "Where are you from?" rather, "What is your native country? You must be coming from the U.K, is it?" You would not be asked, "How old are you?" rather,

"What is your good age?" No one would say, "Let's go." but, "Shall we proceed?" or slangily, "Let's make a move." Quickly you figured out that if you were going to be understood, you had to speak like this, even imitate the pronunciation and accent. Otherwise you would end up repeating yourself over and over until you did it their way.

We had to make frequent visits to Old Delhi to score hash. Even though it was cheap, I still didn't want to score too much because scoring was part of the ritual and always an adventure. Scoring hash is almost always from Muslims. By the time we got to Delhi we were out of hash. We had assumed that it would be as easy to score in India as it was in Pakistan. It wasn't. In Pakistan you were never more than a few minutes away from a place where you could score. In India it was vastly more difficult. Once we asked a taxi driver where we could get some charce (charas). He took us to a whore house in old Delhi.

As we entered we were bade to sit on cushions on the rug covered floor. Minutes later a pasty white, skinny Caucasian junkie slithered down a ladder from a hole in the ceiling. He asked what we wanted, and we immediately realized that he was English and the proprietor of the brothel. We were able to score but by the time we were ready to leave word had spread that two white people were in the brothel. The entire staircase was filled with curiosity seekers. Soon near pandemonium broke out and as we tried to make a hasty exit, we were pawed by everyone on the way out. It seemed like a close call with a very unpleasant experience. This was one of the few times I ever felt like we were in danger in India.

While in Old Delhi, we would get some good inexpensive dal and chapattis at the Sher e Punjab, and whatever necessities were needed at the time, or just sit haggling with Kashmiri shopkeepers even though I had no intention of buying anything. I had to hone my bargaining skills and it was like a sport to both them and me. The game was simple: If you were selling something, you tried to get as much as possible for it. If you were buying, you tried to buy it for as little as possible. The result is that it can take a whole day or even a week of haggling, walking out and coming back or walking out and being called back, to buy a blanket, the seller giving all the reasons why he should get the price he is asking and the buyer giving all the reasons why it should not be so much. Eventually, if it goes on long enough, it will end up with the seller lamenting how he is losing money but because you are a guest in his country or are the first sale of the day (a good omen), or several other good reasons, even though it will be taking food from his children's mouths, he will sacrifice the item to you for the price you are willing to pay. Naturally, he is still making a profit. I got good at this sport. So good that Indians would send me to buy something for them from the bazaar because they said that I bought it cheaper than they could!

Then other days, it would be a journey in the other direction, like the American Consulate to get our mail. In New Delhi, because it is the capital, the consulate is located at the United States Embassy. Mail is a major event when you are on the road. Most freaks got their mail either at Poste Restante (general delivery) or at American Express. I preferred to get my mail at the consulate. The consulate was usually not as centrally located as AMEXCO but they usually had a good restaurant. In any case when you are as stoned as I was most of the time, if you went to the consulate and got your mail that day, you had done a lot. It was an all-day event what with stopping several times on the way to get your THC levels up and all. It was a trip to get wrecked and sit on the top level, front row of a red London double-decker bus, go barreling down a long boulevard and come to a roundabout leaning at an angle that you were sure could not be maintained without tipping over.

It was like a carnival ride, especially when you are stoned. The top left corner of every bus was caved in from hitting the trees that overhang the streets. Sometimes we would hitchhike around town. People with drivers would always stop for white people. But then you had to deal with the twenty questions, the most frequent in Delhi being "Have you seen the Qutab Minar?" I had seen the Red Fort and Jamma Masjid because they are just near Chandni Chowk and you will see them during your wanderings, but the Qutab Minar Complex was on the extreme outside of New Delhi to the south. In order to see it, you had to actually go there. So, if you answered that you have not seen it you got, "You have NOT SEEN the Qutab Minar? You MUST SEE the Qutab Minar." I did not want to go to the Qutab Minar because that would have indicated that I was a tourist and I was not a tourist, but a traveler!

Eventually, I got so sick of hearing that I MUST SEE the Qutab Minar and told the gentleman who had given us a ride to please take us there now. He immediately obliged and I did see the Qutab Minar, a twelfth-Century victory tower made of marble and red sandstone with incredible decorative carved features. It is one of the most beautiful historical sites I have ever seen and I'm glad I was forced to go there. I've been back several times since.

Chapter Ten

Agra and Kanpur

At the end of January we decided to mosey on down the road apiece. We hitchhiked to Agra in half a day, left our bags at the Sikh temple Gurudwara and started walking around the city. The first thing we noticed is that all the windows had bars on them. This is to prevent the monkeys from raiding the houses of food. The monkey population is huge, and they can be extremely aggressive and thieving. They will run right up to you on the street and rip the food out of your hand if they can.

Eventually we ended up at the Taj Mahal. What can be said about the Taj Mahal? It is considered one of the wonders of the world and anyone who sees it cannot fail to be moved. This monument of love literally glows even in the daylight. The architecture, materials and craftmanship are matchless. The vast expanse of pure white marble inlayed with semiprecious stones is a true wonder. But after all, it is a tomb and there is no life to be felt there. Unlike the Golden Temple, which is vibrant with life and feeling.

Agra was a bit touristy, so we moved east by third-class train to Kanpur where we first saw the Ganges River. At the time I was unaware of the spiritual significance of the Ganges to the Hindu population of India. I had little knowledge of Hinduism. I had read about it in high school but I still had the concept of God as "the phantom of the universe" who is "up there" somewhere judging who is good or bad, not that it mattered to me in any way, shape or form; I was, after all, invincible. I was about to get dipped.

Suddenly I was in the valley of the Hindus. There were no Muslims to be seen where hash could be scored or to smoke with. The Hindus that smoked dope were the Sadhus. Sadhus are the so-called holy men of India; itinerants who have renounced all worldly goods and travel about on foot in varying states of nakedness, some covered in only ash. They let their hair and beards grow and smoke hash, or mostly ganja (marijuana) I should say, (hash is expensive) and beg for their food. Wow! These guys had it all figured out. They just wandered around, did nothing but bullshit all day long and smoke dope. And they had the entire population feeling privileged to feed them.

As we pulled into the Kanpur train station I was stuck by how many monkeys you could see everywhere. They literally covered the rooftops. At the station I called a banana vendor over to the train window so I could buy a few bananas from him. He walked over to the window carrying a three-foot stalk of bananas. I told him I wanted four bananas, which he handed me through the train window. I gave him one rupee (equivalent to ten U.S. cents at the time.) Just as I handed him the one rupee note the train started to move out of the station. As he searched for change the train gained speed and he began running next to the train. Finally, he gave up trying to find change for the one rupee and, to my shock, threw the entire stalk of bananas through the train window to me.

As I passed bananas around to the people in the train I wondered if the whole stalk was one rupee, how much was one banana and how did this guy survive when he could sell the entire stalk of bananas for one rupee? The next day we arrived in Allahabad where we got off the train, slept in a gas station overnight, and moved on the next day to Benares.

Chapter Eleven

Benares, the holiest city

There are a lot of really *great* places in the world but there are only a few *unique* places. Benares is one of them. The name "Benares" is a corruption of the real name, Varanasi, derived from two streams, the Varuna on the north side of the city and the Assi on the south side. Hindus also call Varanasi "Kashi," The City of Light. It is an ancient city, visited by the Buddha in 500 BC and mentioned in both the Ramayana and the Mahabharata.

Benares is considered the holiest city in India and all Hindus dream of dying here. They believe that if they die here, are cremated and have their ashes thrown into the Ganges, that the cycle of birth and death is broken and they will have finished the game, breaking the cycle of birth and death and returning to the Godhead state of infinite consciousness. Each year over a million pilgrims come to Benares to bathe in the sacred river Ganges and cleanse their souls. Except for our visit to Sarnath, we never got out of the Old Town, a maze of narrow back lanes (galis) along the ghats (ghats in Varanasi are riverfront steps leading to the banks of the River Ganges.)

The city has eighty-eight ghats. Most of the ghats are bathing and puja ceremony ghats, while two ghats are used exclusively as cremation sites. Most Varanasi ghats were rebuilt after 1700 AD when the city was part of Maratha Empire.) The galis are exciting to walk through but easy to get lost in. Benares is famous for its ornamental brass work, silks and embroideries and glass beads. Shops line the narrow lanes and as you walk through them you can smell the perfume of faded frangipanies, rotting jasmine, burned myrrh, raised dust, dry bovine excrement and fetid water trickling under flat stones outside the buildings. Nobody seems to mind if a bull and cow mate in the middle of the lane, blocking all foot traffic in both directions.

The Ganges river ghats are the main attraction for visitors to Benares; wide steps leading down to the river. The most important Hindu temples and the burning grounds, where body cremations take place, flank the Ghats. Along with the smells mentioned above, the entire atmosphere has a tinge of the scent of burning flesh. There is a constant stream of processions carrying shrouded bodies through the streets to the ghats for cremation. Once there, they are placed on a pile of wood (how much and what type of wood depends on how much can be paid). Then a relative (the oldest son) performs a ritual by circling the pyre, pouring on different substances like ghee, milk, essences, etc. and then setting the pyre alight. Flames rush into the air and the family watches while their loved one's body burns. At some point the body may sit up and will be forced back down by an attendant with a large bamboo pole. He may even have to pop the head with a blow of his bamboo. Eventually the embers (or embers and body parts left unburned, if they are poor and cannot afford enough wood) are pushed into the Ganges. The healthiest dogs in India can be seen here as they dive into the river to fetch parts that have not been completely consumed by flames. Burning goes on day and night.

One day after stopping in the Government Ganja and Opium shop to score some ganja and Bhang, we came to the river to see the sun set. After dark a few Sadhus saw us smoking chillum and came to join us. We shared our smoke and with the English and Hindi words we had in common, they conveyed to us that they were very holy. They beckoned that we should come with them to one on the nearby temples.

We followed and sat with them while devotional songs were sung, and drums and cymbals were played. It was a magical, timeless moment, sitting in an ancient temple on the Ganges while the same songs were sung that have been being sung for centuries. At one point a gorgeous young Sadhu with long matted locks to his waist reached into his bag and handed me a very small book. "This is the answer to everything," he conveyed. I couldn't make out what it was in the dark, so I stuck it in my pocket and folded my hands together before me saying, "Shukria" (sweetness) "Mihrbani" (graciousness). (There is no real word for "thank you.") He beamed back to me impressed with my expressions of gratefulness. We smoked another chillum and parted ways.

We stayed the first night at the Gurudwara and the next day a man invited us to stay at his house in the old city, a lane or two away from the river front. The days were spent wandering the lanes getting stoned and selling the watches we had smuggled into India. They fetched anywhere from Rs. 100-200. Nights were spent at the burning ghats and temples.

One day we decided to go to Sarnath, one of Buddhism's major centers in India. When he had gained enlightenment at Bodh Gaya, the Buddha came to the deer park at Sarnath and delivered his first sermon there under a Bodhi tree. We took a bicycle rickshaw at a cost of one rupee & char annas—about twelve cents to go ten km.

Given its historical importance, I was surprised to see the neglected state of the stupas and the limited collection in the museum, although there were some magnificent pieces. Nevertheless, the deer park was a place of peace and reflection despite the distractions of loud transistor radios and young monks running around.

On the way back I had the driver stop at a shop for a moment and bought a mosquito net to protect us from the massive number of mosquitoes that gorged on our blood at night, making sleep nearly impossible. Considering the incidence of malaria and elephantiasis I considered the twelve rupees I spent on it a good investment and well worth the space and weight it took in my backpack. That net lasted many years and became one of my most important possessions.

We decided to relieve the rickshaw at that point, and he insisted on charging Rs. 16 for the trip back from Sarnath. Since I knew that the price should be Rs. 1.25 I refused to pay more. At that point the driver grabbed the mosquito net from my hand and refused to return it until I paid him. A shouting match ensued that attracted a crowd who had nothing better to do than watch Sahib blow his cool. Just at that moment a road-worker happened to walk by carrying a short-hoe in his hand. I grabbed the short hoe from his hand and raised it over the rickshaw driver's head. He put down the net, I gave him "ek rupiah, char anna," handed the hoe back to the road-worker and walked quickly away, sensing great danger in the air.

We spent that night in ecstasy. After chillums and singing at the temples, we had a glorious night of sleep beneath the cocoon of our newly-acquired mosquito net. Though we could hear millions of mosquitoes buzzing outside, inches away, we were safe and protected from their blood sucking, disease-spreading job.

The following day, after selling a few watches in the bazaar, I noticed a well-dressed official looking guy following us. We tried to ditch him by walking quickly through the small lanes in the opposite direction of where we were staying. Eventually we lost him and returned to our tiny heavenly abode so graciously shared by our host. Within one hour the guy who had been following us showed up at the door. He was C.I.D., Indian secret police. He interviewed us and said he had witnessed us selling watches in the bazaar, a serious crime for which we would surely spend years in jail. We, of course, denied everything.

He did not seem like he was asking for a bribe, nor was he in any hurry to haul us away as the interview took forever, as only Indians can drag things out, detailing the seriousness of the crime. Finally, he said that he would have to search our belongings entirely and would return in half an hour to do so. That ended our plan to stay in Benares for an extended period. We packed everything and were in a rickshaw with the curtains pulled up heading for the G.T. road within fifteen minutes, making a hasty escape from certain incarceration.

We made it as far as Patna that day going off the G.T. road to make our way to Kathmandu, in Nepal. We stopped at a Dhaba or roadside restaurant just after entering Bihar state, one of India's most backward places. The Dhaba is the happening place for drivers of the road. Usually just little mud and grass shacks with tin or leaf roofs under which the owner prepares food and tea at a wood fire over a stove made of dried dung and mud. Dhabas are usually surrounded by charpois (string beds) where the people of the road sit or lie and talk, eat, smoke, and carry on the latest gossip of the road. The G.T. Road Dhabas are vividly alive with throngs of people including jugglers, tumblers, holy men, blind men and mad men, widows, prostitutes, child brides, truckers and the occasional western road bum.

We stayed in Patna at the Sikh temple, which was beautiful and had two vegetable dishes at the langar meal in addition to the usual dal and chapattis.

The next day we made it to Muzafapur, not a far journey but made long by the fact that we had to take many ferries. We stayed at the Sikh temple again before hitching a truck ride to Birganj at the Nepali border, where we stayed overnight in a Hindu Dharmsala.

The next morning, at the border itself, was a line of trucks half a mile long parked by the side of the road, waiting for dawn, the time of departure. We started asking for rides and every truck driver wanted money. Ulli (The German gammler who told me about his trip to India) had told me about this spot and advised what to do. It was the only place I was ever asked for money from a truck driver for a ride. We just kept moving up the line until the first truck in line said he would take us without charging us. We started up through the Himalayan foothills through giant red rhododendron forests, getting colder by the minute. That night we slept in a log cabin a few miles outside Kathmandu and woke up freezing.

Chapter Twelve

Kathmandu

We left before dawn and entered Kathmandu just at sunrise. The truck dropped us off at a square and as we walked away from the truck, I noticed that there was not a living human to be seen and that there were hundreds of dead rats in the street. My first thought was that the entire city had been killed by the plague overnight. I later found out that those were just the rats that died of starvation overnight and that Nepalis are afraid of the dark. They don't come out until daylight.

We walked down the one paved street in town and saw a sign that read, "Hill View Hotel." We took two beds in a dormitory room that had about ten beds in it. There were six or seven other western road bums staying there. These were the first Westerners we had seen since Delhi.

The "scene" was at the Globe Café, a small four-table Tibetan restaurant with just enough room for the ten or twelve freaks who were in Kathmandu at the time to hang out all day, eating buffalo steaks, smoking dope and being hip. Dal and Suzie were a Westerner couple; he was a totally self-absorbed dirty freak and she a sweet Danish strawberry blonde skinny girl who didn't seem to belong there. I heard years later that he was murdered by dacoits.

Eight-finger Eddie was an American, older than the rest of us by at least fifteen years. Apparently, he had a savings that gave him enough interest income to live in Copenhagen in the summer and Morocco in the winter. This was his first trip to India. He had a room that he rented by the month, which gave me the idea to do the same. I rented a room with its own bath for ten dollars a month. Eddie smoked grass and never wanted to smoke hash with us. I heard that Eddie later was in the Goa/Anjuna Beach scene for years and lived his life out there as the guru to the hippies. Eddie died there in October 2010.

We met a French guy who had bicycled from France. He was a former Legionnaire and I don't know how or why he got out of the French Foreign Legion, but he was on his way to Vietnam because he'd heard that Vietnamese women were the most beautiful in the world. There was a tall, husky, clean-shaven American who played the guitar. He was more of a tourist who also just happened to fall into our scene. Legionnaire and Clean-Shaven didn't smoke dope. It made them *not* one of us, but they were harmless, pretty nice guys.

Our new room was on the second story, had colorfully tiled floor and a large beautifully carved wooden window frame with solid steel-hinged wooden shutters. There was no stove, so we had to go around the corner every morning to the Chai Walla to bring back chai. When Legionnaire came over to see it, he gave it a full military inspection. Noting the ceiling was low; he said it was "not guud forr worrk" pantomiming as if fucking in a standing position with a girl astride his hips, humping air.

One day, just before we moved to the new pad, a straight looking middle-aged man came to the Hill View and said his name was Hilmar Pabel, photographer for Stern Magazin in Germany. He had come to Katmandu to go on safari with the king but for some reason that was cancelled so, seeing us and our lifestyle, he wanted to do a story on the Freaks of the Road and asked if he could interview us and take some photos of us in various places in Kathmandu. I told him that would be no problem if the price were right. We agreed to a price, (enough for us to live a couple of months at our current rate of expenses) and he interviewed us and took dozens of photos. I never got to see the magazine, but I have a couple of pages from it that a German friend saw and cut out for me. I also later found out that Hilmar Pabel was a world-renowned photojournalist.

One day while sitting at the Tibetan Globe Café a man came and stood at the foot of the three cement steps leading up to the café itself. He had a large bundle in his hand. When I went out to see what he wanted to sell he set his bundle down on the steps and untied the old cloth rag. Inside was about a kilo of pure Nepali marijuana buds. I didn't particularly like to smoke weed at the time because hash was so available, but he only wanted ten rupees for the whole bundle, so I bought it. It was outrageously good. I asked him where he was from and he said, "From the mountains." No shit! There was no other place to *be* from! Anyway, I spread the bud around to everyone and it was consumed quickly. Every day we would hear someone say, "I wonder when the Man from the Mountains will come back."

I ran out of shit (hash) and had to go score. There was a very short middle-aged Nepali who squatted on the ground before a cloth piled high with weed every day in front of the post office. He was a funny looking guy; scrawny, bow-legged as hell, but always smiling. I went to ask him where I could score hash. He said I should give him the money and he would be right back. I scored a small amount of Temple Ball and knew for sure that he had at least doubled the price. One day I was scoring a pound for an American tourist for which I had again doubled the price. While I was dividing the shit up on the table at the Globe Café, I noticed that the envelopes that it came in had an address on them with arrows pointing to the address and a note saying, "Please come here, please you come here."

Aha! The Charce walla knew I was getting the price doubled and wanted to eliminate the middleman. I went straight to the address, which was a pharmacy above the post office. He had chests full of Temple Balls, big hard balls of hash. There were hundreds of pounds of hash. We struck a price and I scored directly from him after that and just doubled the price to the occasional tourist that wanted to score.

The Ganja Walla who sold in front of the post office figured out where I lived and knew I had hash, which he could not afford himself. Every morning at dawn, on his way in from the Valley to the city, he would stop under the window stringing together all the English words he knew into a song which he would serenade us with until we opened the door for him to come in and smoke hash. "NEVER MIND THE BIBI" was his usual song. I would load the chillum and Uschi would go around the corner to get tea for us all.

One day he told me that she was not a very good Bibi (wife) because her tea was always cold. He thought she had gone to the kitchen to prepare it and didn't know that she went to the Chai Walla in the freezing cold to fetch it for us. The last chillum of the day was smoked in bed before going to sleep and the first of the day was smoked in bed before getting up in the morning.

Kathmandu was also full of Tibetan refugees, the first we had seen since the incredible encounter in the tent at the Golden Temple in Amritsar. They were a beautiful and brave people. Some had walked for months over the roughest terrain in the world, leaving everything to escape Chinese oppression. Despite their desperate situation you would always see a smile on their faces and a proud upright stride. The men wore pants and stood to urinate. The men all wore an earring composed of a thread through the lobe with a bead of turquoise on one end and a bead of coral on the other, just like the Tibetan man I had met in Amritsar. I thought this was totally cool and adopted the custom immediately. Up to that time I had just had a tiny golden ball in my left ear. It had been pierced since New York City.

One day I was sitting on the steps of the Globe Café when a little boy of about eight years old hit me up for money. I was surprised he spoke a few words of English. English was common in India but rarely did anyone in Nepal speak English. He was as cute as can be and said his name was Krishna. I still had a couple of watches for sale so I told him I would pay him if he would take them one at a time to the bazaar and sell them for me. All went well until the final watch was being sold. Somehow, word got back to me that the police had Krishna in jail for stealing a watch. I went to the jail and asked what was going on. They said they had caught him selling the watch in the bazaar so he must have stolen it. I told them that I had given him the watch, that he had not stolen it and that I had asked him to sell it for me. The matter of what the hell I was doing selling watches in the bazaar was handled separately with a small gift to the officers.

I had really taken a liking to Krishna and he had become like a son to me. I thought it would be good to teach him how to make money from tourists without begging. I took him to a bookstore where they sold English textbooks and made an agreement with the owner: Krishna would come here with tourists, they would buy the English textbook for ten rupees and Krishna would return it later for him to buy back for five rupees. Then I taught Krishna to approach tourists, looking clean and cute and tell them that he will give them a free tour of Kathmandu just so that he can practice his English. Eventually they will ask how he had learned what English he has, and he can tell them that he wants to learn more but the book costs ten rupees. It worked every time! He could do it once or twice a day. In a matter of days Krishna was making more in a day than his father made in a week.

One day Krishna told us that his eleven-year-old sister was getting married that morning and begged us to come to his house and share in the wedding party. We walked across Kathmandu City and into the valley. I kept asking how far it was and he kept saying just a little further. After what seemed like an interminable walk (it was probably more like an hour) we approached a small mud hut with a dirt floor.

His wedding party was small, but the bride had not yet gone

to the groom's home. She was a child in women's dress wearing exaggerated makeup. I had to bend over to enter the small doorway. The wedding had already taken place, but Krishna wanted me to share the food. I was really pissed-off that he had forced me to walk halfway across Kathmandu Valley, so I was more or less seething when I sat down on a short stool before a wood fire. The whole hut was smaller than my little room in Kathmandu. Krishna walked over to me and held his hand out. I opened my hand, palm up, and he poured about a tablespoon of dried oatmeal into my palm. I looked at his sweet, beaming, proud face and realized that this was the wedding feast. I have never been so humbled in my entire life.

My anger disappeared instantly as I saw how proud he was that I had come to his family's dwelling and with what love he shared the little that they had. I looked at the dried oatmeal and deliberately ate every grain, savoring it as if God had handed it to me. I held his hand all the way back to the city. The day we left Kathmandu Krishna and I wept in each other's arms.

Another "Krishna" incident happened in Kathmandu, but this time it was another Krishna, the one that my little friend was named after. One day I pulled out the little book that the Sadhu in Benares had given me. It was the Bhagavad-Gita - the Song Divine - a Hindu scripture that forms part of the great Indian epic the Mahabharata ("Great Epic of the Bharata Dynasty"). It was written in Sanskrit with English translation. The Gita is written in the form of a discourse between the two main characters Prince Arjuna and his friend and charioteer, Krishna, who is also an earthly incarnation (avatar) of the god Vishnu, the Preserver. The poem consists of 700 Sanskrit verses divided into 18 chapters. The moment I began to read the introduction I knew that something was happening to me that had never happened before. The words seem to resonate in my heart, not just register in my mind. The introduction starts out by saying:

"Truly speaking, none has power to describe in words the

glory of the Gita, for it is a book containing the highest esoteric doctrines. It is the essence of the Vedas; its language is so sweet and simple that man can easily understand it after a little practice; but the thoughts are so deep that none can arrive at their end even after constant study throughout a life-time," which was exactly what I experienced when reading the Gita for the first time. I knew, deep in my heart, that there was way more to this than I could immediately grasp. I had never had any intellectual deficit or lack of intelligence that had prevented me from understanding even the deepest western philosophy. But this was different. I felt compelled to re-read it repeatedly. This started a quest that lasted over the next year to find the meaning of life from a small book. I remembered Pop Schedel, my high school teacher, asking me if I knew what existentialism is. I had looked up the definition and he gave me a golden toothed sly smile while saying, "You never know," when I asked him what it meant that, "man's essence precedes his existence." Was I about to finally figure it out? My intuition told me the answer was yes.

We got a truck ride to Raxaul, which is the Nepal/Indian border town, then took a train overnight to Patna. The next morning, we hitched a truck ride through Bihar, again on the Grand Trunk Road, traveling through Bengal, sleeping in the truck that night and arriving in Calcutta the next day.

Chapter Thirteen

Calcutta

We crossed Hugli River, a branch of the Ganges, on the Howrah Bridge, witnessing the sorriest state of humanity I had ever seen: beggars dressed in filthy rags and children barely covered and nothing but skin and bones. We got a room at the Kalighat Sikh temple, put up our mosquito net, took a shower and headed for Chowringee area in Central Calcutta. There we found the Maidan, the world's largest urban park covering over 1,300 acres. We didn't stray too far into the park itself, mostly sitting on the edge near Chowringee where the happenings are, smoking endless chillums, one after the other, day after day.

Calcutta's streets were mostly narrow and in very poor condition. Motorized transportation was rare. Here I first saw human-pulled rickshaws. It was extremely hot. I have never seen so many undernourished people in my life. There were beggars everywhere.

They had a streetcar system that we used to go about town, especially from the Sikh temple to the town center. One day while waiting at the streetcar stop, I saw a gunny sack lying on the sidewalk. I noticed a leg and foot of skin and bone sticking out from under it. I waited for it to move but it did not. Just then two men dressed in rags pulled up in a cart, lifted the dead body and threw it onto the cart and took it away. Their job was to pick up the bodies of those who had died overnight on the streets.

We stayed at that Sikh temple and the chief priest talked with us. We were flat broke when we got to Calcutta and told him so. He had this wooden money box, and every morning when we went to see him, he opened the money box and gave us two Rupees for the day; a rupee each. He also gave us a note to give to the Chai Walla down the road for free chai. And then we took the streetcar without buying a ticket to Chauringee and bought and sold newspapers.

In order to get some cash, we purchased a small stack of *Times of India* newspapers and in Chowringee we approached the best dressed men we could find and asked them to buy a newspaper. We had paid maybe fifty paisa, and we told them they could pay whatever they wanted and most gave us ten rupees.

We had student IDs printed at a local print shop with the name "Johann Wolfgang Goethe University" on them, and a rubber stamp made of the same. We forged student ID cards, which we turned in to Garuda Airlines and got fifty percent off the ticket to Bangkok. We then made more ID cards for other travelers and sold them. The "portrait scheme" was created so that we could get permission to buy the airline tickets in rupees. To prove that we could only earn rupees, not dollars, we got some guy to come with us to the Reserve Bank of India to testify that he had purchased a portrait which I painted of him and that he had paid us in rupees, thus we gained the permission to buy the already discounted air ticket with rupees.

Since we were planning to go from Calcutta to Bangkok one of the things we had to do was to get a Thai visa. There was only one way to go and that was by air. The plane stopped in Rangoon but since Burma did not allow tourism and the plane landed on one day and left on the next, one had to get a 24-hour visa for Burma. Plane fares were expensive by our standards and we wanted to pay in black-market rupees and not dollars, which would have been double the cost. We were told that the only way we could pay in rupees was to get a letter from the Reserve Bank of India stating that we had their permission.

The bank told us that we would have to prove that we'd gotten the rupees from a source other than having brought them into India or bought them with dollars. One day, while contemplating how to accomplish this, a young Bengali struck up a conversation with us in the Maidan over a chillum. He asked all the usual questions but also happened to ask me when my birthday was. It happened that it was my birthday on that very day. He said he would be right back.

He returned after a short time with a package that he said was a birthday present for me. I opened it and found a western style white shirt. By this time, I wore only Indian clothing mostly white Punjabi style pajamas and either a white Lucknow Kurta (shirt) or a saffron colored shirt which I had tailored in Benares. I told him I could not possibly accept such a generous gift from someone I didn't even know. He begged me to accept so I told him I would accept it on one condition, that he sign a statement that he had purchased a painting from me that I had myself painted for exactly the amount I needed for the plane fare to Bangkok. He agreed, and the letter was executed.

I took the letter to the officials at the Reserve Bank and they said that this letter proved that I had not brought the rupees into India or purchased them while there. They said that unfortunately, it was not legal for foreigners to earn money while in India without a work permit. I told them that I did not actually earn the money or sell the painting, but that it was a gift to my friend and that he had also made a gift to me of the money that I needed to leave India. After a few days of haggling and they making every possible hint that I could make a gift to them also (which I pretended not to get), they finally gave me the permission. Persistence pays in India. If you can outwait the other guy, it usually works.

The Reserve Bank was quite a scene. The officials sat behind large desks with piles of file folders lined up against the wall behind them one after the other in pile that required ladders to reach the top. This was their idea of organization. Another amusing entertainment during my days at the Reserve Bank was to watch Bengalis enter the bank as if they had business to do and take a ride on the only escalator in India. They would try to be nonchalant, take the escalator up to the first floor and walk back down. They would glance around and, if no one was noticing them, take another ride.

With visas and tickets in hand we could now relax and enjoy the days. Showers had to be taken early in the morning because the metal tank that held water was on the roof of the Sikh temple and by noon the water was so hot you could not bear to bathe with it. Temperatures were going over 40 (104 F) degrees every day.

A few days before leaving Calcutta, we were sitting at the Maidan and a baby chipmunk came up to me, begging for peanuts. I picked him up and put him in my shirt pocket. The pockets of the kurta are sewn into the side seam at the bottom. I fed him, and he lived in my pocket. He was my new pet.

I had been stoned twenty-four hours a day for over a year at this point. Although I was still thinking clearly, I took chances that were outrageous. For instance, one day it was so hot that we decided to go sit inside the American Consulate where it was air-conditioned. Before long we realized that we were getting behind on our hash smoking, so I mixed up a batch and filled a cigarette in the Pakistani fashion and we smoked hash in the lobby of the air-conditioned American Consulate. Hash smoke was billowing throughout the consulate and we were acting as if this was quite ordinary.

The next step was to figure out how to get a kilo of hash and a kilo of weed across the Burmese and Thai borders without getting busted. We only had one small backpack each, and with our toiletries, a change of clothes, sleeping bag and mosquito net, it just wouldn't fit. Besides, it is impossible to conceal something that would have taken up half the backpack. I decided to put it all in a small pishvi, a shopping bag made of jute, put a towel over the top with a bar of soap, toothbrush and toothpaste on top, and just carry it in hand.

We took a bus to Dum Dum Airport to the north of Calcutta and boarded our flight to Rangoon. Goodbye India, for now.

Chapter Fourteen

Out of India: Rangoon

After a very short flight to Rangoon we landed and were told that if we took our bags with us, we would be required to go through customs but since we were scheduled to leave early the next day, we could leave our bags at the airport and avoid customs. No decision there! I just took my pishvi in hand and walked straight to immigration. I set the bag down on the floor and leaned it against the counter out of view of the immigration officer. I gave him my passport and immunization record. While he was examining my passport, the chipmunk scampered out of my pocket and up my shirt and sat on my shoulder. I quickly grabbed him and stuck him back into my pocket, avoiding discovery.

The immigration official examined my papers and started shaking his head and saying, "Hmm." He looked up at me and said, "Mr. Hamilton, would you mind stepping into that room over there," gesturing over my shoulder. My heart went into my throat. I thought, "This is it. I'm busted on the Burmese border and will never see the light of day again." The official then said, "You won't believe this, but your cholera shot expired yesterday and before we can allow you to enter Burma it will be necessary to give you a booster shot. If you don't mind stepping into that room, it will only take a minute and, of course, there will be no charge."

"No problem!" I replied. I picked up my pishvi walked into the room, got my shot and walked out into Burma. We boarded a bus that drove us into town by way of Cocaine Road. Wow, this place was so hip, even the street names were cool!

We checked into a hotel on Shwedagon Pagoda Road. By the time we had checked in and eaten it was dark. We wandered outside and started chatting with a taxi driver. He asked if we had seen the Shwedagon Pagoda. When we replied that we had not he said he wanted to take us there; it was a short distance, but we should go in his taxi. I had never even heard of it.

We agreed but first he had to buy gas. Apparently, gas was so hard to get and so expensive that the taxi drivers waited until they got a fare, and then bought the gas on the black market from guys on the street with cans. We got a gallon of gas and drove to the pagoda. It was the most incredible stupa I had ever seen. It was a gilded from top to bottom and over 300 feet tall with a 76-carat diamond at the top of its vane. According to legend, the pagoda is 2,500 years old. Archaeologists believe the stupa was actually built sometime between the 6th and 10th centuries by the Mon king and his people, but this is a very controversial issue because according to the records by Buddhist monks it was built before Lord Buddha died in 486 BC.

Chapter Fifteen

Nightmare in Bangkok

The next morning, we went by bus back to the airport, collected our baggage and boarded the plane for Bangkok. In Bangkok we found a small hotel, the Thai Song Greet, near the Walampong, the main train station. It was only a dollar a night. It was bloody hot in Bangkok. *Never* go to Bangkok in April!

Everything was different from India. The people were less friendly, inquisitive or even interesting, for that matter. It seemed that they could only see dollars when they saw us. Each shop had a little fake tree with Bhat tied to the branches. It was a little money tree. I guess it was supposed to bring good business or something. About forty percent of Thailand was Chinese. The food was completely different than we were used to. The iced coffee was great, though. I drank them all day long. We ran into a few westerners that warned us against the local whiskey (not that we would have been as un-hip as to drink alcohol anyway). They said that a few people had become temporarily blind or paralyzed from it. There were a lot of U.S. soldiers on R&R from Vietnam in town; I guess that's why the locals saw only dollars when they saw us. I was still dressed in Indian clothing and hadn't shaved or cut my hair for over a year.

With the money we made selling hash in Kathmandu and then converting it to dollars, we had about five hundred dollars. Since we were planning to go to Japan and then back to California, I figured I was going to need more. We bought travelers checks, had someone cash them, and then reported them stolen, doubling our money. I realize that this is completely unethical and dishonest but at the time, as you can tell from some of the other tales I have related, we were young, foolish and, at times, stupid. At the time it didn't cross my mind that it was not ethical. They had all the money and we had none.

Thailand was more expensive than India. We were spending more on our hotel every night than it had cost for two to live a whole day or two in India. I wasn't worried, though because I just never worried about money.

We had short visas and before I knew it, the expiration was only two days away. I had been spending my days getting stoned and taking five or six showers a day just to stay sane in the heat. Anyway, we went to the immigration office to extend our visas. While waiting to be seen by an official, we met a large, middle-aged American who said he was the distributor for A.M.F. in South East Asia. He had formerly owned Air Lao, which had been federalized, and he'd lost everything. He said he was driving to Penang in Malaysia and would be happy to give us a ride in his big Cadillac.

The corrupt official interviewing us for our extensions said we would have to prove that we had at least $150 USD before he could extend our visas. I said we had it, but he wanted to see it. I laid the money on the table and he put his hand on it. I put my hand on top of his and removed the money. He wanted it as a bribe to extend our visas. He said he would not be able to extend.

I said fine, and that we would leave Thailand immediately. He asked how we intended to leave. I replied that we would go by road to Malaysia to which he replied that since my visa was only good for two days and it would take at least three days to reach the border, he may as well just put us in jail now. I said he could not put us in jail now, as we were not yet in violation.

"Fine! You want your visa extended? I will extend it for you." The tone of his voice scared me. He picked up both passports and walked out of the room and down the hall. He was walking out the door with our passports, our only valuable possessions.

I walked down the hall after him, came abreast of him, grabbed the passports out of his hand and we ran out of the building. Fortunately, the American with the Cadillac, whom I had by now nicknamed Web (because the monogram of his initials on his shirt was W.E.B.) was just pulling out of the parking lot. We jumped in the back of his Caddy and asked if the offer was still good for the ride to Malaysia and he said yes. We drove off with the official giving chase.

We stayed overnight a Web's girlfriend's house and loaded the Caddy the next morning and hit the road south. Now this was traveling in style! We stayed in a Hotel in Huahin that night. After giving me enough time to take a shower, there was a knock on the door. I opened the door and there stood a cute young lady, maybe sixteen years old or so, a Thai prostitute. She worked for the hotel and was part of the hospitality. She didn't seem to mind in the least that my wife was in the room when she offered her services.

The next day was pretty much the same except that the Ullu (jungle) got more dense. The road was now just a path of dirt through the jungle or hardwood forest. Where the road stopped, the jungle began. There were chameleons six feet long hanging from the sides of trees, elephants crashing around, and a cacophony of jungle sounds. We stayed that night at a hotel in Ranong. The same scene was repeated with another young Thai prostitute. The next day the road became really wet and we got stuck repeatedly in the mud, having to be pulled out by a bulldozer or an elephant, each time at some expense. I was told that some vehicles get so mired in the mud that they were abandoned.

Once while being pulled out of the mud by an elephant I looked out the window and saw a bus that had come from the other direction up to its axles in mud. Just then I saw a long white neck craning out the window to examine the situation. It was Roger, my long-lost brother from Germany! We scampered out of our respective vehicles and embraced while ankle-deep in mud. He said he was on his way from Borneo to Bangkok. I told him that Bangkok sucks and he should get in the car and go to Singapore with us, which he did. He was out of dope and was happy to find that I had a kilo of hash and a kilo of weed. That night we stayed in a hotel in Pang Nga. The same scene repeated itself with the hotel hooker.

The next day was still yet more jungle, still yet more mud, still yet more being towed and again, at the hotel in Hadjai, near the Thai/Malaysian border, more gorgeous Thai hookers even cuter and younger than those before. Though our visa had expired, they were all but asleep at the border and gave us a routine stamp. We had escaped.

Chapter Sixteen

Malaysia and Saigon

There was a noticeable difference as we crossed the Thai/Malaysian border. First, the roads were better than I had seen since leaving Germany. It was no Autobahn but there were two full lanes with a line down the middle of smooth paved asphalt. Web told me that since rubber was one of the main crops in Malaya, the roads were rubberized; that's why they were so smooth. Web cranked up the Caddy, cruising at speeds at which I had not traveled for over a year. It was a little scary, but exciting. The landscape was completely different, too. To the east about twenty kilometers was the Andaman Sea at the point where it becomes the Strait of Malacca, separated from us by a huge swamp forest that made the first town we visited inaccessible by sea. Alor Star (or Alor Setar - I saw it spelled both ways) was a neatly laid out town on the West Bank of the Kedah.

We stopped for breakfast and traveled further toward Butterworth through the extensive paddy rice fields of the Kedah plain with Web giving me an education about Malaya on the way. "Remember, the Chinese own the businesses, the Malays hold all the government jobs and the rest of the Malays are either rubber tappers or fisherman." By noon we were in Butterworth, on the northwest coast of Malaya. It lies on the Perai River and faces George Town on Penang Island. It is a railhead for goods like rubber and tin leaving the area and oil coming in. It was only a two-mile ferry ride across the Penang Straight to George Town. Penang is a free port, which generally means you can buy anything from anywhere at about the best prices on earth. There is also a certain underworld intrigue and undercurrent of shady business that accompanies all the free ports I have seen, a certain aliveness that comes with the territory. It was the first and only place I had been where the purely Chinese architecture was completely preserved.

Web left us off at the Sikh temple. I was sad to leave Web. He was a nice guy and reminded me of my stepfather. I wasn't sad to leave the horrible stench of the king fruit (durian) that permeated the entire Caddy. Web's girlfriend had brought a case of it from Bangkok for her relatives in Penang. It smelled like rotten eggs the whole trip!

After leaving our backpacks at the Sikh temple, we explored George Town, got high in the park, and had mei (noodle) soup lunch from a street vendor. Penang "Betel Nut Island" is an extremely culturally diverse spot showing influences of the earliest Indian settlers and the subsequent Portuguese, Dutch and British settlers. Two hundred years ago it was a jungle. It was ceded to the British East India Company and became a major trading port for tea, spices, china and cloth. Rich traders built their villas there and sent their children to school. In the narrow streets of the old fort section of George Town the architecture is purely Chinese. Also, on the outskirts of George Town are major tin-smelting facilities, rice and coconut oil milling, and manufacture of soap, rattan and bamboo articles.

It is a bustling town, very clean, organized, and friendly. The food was cheap and delicious. We stayed a couple of days. The weather was a relief; it was clean, the food was good, the Sikh temple was free, and we had plenty of hash. We were set.

Leaving Penang, we were back on the road hitchhiking again for the first time since India, this time on good roads in a beautiful tropical climate. We got to the town of Ipoh that evening. It is the nation's tin mining capital, located in West Malaya on the Kinta River on the flat plain in the Kinta Valley just west of the Cameron Highlands. It is surrounded by steep hills, except to the south. It is named after a local tree whose poisonous resin was once used by Aboriginals for hunting. The countryside was pockmarked with huge sandpits from which ore had been extracted. The foothills were covered with rubber plantations. The town was spacious with a rectangular layout. We stayed at the Sikh temple.

The next morning, we got as far as Seramban and parked ourselves in the Sikh temple once again. Seramban is located on the Linggi River on the Strait of Malacca. It originated as a tin mining settlement, but rubber production was now the town's main activity. We saw extensive paddy rice in the valley of the Main Range to the east. The Singapore-Kuala Lumpur road passed through the town.

May Day of 1965, we went to Port Dickson, only a forty km hitch. Port Dickson used to be used as a major port to export tin but was now largely a seaside resort with a fishing village.

We could see oil refineries along the sandy coastline with tankers anchored offshore. We met a nice Chinese man named David Lim. He took us to his house and offered to let us to stay as long as we wished. In the evening he put on a feast for us, the likes of which I had never seen: a twelve-foot table full of thirty different dishes.

David was extremely nice to us considering he was a completely straight Chinese businessman and we were total freaks. I think one of the things that gave us an advantage over other travelers of our type was that, unlike most, we kept ourselves extremely clean and well-groomed in spite of the fact that I had long hair and a beard. Roger was one of the few road bums that looked "normal." One of the first things David asked us was if we were "R.C." I had no idea what he was talking about. "Roman Catholic" he explained, "Are you R.C.?" He was R.C. and hoped we were too.

We stayed a few days with David and his family and had a great time. He taught us a lot about the history, culture and politics of Malaysia. One of the things he told us was that the "real, old Malaya" was on the east coast. We decided that after going to Singapore to book our passage to Japan, we would visit the east coast.

May 5th, we started for Singapore and were picked up by a British couple from K.L. in a Land Rover. He was a Sergeant in the British Air Force, stationed in Kuala Lumpur and she was his wife. They were very nice and when we told them we were planning to stay in Singapore for a few days and then travel north again they invited us to stay with them for some time. They were on their way to Singapore to attend a going-away party for the Commanding Colonel. They gave us the name of their hotel and we set a time to go to their hotel to finalize plans to ride back to K.L. with them.

We checked into the Queen Street Sikh temple. It's a classic. And one of those Asian traveler bottlenecks where everybody comes through sooner or later. I loved Singapore. One degree north of the equator, the weather was perfect. I thought I could live there. A free port, it was bustling but funky. The most cosmopolitan place I had seen. The mix of Chinese, Malay and Indian along with legendary free-wheelin' "Sin City" status it held was intoxicating.

Parts were bordering on modern; other parts were old and ramshackle. The Mercedes Benz on the street next to the bicycle rickshaws was emblematic of the city itself. My world was of the bicycle rickshaw or trishaw. Across the street from the Sikh temple was a Chai Walla (tea stall) on wheels with five or six low wooden stools. This was our hangout. We would sit here for hours on end drinking tea and smoking hash and talking with fellow road bums. The travelers on this side of the Bay of Bengal were mostly English. It just seemed like when an Englishman headed east, the logical end was Australia. Not just the "overlanders," immediately identifiable by their boots, shorts and hats, but also the road travelers from England seemed to end up in Australia. We would occasionally bump into an over-lander, but they hung out in different places than we did. They were like campers on the move. They annoyed me and I felt they were poseurs. I took pride that I wasn't one of them; I was a real traveler with no end goal and no timetable.

Queen street, ahhh Queen Street. The Chai Walla was a breath of fresh air. I hadn't had real chai since India: rich, strong, sweet, nourishing. At the end of the block was Bugis Street, by day food stalls, by night a hooker's paradise. The Chinese whores were beautiful ranging in age from fourteen to fifty. The fifty-year old ones were usually pretty worn-out looking but probably cheaper. It was a haven for ladyboys.

Our food came mostly from street food vendor's wheeled carts. Chinese noodle soup stalls were a constant, as were the fruit carts. Huge varieties of tropical fruits cut up, on skewers, resting on a bed of ice were to be had for pennies. You could buy a whole pineapple artfully skinned and quartered before your eyes for a nickel.

We went to the hotel to meet the sergeant and his wife to arrange to go back to K.L. with them. They were in their thirties. He, I don't remember very well; I didn't have much contact with him. She was a tall and large but not overweight woman and quite attractive. They were getting ready for the going-away party for the colonel. She was wrapped in a towel and he was in the other room bathing and getting dressed. As we sat and talked, I rolled a cigarette between my fingers, emptying the tobacco into my other palm. I heated a big chunk of hash, mixed it with my thumb into the tobacco in my palm and refilled the cigarette. I lit it up, took a few hits and passed it to Uschi. She took a couple of hits and passed it to the Natalie. Natalie started smoking it like she had seen us smoke and didn't pass it on. I asked her if she was going to pass it and she said, "No, I'll smoke this one. Make another for yourself."

I mixed another batch and lit another and continued getting high. After we finished smoking, the sergeant returned to the room and mentioned to Natalie that she had better get a move on or they would be late for the party and it would look bad. She got the giggles and started laughing at him and told him how ridiculous he looked in his "monkey suit" and how stupid he sounded saying they would "look bad." "Who gives a damn about that stupid colonel anyway? I'm not going, you look and act like a perfect ass!" He realized that she was stoned out of her mind and tried to guide her from her chair to the bathtub. My last view of her that night was of her naked in the tub laughing hysterically.

The next day Uschi, Roger and I went back to their hotel to meet them for the trip north. Neither one of them said a word about the party and neither did I. The trip to K.L. was uneventful. We arrived at their home on the base. It was a nice little cottage with a nice yard and lawn. I spent the days in her library reading about Malayan mysticism (really, it was about the Malay Bomos, witch doctors), listening to their stereo, wrestling with their Great Dane on the lawn, and smoking hash. Natalie took quite a liking to the hash and was by my side day and night for the chance to get high again. Pretty soon Sarg started complaining that his tea (supper) wasn't ready when he came home and pretty much nothing else was getting done either. He would ask what we did today, and she would say, "Oh, we went horseback riding and got high." Eventually he told her that she had to get rid of us. She wept in my arms as she told me. "How will I get high if you are gone, where will I get more hash?" It had only been a few days and in her mind, she was hooked. I gave her a big chunk of hash and we moved to the K.L. Sikh temple. We stayed there one day and the following day we hitched to Kuantan.

Kuantan is on the eastern coast of the Malay Peninsula at the mouth of the Kuantan River, on the South China Sea. It is the most important east coast port, shipping tin, rubber and copra south to Singapore for export. It's the only east coast town with a direct road link to Kuala Lumpur so it is a transfer point for westbound travelers. If you visit the east coast, you pretty much must go through Kuantan.

Traveling north through Pehang State along the South China Sea, the region's thinly settled population is Maylay, Chinese, and semi-nomadic Aboriginals. Pahang is mostly dense jungle but there are several rivers resulting in deltas and plains. Malay farmers and fishermen live along the rivers and coast. Along the coast is a twenty-mile wide expanse of alluvial soil. The villages are Malay fishing villages, quite primitive and idyllic. The beaches are beautiful, empty of population and dense with coconut trees up to about twenty feet from the water. You could see the fishermen with their boats pulled up onshore tending to their nets, seemingly oblivious of the beauty of the place they inhabited. The coconut harvesters with their trained monkeys who they sent up the trees to knock down the coconuts were a ragged poor bunch and I never saw them together. It was just one man and his monkey. I guess "birds of a feather flock together" because I have never seen any of these groups interact with one another.

The next night after our stay in Kuantan we slept on the beach near Besarah where we met a Canadian named Dave. He had a pet baby gibbon named Boomer. We had a ball laying in the shade of the palm trees, swimming in the warm waters of the South China Sea, playing with Boomer on the beach and, of course, smoking hash all day and night.

The next night we stayed in a church in Kuala Trenganu where we were invited by the priest to stay.

Now we had entered Kelentan State, in northeastern Malaya. Its border with Thailand is mountainous jungle. Our last stop was Kota Bharu, the capital of Kelentan on the east levee of the Kelantan River. We stayed for a couple of days, the first night at the home of an Irish priest and the next night at the Sikh temple.

The next day we headed south, stopping at Kuantan again

and the following day back to Singapore. Once again ensconced at the Queen Street Sikh temple, we enjoyed Singapore again with all its luxuries. Ahhh...back to the Chai Walla again. We had five days in Singapore before boarding the Messageries Maritimes (M.M.) Line's *Laos* for Saigon, Hong Kong and Kobe, Japan on May 24, 1965.

The first dinner on the Laos was the first western food I had eaten for many a moon and even though we were "economy class" (seventy-five dollars from Singapore to Kobe), it was delicious and always ended with a cheese course of Camembert and Brie. Before the first meal, the maître de stood before us and in a very thick French accent announced. "Zis ees economee, you do not want…you get!" I was perfectly satisfied. The cabins were segregated with four men or women to a cabin. The first night we slept at sea and the following morning when we awoke, we were entering the mouth of the Mekong, heading toward Saigon.

The Mekong delta is huge, and it takes about two and a half hours to get to Saigon. After we docked, we went into Saigon. It was wartime and that was evident everywhere from the military vehicles and personnel to the sounds of bombs going off in the distance. We went into a bar to get a cold drink. It was a long thin railroad-car type place with small tables lined up along a wall. We ordered colas and the large American black man that waited on us said, indicating with a head nod toward Uschi, but looking me straight in the eyes, "Some of the people think it's weird, you bein' here. Now me, it don't matter, but the people, you understand… the people." I turned around in my seat and looked beyond the bar where I saw a line of very young and beautiful Vietnamese hookers standing at the curtained entrances of booths just big enough for a bed and separated only by curtains. We were in a whorehouse! I left a couple of bucks on the table and we split.

The first thing I noticed in Saigon was that the women were incredibly beautiful and well-groomed. They were tall and thin with beautiful complexions and invariably pretty feet. They walked with a self-assured stride. The Legionnaire in Katmandu had told me that he was on his way to Vietnam because they are the most beautiful women on earth. Now I saw it with my own eyes and could definitely not disagree.

As we walked down the street, I could see the French influence, everything from French lingerie shops to sidewalk cafes. Even in a city in the middle of war, it was beautiful. I was amazed how happy everyone seemed to see us and amazed at their cheerfulness evidenced by the smiles on their faces. We passed the U.S. Embassy, which was blockaded under heavy security. Any cars going in were searched thoroughly even using mirrors on poles to look at the underside for bombs.

That night we slept onboard the *Laos* in port. On deck we could see bomb flashes in the distance and hear their sound a few seconds later. It reminded me of watching lightning when I was a kid but way more solemn.

Uschi was just as curious and observant as I was and we were both totally devoted to each other. I think she got a little road weary earlier than I did and at times I thought she felt like I was dragging her around the world for no reason, which I guess I was. It would take a long time for her to be thankful for it. We were great companions at the time with a shared sense of adventure, wonder and romance.

On the way to Hong Kong an interesting thing happened that sealed my friendship with the purser. He always stood in the dining hall with his hands locked behind his back, watching everyone eat at dinnertime. One evening I saw that he was missing. I immediately thought about Boomer the Gibbon in my cabin. We had given him a sleeping pill, put him in a backpack and smuggled him aboard. I went immediately to my cabin and there was the purser, chucking Boomer under the chin. He looked at me, smiled, and said in French, "The ape is O.K. but" and then pointing to the opium pipe on the counter, looking more solemn, said, "Attencion feur."

After two days of sea travel, we landed in Hong Kong on the Kowloon side. As we walked along Navy Street, the hawkers were everywhere. "A1 Johnny?" A1 is the best class of heroin. (There is A2 and A3 too.) It is pure heroin in powder form. It is so pure that they smoke it in a bong. We didn't buy any. Hong Kong is a free port also but didn't have the charm for me that Singapore had.

We explored Kowloon, taking a funicular to the top of Victoria Peak. This was the first time I discovered that I have a fear of cables. It was a small, open train-like affair, on tracks, hauled up the hill by a cable. At each stop it would bounce forwards and backwards a few times and you could see the cable stretch like a rubber band in front of the train. I was certain it was going to give way and we would go sailing backwards down the hill. We took the bus back down. That night we slept onboard and sailed for Kobe the next day. It took four days to get there.

Chapter Seventeen

Neat & Tidy Japan

When we landed in Kobe, we headed down the gangplank and I could see into the huge open sheds of the Japanese customs. They were tearing everybody's luggage apart. I had a kilo of hash and a kilo of grass in my backpack and panicked. We did a U-turn and went back to the purser, with whom I had struck up a friendship and told him how we had to go straight to Tokyo by hitchhiking and since it was evening and we had no place to stay in Kobe, I would be extremely grateful if we could sleep onboard that night and leave the next day. He agreed. The next morning when we walked down the gangplank into Japan. There was no one in sight. We walked past a small hut where two customs officials asked us if we had any whiskey in our packs and we said no. They motioned us to go ahead. Whew! Another border successfully navigated. It was June 3, 1965.

We were amazed at how modern Japan was. But everything was little! The cars were little, the café tables were little, and the chairs were little. Virtually no one spoke English or German. All the people who picked us up hitchhiking wanted to give us something…some little gift, even if it was a pack of cigarettes. Everything was clean and neat. That night we made it to Nagoya, where we slept in the Catholic Church. The next day we arrived in Tokyo and, I do not know how we found it, but ended up at the Otsuka Youth Hostel. It was a typical Japanese house in a nice neighborhood but there was no one there! I mean no one! So we just picked a room and moved in. That evening another guy moved in and asked where the officials were.

When we told him that we had not seen anyone, he moved in too. He was an older American guy who was genuinely nice and very talkative. He told us he was a fencing master who had taught all the Hollywood swashbuckler actors how to sword fight. He carried an umbrella, a lethal weapon in his hands. We stayed there for four days while we looked for a pad to rent and never saw an official of the Youth Hostel.

We found a place that would rent to gaijin (the Japanese word for foreigners "strange souls") and rented it. It was a four-and-a-half tatami room (9 shaku × 9 shaku ≈ 2.73 m × 2.73 m) with a closet, a sink and cook plate. The shared toilet was at the end of the hallway. The floor was tatami mat. You always took your shoes off before entering and slept on futon pads that were rolled out on the tatami floor at night and rolled back up and placed in the closet in the morning.

In the meantime, we had found the cool part of town, which turned out to be the Shinjuku area. Shinjuku is a major subway station surrounded by hundreds of restaurants, coffee houses, and thousands of tiny shops. Each coffee house specialized in a music type: classical, jazz, Brazilian, etc. And they had outrageous sound systems. We hung out at the two best jazz coffee houses and the Fugetsudo, a classical music coffee house. We were extremely popular as foreigners on whom the Japanese youth could practice their English. Many of them could read English but could not speak.

Also, we were completely different-looking (freaks) from anyone they had ever seen or heard of. We noticed right away that people tried to avoid contact with us. They were not nearly a gregarious as Indians. We would walk into a small shop where ten people were working (all stores seemed overstaffed) and suddenly everyone disappeared. It was probably because they feared embarrassment at not understanding us.

We made friends with a pill freak named Kyoshi and his girlfriend Fumiko. She was a young girl with an incredibly beautiful face. Unfortunately, she was a worse pill freak than Kyoshi and spent most of her time unconscious on the bed. Kyoshi tried hash for the first time and loved it and partly weaned himself off the downers. He loved to play pachinko (a Japanese pinball-like game that you play for prizes). We would smoke hash at his pad and he would bum a few coins, go running out the door and come back later with sweets and ice cream he had won at the corner pachinko parlor. Before we left Tokyo, we gave them our address in Frankfurt. Unbelievably, when we eventually returned to Germany, we found out that they had taken the Trans-Siberian Railway and come to Frankfurt and looked up Uschi's sister, Otty from the address we had given them. Otty's mother-in-law and father-in-law took them in but when they could not tolerate Kyoshi's harsh treatment of Fumiko (he beat her), they threw him out on his ear. She met a German guy, got married to him and become an upright citizen. God only knows what ever happened to Kyoshi.

One thing we realized right away was that Japan was awfully expensive compared to India and Southeast Asia. Our pad was only a hundred bucks a month but food and everything else was incredibly expensive. For example, a pineapple (for which we had just been paying five cents American in Malaysia) cost about a pound sterling (at that time $2.80). We were going to run out of money soon, so I mailed the kilo of hash to my brother in New York City, which he sold and sent me the cash in five hundred-dollar bills. Sending five hundred bills was less detectible than sending many one-hundred-dollar bills. I traded the weed, which we never smoked anyway, even though it was dynamite stuff, to an American airman stationed in Japan for his stereo system and three records: John Coltrane's *My Favorite Things*, a Clifford Brown album and a Ray Charles album. To this day I know every note of every tune on those three albums. We had to find a way to make more money to survive so we decided we would do some chalk painting on the sidewalks and take contributions from passersby. We selected a good spot where there were plenty of well-dressed people.

We chalked a map of Honshu Island (the main island of Japan where Tokyo is located) and hit the jackpot. We could easily earn ten quid (about $28) in an hour or two. Unfortunately, the spot we selected was in front of the Diet, the general assembly building for the government of Japan, and were told to move after a few sessions.

Never mind, it did not seem to matter where we chalked, the map of Honshu was a huge hit and we cleaned up wherever we went. Eventually we discovered that people left money even before we started with the chalk drawing, so we had Kyoshi write a note in Japanese on a piece of cloth which said, "We are students and have traveled one year from Sweden. Please give us tomorrow." The last sentence is a Japanese idiom. We would just sit on the sidewalk, put out our sign and the money dropped like manna from heaven. We had to endure lots of strange questions, like a young boy shyly asking, "We wonder, do you see everything blue?" They wondered because we had blue eyes. I just smiled and answered politely and would get somewhere between a hundred and a thousand yen. (The exchange rate was 360 yen to one dollar at that time.)

One day a blue limo with "Corps Diplomatic" plates pulled up and a blonde-haired, blue-eyed man stepped out, dressed impeccably in a blue suit and tie and said, "God dag," "Hello" in Swedish. We told him that we did not speak Swedish and he asked about the sign. We said that it was true that we had traveled one year from Sweden but that we were not Swedish. He said that someone had called the embassy and that he was concerned that two Swedish students needed help. He asked us to change our sign to say that we were either American or German, which we had told him we were. We agreed to change the sign.

Anyway, it was no less than panhandling without verbal communication. It worked great and we lived high on the hog while in Japan. We didn't really like doing it; it was like a job so we would go out and do it until we had enough for what we wanted to buy (dinner, a pineapple, and a couple of packs of smokes or whatever) and then quit for the day. By night we would get stoned and hang out in coffee houses or go to Kyoshi's and get wrecked.

Our first day in Tokyo at Fugetsudo Coffee house, something happened that changed everything for Roger. He had a sense of doom from the moment we got to Japan. While we were having coffee that day, a young Japanese boy approached us and asked, "Why did you come to Japan?" Roger understood "*When* did you come to Japan?" He answered, "I came today." But with his British accent it sounded like, "I caim todai." The boy understood, "I came to die." He said, "You came to die?" in total amazement. Roger took this as a bad omen and was sure he would never leave Japan alive.

He was too proud to earn money the way we did so he applied for a job at a Japanese rat extermination company. They showed him a training film that showed them catching rats by hand and he totally freaked out and had nightmares. He was completely at a loss about what to do next. We were supporting him with the money we were earning. He said he had to get out of there, so I packed his bag and said, "Let's go. You are stowing away on the next ship back to Singapore." I had checked the steaming schedule in the English newspaper and there was a ship leaving Yokohama that day, so I hauled him off to Yokohama Port and shoved him on board.

While in Tokyo I read *Autobiography of a Yogi* by Paramahansa Yogananda. Through it I became more aware of the Master Disciple relationship and the fact that there are real Masters of spirituality and not just ganja smoking Sadhus. One thing I read that resonated was that Mahatma Gandhi maintained silence one day a week. I decided to try it myself and toward the end of my stay in Japan started maintaining silence one day a week and found that I enjoyed it.

I started reading The Bhagavad-Gita again and found that it touched something deep inside me. The words were so simple and sweet that anyone could understand them, but the meaning seemed so deep that I felt that I would take a lifetime to comprehend, just as it was written in the forward. I read it over and over. It eventually changed my life.

In the Bhagavad-Gita Lord Krishna is going into battle. It is a description of the conversation between Lord Krishna and his disciple Arjuna. The essence for me was that Arjuna was asking Krishna, "considering that these are my own people against whom I am going into battle, am I not better off to lay my life down before them, than to kill them?" Krishna tells Arjuna, that he, Krishna, is the doer of all things and that he, Arjuna, is merely the instrument of this doing. He tells Arjuna that these people are already dead by his will. The actual killing of them is only the shadow on the Earth of his will. There follows a discourse describing Krishna's Being as that of the Avatar (The Christ). This was my first exposure to God as omnipresent. Growing up, going to church, for me, God was like the phantom of the Universe, sitting on a cloud somewhere, writing down who was good and who was bad. The good ones go to heaven and the bad ones go to hell. My mind was blown. Krishna tells Arjuna that the goal of life is to become united with God and describes the various paths. I began to feel a burning question within myself. What was *my* path?

When we first came to Japan, our plan was to go to on to California. After a short time, I felt that Tokyo was as close as I wanted to get to the West for a while. It was all moving too fast for me and I was feeling a longing to return to India. I began to feel a certain frustration within myself. I began to see my life as if from above, looking down. It seemed like looking down on an ant colony. I saw myself scrambling around the world, looking in place to place, under every rock, "Hey, Mik, are you under there?" It seemed like no matter where I went, I took my limited self with me. I grew more and more frustrated and the questions within me grew louder and more persistent; "Who am I, what is my path?" I had questions but no answers. I discussed this with Uschi and she shared the same feeling of seeing us from above looking like ants aimlessly wandering around an ant hill. It began to be a mutual frustration. We wondered, how will this all end.

The more I read Bhagavad-Gita over and over incessantly, the more the question, "What is my path?" grew inside me. I knew I had to find the answer to that question and I somehow knew that I would find it in India. I was starting to question myself and my motives.

I don't remember our exact discussions at the time about returning to India but I'm pretty sure Uschi did not want to go back to India. Even as a little girl in Germany she was sure she would live in America. I just told her that I didn't know why, but I absolutely had to go back to India.

September 21st, 1965, we boarded the M.M. Line's *Viet Nam* back to India. We backtracked the same route to Hong Kong, Saigon, and Singapore, that we had taken to bring us to Japan, arriving on October 1st in Singapore.

Chapter Eighteen

Singapore, Again, and Cambodia

We decided not to go straight to India and got off in Singapore. We had some cash at the time that we had made in Japan, so we checked in to the Sin Chew Hotel at the corner of Albert and Queen Street. That way we could smoke hash in our room, which we could not do at the Sikh temple.

Our first trip to the Chai Walla was a happy reunion with Roger who was sitting there taking chai. He was with an American named Ray Ordas who he had met on the ship that he stowed away on. Ray had taken Roger under his wing on the ship and given him food he sneaked from the table. They had made friends with a cycle rickshaw driver named Chan. Chan was in his early twenties and was an opium addict. They had both gotten into smoking A1 and pure morphine.

We scored a huge rock of pure morphine and started smoking it several times a day. Every time we tried to go out of our room, we would wander a few blocks and suddenly "realize" that, "oops, guess what? We're back in front of the hotel again. Well, what the hell, we may as well go in and smoke a combo." I would take a stool and put out piles of tobacco, hash, opium and morphine, scrape a little from each pile together and mix it, put it in my chillum and fire it up. That was a "combo." In a very short time, we were addicted; addicted in the meaning that we were no longer taking it to get high, but to stay well. As soon as the effects of the opiates started to wear off, we would begin to get sick and the only cure was to take more. We were consuming huge amounts of hash, opium and morphine.

One day Chan said, "Today we must go to Mariamman Temple to see fire walking." He explained that once a year the Hindu followers of the goddess Mariamman thanked her for her boons during the preceding year by walking on fire. Chan cycled us there. We entered the temple and saw a pit about two meters wide by six meters long and perhaps half a meter deep. In the pit were three stacks of logs standing on end with the tops leaning in toward each other. There were fifteen to twenty logs, each about five meters long, in each stack. They were set afire and as they blazed; they fell down into the pit where workers with long poles evened them out. After some time, the fire disappeared and there was a thick bed of orange glowing coals covered with white ash. The heat was still so intense that it would have melted the film in your camera even at only a few meters away.

In another courtyard the priest was preparing the firewalkers by shouting incantations, slapping them with leaves, wrapping ropes around them, and putting them into a trance state. I was told they had prepared by fasting for twenty-four hours. The firewalkers were almost all boys in their late teens or early twenties. In the meantime, right next to this, was a priest piercing the skin of an older man's body with long skewers. On the torso he would take a fold of skin between his thumb and forefinger and push a sharpened steel rod about six mm in diameter and two meters long right through the skin to the middle of the rod and then leave it there and put another in a few centimeters away so that the entire torso, front and back, was covered with steel rods piercing the skin at regular angles to make a pattern that accommodated a steel framed harness. Through the tongue, lips, forehead, and cheeks smaller skewers were used. After the harness superstructure was put on, the two men danced around the temple grounds in ecstasy. When they were finished, the superstructure was removed and one by one the skewers were removed by the priest and ashes rubbed over the place where they had pierced the skin. I was standing a little over a meter from this and could not see a drop of blood or a hole where the skin was pierced after the ashes were applied. It seemed like a miracle.

Now it was time for the fire walk. The young men stood at one end of the pit and one after another ran as fast as they could through the red-hot coals. At the end they were doused with water. I was standing right there and did not see a single burn or blister. The highlight was when an old man with white hair and beard took a small child onto his shoulders and leisurely strolled through the coals. He looked like he was in ecstasy. He had no burns or blisters. I could barely stand the heat from a few meters away.

The following day we were sitting at the Chai Walla when the neighborhood Chinese started some celebration. They were in costumes and stuck long skewers through their cheeks, passing through their mouths and extending out the other side so that half was on one side and half on the other. There was lots of blood and their preparation was opium, not fasting. They danced around in a parade-like fashion for some time like this, beating drums, clanging cymbals and blowing horns in a cacophony of sound that was ear shattering and seemed to have no organization. It wasn't music; it was just each one doing his own thing, making noise. It was gross compared to what I had seen the day before. I never did get any explanation as to why they did this.

We had bought a camera the last time we were in Singapore and for that reason had a few photos that we took on our trip to the east coast, Japan and again this time in Singapore. We planned on smuggling the camera into India and selling it for a good profit.

After two weeks of this we headed north with a huge stash of opium and morphine. We still had plenty of hash. Crossing the Jahore Straight to Jahore Bahru, we were back on mainland Malaya. We hitched up the west coast to Malacca where we stayed in the Sikh temple for a couple of days, one day in Ipoh at the Sikh temple and two more days in Penang. We stayed two days in Taquapa in a hotel and then took a bus to Bangkok. In Bangkok we checked back into our old haunt, The Thai Song Greet Hotel. We stayed in our room for several days, never venturing farther than the corner to get something to eat and that even rarely. We were totally hooked and would sit in our room and smoke combos all day and night, eating very little. We decided to go to Cambodia.

We hitched to the Thai/Cambodian border and slept in the police station in Sisephon. The next day we hitched to Siem Reap and checked into the Angkor Wat Hotel. In retrospect it was completely stupid to be traveling in Cambodia with an American passport at that time. There was a war going on and the Pathet Lao would board busses, ask for passports and if yours was blue they dragged you off the bus and shot you in the head. We heard these stories immediately on entering Cambodia and immediately stopped speaking a word of English and only spoke German for the remainder of our time in Cambodia. We discovered that just a few miles from Siem Reap was one of the wonders of the world, the Angkor Wat ruins. I had never heard of them. We hired a cycle rickshaw to take us there and I have to say that, even as stoned as I was at the time, and as opposed as I was to visiting "historical sites," my mind was blown by Angkor Wat. At that time Ankor Wat was completely devoid of tourists. We were the only people there.

At Angkor Wat, we met two Germans in their twenties who had hitched all the way from Germany. They were clean cut "Nazi boys" by their own description. They went only by their last names, Buettner and Schieke. They were always laughing and happy. They told us how they would ride through Persian villages standing in the backs of trucks giving the "Heil Hitler" sign and the Persians would cheer them. They loved Persians because the Persians loved Hitler.

We stayed two days and then took the northern route by

truck to Phnom Penh. We checked in to the Hotel Asie, where we stayed for four days, getting "well" with drugs. I never smoked weed but had heard that the Cambodian weed was a "must try" I bought fifty cents' worth, which was a good quarter pound and a bamboo bong. The weed was OK but not for me. I loved my hash and combo. I threw the weed away and kept the bong.

We hitched the southern route through Cambodia back to Thailand, sleeping in a schoolhouse in Battam Bang. At the Cambodia/Thai border I did one of the stupidest and most dangerous things I had ever done. In my drug haze, I took a huge risk, though at the time, I didn't even think it was that risky. The bong would not fit in my backpack; it was too long, about half a meter. So, I laid it across the top of the pack and secured it with the top flap of the pack, leaving it stick out about four inches on either side. It was obviously a bong strapped across the top of my pack! When we got to the border and went in the customs shack, they told us to put our packs on the table. The customs official ordered Uschi to open her pack so it could be searched. After searching her pack, he came to me and said, "Open, you open." Knowing that the bottom half of my pack was filled with drugs, I didn't hesitate for a moment. I picked up my pack, slung it over my shoulder as if I didn't understand him and walked out of the customs shack and into Thailand. They were so shocked that they didn't say a word. My heart was in my throat. Imagine what a Cambodian prison is like! They would have put me in jail for years—unless I bribed them, of course.

We hitched back to Bangkok and checked back into the Thai Song Greet. I hated Bangkok and swore after my visit that I would never return. Now here I was again for the third time!

We stayed for five days, doing dope day and night, then headed back south toward Singapore to be there for the next MM ship to Colombo. We stayed in a Hotel in Hua Hin and no sooner had I taken my shower than a young hooker came to the door and asked if I wanted to fuck her. Right in front of my wife! All Thai hotels that I had stayed in had their own hookers and they would usually wait until you had time to clean up and then knock on the door and ask if you wanted to fuck. No matter that your wife was standing in earshot of the conversation. It was quite matter of fact. I would just smile and say, "No thank you." Then they would give the price and ask if I was sure. If you assured them that you were certain, they would just smile and tell you to call if you wanted them. It was all quite harmless but a little bizarre.

We took the night train to Hajai and then hitched to Ipoh. By November we were firmly ensconced in the Bugis Street Park Hotel in Singapore, wondering what the hell had happened to the last month and a half. It had disappeared into a morphine haze. The stay at the Bugis Street Park Hotel only lasted two days because the Chinese would stand on ladders and look through the transom and spy on us, so we moved back to the Sin Chew.

I had been hooked long enough that I knew it was dangerous. I'm not talking about the hash. That was a fact of life for me and didn't mess with my health and perception. But the opium, and especially the pure morphine that I had been smoking for a couple of months, was beginning to take its toll. I had barely eaten in two months and weighed less than a hundred pounds. I remembered Schieke in Cambodia looking at me one day, cocking his head to the side and saying, "Mensch, du bist nur en Hemd." Man, you're nothing but a shirt. (I was still wearing the Lucknow kurta, a blousy style white Indian shirt.)

At the same time, I was reading the Bhagavad-Gita day and night and the question, "What is my path?" was growing bigger and more constant in my mind. In fact, it was becoming an obsession.

In Bangkok we had heard that a friend of ours, whom we had known from the European gammler scene, Ruth Brustman, was in Singapore. We had also heard that her husband Peter (they were both Austrian) had flipped out on acid and jumped off the roof of the Y.M.C.A. in Baghdad and killed himself. We went into the Sikh temple just as they were closing and, sure enough, Ruth was there. Since the temple was closing, we went to the Chai Walla. I noticed a clean-cut westerner follow us out the door. He followed us to the Chai Walla and sat down on a stool next to us. I mixed up a batch of hash and tobacco and filled a Moroccan sepsi pipe (a small clay pipe-head that fit on the end of a turned wooden pipe stem), lit it up and passed it around. When it came back to me, I filled it again and offered it to the stranger. He said, "No thanks, I'm trying not to use drugs." I thought that was very odd. Everybody I knew was trying to smoke as much hash as possible and here was a guy saying that he was trying *not* to take drugs. He introduced himself as Steve Simon, from Miami. He seemed like a nice guy. He was short-haired, had a three-day beard and beautiful eyes. He smiled a lot.

When I asked him why he was trying not to take drugs he told me that he had heard of a spiritual master in India named Meher Baba and that he was on his way to India to see him. This Meher Baba had told him not to use drugs. He had been a junkie. He said that he thought Meher Baba was the Avatar. I told him that I had met hundreds of Babas in India, and they were all fakes. I wished him luck but told him not to get his hopes up.

The next day I went to the American Consulate to check my mail and my buddy, Chris West (the guy who saw me off in New York) had sent me a letter. In the letter were four hits of Sandoz LSD 25. I had never taken psychedelics except for peyote. When I went back to the Chai Walla, Steve was there. I told him about the acid and he said that he had tripped dozens of times on acid and the one thing he recommended was that I fast for at least twelve hours before dropping and that I have a guide for my first trip. He said that he would be my guide if I wished.

I dropped the acid that evening and experienced something

I had never experienced on any drug before. The hallucinations of colors and the other entire phenomenon were not what really got me, though. That was nothing. It was that I went beyond the senses, left my body and experienced the nothingness. I felt a oneness that was not mathematical (mathematically there is always a second.) When I started to come down a little, Steve guided me and told me a story that was a creation analogy. He said that he had read this in Meher Baba's book, *God Speaks*.

The analogy went something like this: All creation is illusion; it only appears real to the individualized consciousness. In the beginning was an infinite ocean. It had no shore, no surface and no bottom. The ocean was the infinite ocean of consciousness, God. It was not even aware that it was an ocean. In this ocean of infinite consciousness, a whim surged. The whim was to know itself. The nature of a whim is beyond reason, so it does no good to ask why the whim arose. The whim came in the form of a question. The question was, "Who am I?" The immediate answer should have been, "I am infinite consciousness." But the question, being finite, escaped from the most finite point in the infinite. The ocean would not be infinite if it did not also contain the most finite, and from this most finite point (the Om point or creation point) in the infinite, escaped the question. Thus, instead of the answer being, "I am infinite consciousness," the answer was I am the most finite consciousness. Thus, duality and the evolution of consciousness came into being, like bubbles on the surface of the ocean that think they are individual drops, when in fact they always were and always will be ocean.

This story would have blown my mind in any state of consciousness but on acid, I had the experience of living it.

The next day I came down and felt I would never be the same again. I felt I had experienced Oneness.

Steve explained that he did not have enough money for his ticket to Bombay. He had about half of what he needed. We gave him the rest of the money and decided that we would stow

Ruth away.

On November 20th, one week after meeting Steve and six days after my first acid trip, we boarded the *M.S. Laos* for Colombo and Bombay. We had paid our way from Kobe to Bombay but were breaking our trip at Singapore and at Colombo. My old buddy the purser was still on the *Laos* and was very happy to report to me that they were not full so he had set aside a cabin for my wife and me. This made us very happy because we would not have to deal with other people in our cabin and we could easily stow Ruth away.

The day we boarded the *Laos,* I threw away all the opiates I had and went cold turkey. The four-day trip to Colombo, Ceylon was pure hell. I was cold turkey and sick. But I made it. By the time we reached Colombo I had kicked the opiate habit.

One funny thing that happened on the way to Colombo was this: We had told Ruth that she could, under no circumstances, leave the cabin. We sneaked the cheese course from the table at each meal and brought it to her. She got cabin fever and went on deck. While she was sunning herself on deck, the purser walked up to her, stood for a moment looking at her, turned and walked away. From that moment on, there was always extra cheese and bread at our place at the table.

The boat docked in Colombo and we spent the day with Steve sitting on a huge rock at the edge of the Indian Ocean. I remember seeing the waves come in, fill the tide pools in the rocks, and then go back out again, leaving them empty. I experienced myself as the rock. As the waves came in and filled me, I felt the joy of fulfillment and the fear of future emptiness. As the tide went out and left me empty, I experienced the pain of emptiness and the joyous anticipation of future fulfillment. I felt I knew what it was like to be a rock at the edge of the sea. It was a timeless moment for me and Uschi, the ocean spray blowing over us in the wind.

Steve told me he was going to Poona, India to see Meher Baba.

I hugged him and felt that our hearts had touched. I wished him luck and again told him not to get his hopes too high; he would probably be disappointed. All I knew of Meher Baba was that he did not want me to use drugs, (Steve told me that Meher Baba told him to tell everyone to stop using drugs.), he lived in Poona, and Steve thought he was the Avatar, plus the ocean creation analogy. We parted with tears.

Chapter Nineteen

Colombo, Ceylon

The first night in Colombo, we found a youth hostel and stayed five days, then checked into the Y.M.C.A. on November 29th. We were stoned on hash and trying to figure out what to do with ourselves. Deep down inside myself I felt like we should have just gone on to Bombay. I was missing India so much. I was confused, frustrated and lost. I felt like I had big problems for the first time. The question kept burning inside me, "What is my path?" I knew that there was a truth to find and I felt deep down inside myself that once I got to India, everything would be O.K. and my current desperation would go away. I also felt that if I just kept reading the Gita I would find the answer to my question. I read day and night in between smoking hash.

We wandered around Colombo, a beautiful tropical city with beautiful people. We couldn't find a good cup of chai anywhere. They explained that it was because they exported all the best tea. We went to the gem shops and sat at a table where the merchant would pour out piles of diamonds, rubies, emeralds, and pearls onto the table for our perusal. Behind us stood four guards, watching our every move.

We felt we should at least see some other part of the island so decided to go to Kandy. We hitched to Kandy and met a Buddhist family who took us home with them. We stayed with them for three days. One day we visited the Temple of the Tooth, which houses a tooth of Guatama the Buddha. The man of the house saw that I was wearing saffron colors and reading the Gita. He asked if I would like to meet a German holy man. I said yes, of course. I was looking for answers and maybe he had some. We were told that he lived in a cave for many years, but we would have to walk along a jungle path for several miles to meet him. We bought some bananas to take to him and Uschi and I set off on the path through the jungle. After about a quarter of a mile my legs started burning. I looked down and there were dozens of leaches on my legs and feet. They were only about two centimeters long, but they hurt like hell. I wiped them off and continued. Every ten steps we would have to stop, and wipe leaches off. After about one kilometer we came across a beautiful bungalow. We saw a white man sitting on the veranda. Sure, enough it was the "German holy man."

The bungalow wasn't exactly a cave and he wasn't exactly a holy man. He was a Buddhist scholar living in a bungalow in the forest translating Buddhist Sanskrit and Pali texts. He had every amenity, typewriters, radios, etc. I told him I was a seeker of Truth. He told us to sit and then began a discourse: "Center yourself and feel your body. Do you feel the weight of your hand on your thigh?" He went on like this for half an hour. After each sentence he would ask, "Nuh?" This was an irritating German affectation for, "you understand?" like I was idiot. Anyway, I got tired of this pompous ass after a bit and told him we had to be on our way. "You must find serenity and be at peace and calm in every circumstance," he said. "NUH?" We walked out onto the patio where there were two monkeys fucking. He totally freaked out and grabbed a big stick and started screaming and chasing them. So much for peace and serenity in every circumstance! Uschi and I laughed our heads off watching him try to get rid of the fucking monkeys and got the hell out of there.

Back in Colombo we checked in to the British Soldier's and Sailor's Institute. It was very clean and cheap. We sat on the front porch and smoked hash endlessly. The first evening I was walking to the toilet when I saw a longhaired, flat footed, blond westerner shuffling across the lobby with a copy of *On the Road* sticking out of his back pocket. We struck up a conversation and

I realized I had just met a hippie for the first time. His name was Kirk. He had a backpack full of psychedelics, Owsley purple double-dome L.S.D. (as pure as Sandoz) and a ton of psilocybin. We dropped acid that night and I walked outside to the corner and sat in front of a twenty-foot-high golden Buddha statue watching its head turn into diamonds, emeralds and rubies. Not a very significant trip.

The next day three clean-cut Americans came to the Institute for lunch and introduced themselves to us. They said they worked for Arthur C. Clarke and lived at his house. They told us all about Arthur C. Clarke's latest project, *2001, A Space Odyssey*, the movie. That sounded cosmic to us. The subject of acid came up and they said that Arthur wanted to try L.S.D. and would we come to stay at his house for a few days and turn him on. Uschi and I were up for it and so was Kirk, so we checked out and went with them. When we got to the house, we found out that Arthur was not there. He was in the West working on the movie. These guys just dropped his name so they could take acid. Oh well, we had nothing better to do and the house was incredible.

We dropped acid with them that night and they turned out to be total idiots. One of them said, "I know who you guys really are." Pointing to Kirk, he said, "You're Paul." Then, pointing to me, he said, "And you are Peter." (Meaning the Disciples of Christ.) I sarcastically said, "Right, and we are going to take you by the hand and lead you to the pearly gates."

I was really starting to peak so I went out into the yard and sat on the grass. It was like a launching pad and I soared up into the universe, exploring the cosmos. Suddenly time and space disappeared and there was nothing. The instant I had a thought the nothingness disappeared, and duality reappeared. I realized I could not fight the thoughts away and had to just let them go. It was the closest feeling I ever had to experiencing Oneness. The only problem was that it didn't last. But the memory of it lasted.

While staying at Arthur's house, one day, reading the Gita something jumped off the pages at me. Why had I not seen it before? Chapter XII. Arjuna is asking Krishna: What is the best path?

Arjuna said: "The devotees who, with their minds constantly fixed in You as shown above, adore You as possessed of form and attributes, and those who adore only the imperishable, formless Brahma, —- of these who are the best knowers of Yoga?" (Union)

Sri Bhagavan said: "I consider them to be the best Yogis who, endowed with supreme faith, and ever united through meditation with Me, worship Me with the mind centered on Me. Those, however, who controlling all their senses, and even minded toward all creatures, constantly adore as their very self the unthinkable, all pervading, imperishable, ineffable, eternal, immobile, unmanifest and immutable Brahma, they too come to Me.

"Of course, the path of those who have their mind attached to the Unmanifest is more rugged; for self-identification with the Unmanifest is attained with difficulty by those who are centred in the body.

"On the other hand, those who being solely devoted to Me, and surrendering all actions to Me, worship Me (the manifest Divine), constantly meditating on Me with single-minded devotion.

"These, Arjuna, I speedily rescue from the ocean of birth and death, their mind being fixed on Me."

OH MY GOD, there it was! I knew the answer was in there! THOSE WHO WORSHIP MY MANIFEST FORM, THOSE I SPEEDILY RESCUE FROM THE OCEAN OF BIRTH AND DEATH!!! That was my path! I had the answer to my burning question but now a bigger problem arose; how to worship His manifest form. And a bigger and more desperate question arose along with it. "Where are you?" The question that haunted my mind incessantly for months now disappeared in a flash and was replaced with another question repeating itself over and over in my mind day and night. WHERE ARE YOU?

We stayed at the house for about three weeks and never saw a sign of Arthur C. Clarke, but I bonded with Kirk. He was a brother. On November 28th we went back to Colombo and the next day boarded the M.S. *Viet Nam* to Bombay. Kirk was going to go by land and ferry to South India. We parted ways physically.

An interesting and funny side-note: While sitting on the veranda at the B.S.&S. Institute smoking hash day and night, I was peripherally aware that across the street was a wholesale drug warehouse. It had a neon sign that flashed in red once every second or so. The sign read: "DRUGS LTD." So for weeks on end I was seeing out of the corner of my eye once every second," DRUGS LIMITED, DRUGS LIMITED, DRUGS LIMITED."

On New Year's Eve, 1965 we sailed into Bombay harbor. I saw the Gateway of India and my heart pounded. I decided that I could not find the answer to my burning question in a drug haze. I gathered all my drugs and paraphernalia, pipes, chillums, etc. and threw them out the porthole into the Bombay harbor. I had kicked opiates and I could kick hash too.

Chapter Twenty

Finally, Back to India

Bombay was eye candy for me. Ahhh… back in India, the Motherland, home. Now everything would be O.K. We checked into a filthy ten-rupee-a-night hotel, The Punjab Hotel, making sure there were no bedbugs. We dropped off our backpacks and wandered out onto the streets of Bombay.

I saw a dried-out fountain and sat on its edge watching India go by. It was like heaven. I looked to my right and saw a young Indian Muslim wrapping a rag around the mouthpiece of a chillum. He cupped it into his hands, touched it to his forehead as in a religious offering, and fired it up as someone held two burning matches over its opening. I smelled the most delicious hash I had ever smelled. He offered the chillum to me and I took it. I had a deep drag and it felt so good. I hadn't smoked in hours…. probably the longest I had gone in years. It was the most delicious hash I had ever tasted. That was the end of my resolve to go straight for the moment.

He said it was Bombay Beauty, a black Kashmiri hash that is very moist. It came in little balls about the size of a goat turd. The Hindi/Urdu word for ball is "gola" so the hash dealer who made regular rounds was called the "Goliwalla." One ball cost a quarter rupee, char anna. You could get five balls for one rupee. We sat for days and nights in the dried-out fountain with these guys smoking Bombay Beauty. Occasionally we would take a Victoria or tonga to Haji Ali.

Haji Ali was a pilgrim to Mecca whose body had washed ashore after a shipwreck. Having had a tomb built for him by local Muslims immortalized him. The tomb itself is in the sea and has a causeway from the land, which can only be negotiated at low tide. Along the walkway approaching the causeway there are several tents. Inside the tents are the Muslim hash dealers and smokers. We sat in their tents and smoked chillum with them for hours on end. Once, a Hindu Sadhu came into the tent wearing a white kurta and white lungi. They told us that he was very holy and the proof of this was when he took off his shirt and exposed his forty-year-old lean brown body. He took a lit chillum, held it in his cupped hand and crossed his arms over his chest so that his hands were lying on his shoulders and his elbows were crossed just below his chin. He formed an air pocket with his arms against his chest, lowered his mouth to the inside of his elbows and began sucking. The air pocket leading up to the chillum cause it to fire up and smoke furiously. Great applause was heard and "waaah," how holy he is!

While sitting at the fountain we got to know the Muslims there. There was one whom I liked very much. He had a wife and several kids (though he was only in his early twenties) who lived in the chawl across the street. He slept at the fountain to make more room for the family and because it was cooler in the evening.

At night big bandicoots would run across our feet as we got high. Uschi and I had this ongoing conversation about where to go and what to do. I had explained to her that I must find the manifest form, or I could not live. We would have to find a guru. So, we bantered back and forth, "Let's go here and let's go there." Finally, my friend Mohammed said, "You must go to Hyderabad." Naturally, he would think of Hyderabad because of its heavy Muslim population and its reputation for its Muslim holy men. So, we decided that Hyderabad it would be. We hitched on our way towards Hyderabad and made it to Poona the first night. I was getting more and more desperate and less and less able to cope with the world as the question, "Where are you?" burned in my brain.

We checked in to the Dreamland Hotel near the Poona railway station and had tali for dinner. (Tali is a tin plate with various cups full and piles of different foods.) This being a Hindu hotel, the food was "pure veg." One tali cost one rupee (ten cents). After dinner, it dawned on me that this was the town that Steve Simon had told me that Meher Baba lived. The next morning, I asked the hotel owner if he had heard of Meher Baba. He said, "Of course, everyone has heard of Meher Baba. Just go along Bund Garden Road until you come to Guru Prasad and you will see him there. It's only two furlongs distance." (If you ask for directions in India, it's always two furlongs distance.)

We got a rickshaw and told him, "Bund Garden Road, Guru Prasad." He pulled over in front of a huge palace. There was a wrought iron gate with a long driveway bordered by shrubbery. I could see spacious gardens in bloom and large fancy Italian statuary. There was a large portico in front and a wide veranda. I remember thinking, "This cannot be the place; holy men do not live in such palaces." Then I saw a sign on the gate pillar: GURU PRASAD.

We got out and as I was looking at the palace, I saw an old, thin, bent, very dark-skinned man walking along the driveway toward us. "Is this Meher Baba?" I thought. As he neared, I felt something inside me that was strange and foreign. He walked up to me and I thought, "If he speaks to me, I will not be able to answer." He put his face directly into my face and looked into my eyes. I was dumbstruck. I could not speak. Softly, I heard his voice say, "Baba?" I felt a wave of heat go from my tailbone to my brain as the name "Baba" seared into my heart. I had never felt such a feeling before. I knew I had just heard the only real word of my life. Barely audibly, I answered, "Yes, Baba." "Baba is not here," he said. The realization of the name I had heard disappeared as fast as it came, and I did not remember that experience in the driveway of Guru Prasad for many months after that.

The old man instructed us to go to the Poona Meher Baba

Center and ask for K.K. Ramakrishnan. We took the rickshaw there and walked into the hall of the Center. There I saw my first image of Meher Baba. It was a full-length, bigger-than-life photograph of Meher Baba.

I was astounded. I said, "He's got a mustache." All the holy men I had met had full beards. I remember Uschi saying, "And look at that nose!" We started wandering from photo to photo on the walls looking at his pictures. As we were doing this, K.K. Ramakrishnan walked into the hall and introduced himself. We told him that we had come to pay our respects to Meher Baba. He said that Baba was in very strict seclusion and no one could see him, not even his closest ones. He said that recently Baba had made an exception for a young American who had come. The young American had found out that he could not see Baba and had lain on the floor of the hall here and cried for three days until Baba finally called him to come to Ahmednagar to see him. I said, "That must have been my friend, Steve Simon." He confirmed that it was. He said that he would send a telegram to Baba to see if he would allow us to see him and that we should come back after one or two days' time.

We went back to the hotel and who did we see? Lo and behold, it was Kirk. He had come by land from Ceylon through south India and by pure "coincidence" checked into the same hotel as we had in Poona! I told him about going to see Meher Baba. He said, "Great, wanna drop some psilocybin?" "Sure," I replied. We dropped and within an hour I was puking diamonds, emeralds and rubies. Sacred mushrooms are a totally different type of trip than L.S.D. During that trip all I could think of was, "The mind is stronger than the drug."

Every time that sentence would pop into my mind, I would feel clear-headed like I was not tripping at all. The next morning was the first time I had ever felt guilty about taking drugs. I remember thinking, "I went to see Meher Baba and the only thing I know about him for sure is that he doesn't want me to take drugs. Steve may think he is the Avatar and that I know nothing about, but I do know that he doesn't want me to take drugs." I thought it was strange that I felt guilty.

I told Uschi that I liked Poona. It was clean, pretty, not crowded and had a nice temperature. I thought it would be nice to stay for a while. We contacted a family that had a house for rent. We negotiated for most of a day and finally they said no. Despite our assurances that we were vegetarian, they were afraid that we would bring meat into the house and defile it forever.

I said we should go on to Hyderabad right away. Uschi asked, "What about seeing Meher Baba and returning to see the result of the telegram?" I said that even if Meher Baba was the real thing, I did not deserve to see him because after going there to ask permission to see him, I had done the one thing that I know for sure that he doesn't want me to do. "Let's go." We stood on the Sholapur Road and a Jeep picked us up. The friendly driver noticed that I was wearing saffron colors (the color of renunciation) and asked us where we were going. "Hyderabad," I replied. "Why?" he asked. "I don't know," was all I could say. "Let's take tea," he said as he pulled over to a tea stall by the side of the road. We had tea and did not speak. Finally, he looked me in the eye and said, "Sahib, go back to Bombay." My only reply was, "O.K." This is how aimless and mindless I was. We crossed the road, put out our thumbs and hitched back to Bombay.

We were back in the Punjab hotel and the fountain for another week of "Where shall we go, what shall we do?" Finally, I said that since we could not agree upon what to do next, that I would decide. I decided that we should go back to Delhi. We had liked Delhi and we knew our way around there. We went by train to the outskirts of Bombay and started hitching.

The first truck that picked us up was going to Ahmadabad, the totally wrong direction to go to Delhi. Being as aimless as I was, I said fine, we will go to Ahmadabad. That night as we were driving along the windshield suddenly shattered. The driver and his companion grabbed long pipes and jumped out of the truck. No one could be found and when they got back in the truck the driver told us that it was a dacoit attack. We saw the beautiful state of Gujerat along the way, especially Surat on the Gulf of Cambay and Baroda. In Ahmadabad we stayed at the Sikh temple and the next day went to Udaipur in Rajasthan. We stayed at a tourist bungalow there.

It is nearly impossible to describe my state of mind at this point. I was very thin, had long hair and beard and wore saffron kurta and lungi. The question, "Where are you?" seemed to have taken over my entire being. I could barely function. I spent the entire day buying bundles of greens for five paisa and walking around feeding the cows on the streets. I was like a hollow shell that you could see but I wasn't there. I was walking around doing things, but my mind was obsessed with only one thing: the question. Uschi was quite worried about me at this time and rightfully questioned my state of mind and sanity.

We started north on the road to Ajmer and Jaipur. Somehow, we got off the main road and got lost in the mountains. I didn't notice or care. Eventually a man in a Jeep picked us up and said he was going to where this road met the main road to the north and he would take us there. He noticed I was wearing saffron and reading Gita. He asked my path and I told him my path was Bakthi. (Devotion) He said it was also his path.

As we approached the town, I saw a sign that said Nathdwara. He said that he would take us to the main road but first he would have to stop by the temple for his puja, did we mind? At this point I was so absorbed in the question that I didn't even hear him consciously. But I did realize that the temple he was talking about was a very famous Krishna temple (there are only a few Krishna temples), the temple of Sri Nathji. He pulled up to the temple compound and stopped and got out. "Do you want to come with me?" he asked. I got out and followed him through a catacomb of hallways.

We entered the temple and I saw hundreds of people in mass confusion shouting and doing weird things with ghee, milk, rice, waving their arms around, etc. I didn't want to see anything, so I sat on the floor with my back against the wall, cross-legged and put my head down. Suddenly I saw several pair of bare feet in front on me pointing toward me. I looked up and there were several men with red dots on their foreheads. One of them asked, "Are you a Hindu?" in a very forceful voice. I replied softly, "Brother, I am a lover of God." He said, "You are not a Hindu, you must go out. Go out, go out, go out immediately." I looked up again and said, "No." Again he repeated, shouting, "Go out, go out!" I looked up again and said, "I don't care if you cut me into a thousand pieces, I am not going out." Again, he repeated the same shouting refrain. Suddenly I had a change of heart and thought, "Why should I ruin their celebration?"

I stood and left the inner sanctum and started walking back through the catacombs. I heard a voice in my head say, "They just kicked God out of their temple." I did not take it personally and did not feel that way because it was me that they kicked out. It was nothing more than a voice within that said those words that I heard.

When I got out to the dusty, earthen compound I looked over and saw Uschi sitting in the Jeep. I walked toward the Jeep and felt something swell up inside me like a balloon filling with water. The question, "Where are you?" that had been repeating itself inside my head for all this time swelled to such proportions that I could not contain it for another instant. I raised my hands to the heavens with outstretched arms and screamed at the top of my voice, "WHERE ARE YOU?"

In an instant I was struck to the ground on my knees by an explosion inside my head that said, "BABA." I could not rise; I was blind to the outside world. The question disappeared and was replaced by, "Baba, Baba, Baba, Baba, Baba, Baba." Uschi got out of the Jeep and pulled me to my feet and guided me to the Jeep. I was stunned and dazed. I could not see, could not hear, and could not speak. All I could do was listen to the name inside my head. When the driver came, Uschi told him to take us to the railway station, seeing that I was in no condition to hitchhike. We boarded a third-class train for Delhi. It was packed with humanity. I crouched on my haunches against a wall and stared fixedly, without blinking, into space hearing the name repeat itself constantly in my head. An ancient white bearded Sadhu sang the 101 names of God all the way to Delhi next to me.

From the train station we shared a taxi with a couple that took us to their home. I don't remember what they looked like or who they were or where they lived. The next day we checked into the Meva Hotel near Chandni Chowk in Old Delhi. For several days I lay on the bed staring straight up into space hearing the name, taking only water. After a few days I began to come around a little and could think and speak again but the name was still there. I realized I was pretty messed up, but I still did not realize what had actually happened. I was blaming Meher Baba for my condition of stupor. I did not realize that I had cried out for Krishna and He had answered.

I told Uschi that something had happened and Meher Baba was controlling my mind or had some part of me that I had to get back so that I wanted to go there to him right away. She said that we had missed our chance; maybe if we had returned to find out the reply of the telegram, we might have been able to see him, but now it was too late. She said we should go to Rishikesh and there we would find a real guru.

That night I had a dream. If I knew what a vision was, I might call it a vision. Maybe it was a vision, I don't know; I've never had a vision before this or after. It was like a dream except that I was not asleep. It was clearly visual and in color. In the waking dream, Uschi and I were walking down a mountain path. It was a rocky type mountain with no trees. The path was rock and was barely discernable as a path, but I felt that if we were careful and looked before every step that we could get to the end of the path. I knew that Meher Baba was at the end of the path. I looked down to the rocks below my feet and I saw dozens of orange snakes. I recognized them as the Sadhus, Yogis, Swamis and Gurus in their saffron colors. I said, "Uschi, look out...snakes... don't stop or they will bite us, and we will not make it to the end of the path." She fell to her knees and the snakes started crawling over her legs. That was the end of the dream.

When I told her about it the next morning she said, "Yes, we should go to Meher Baba." Then for the first time, I realized what had happened. I had cried out for Him and He had answered.

I washed my saffron clothes and dried them on the balcony, folded them neatly and put on a white Kurta and pajama. We headed down Chandni Chowk and I gave the saffron clothes to the first beggar I saw. We took a Harley Davidson rickshaw to the post office in New Delhi and I wrote a telegram to Meher Baba. I didn't know the address, so I just wrote, "Meher Baba/Ahmednagar." It turned out that this was Meher Baba's exact telegraph address. I also had no return address, so I used the postal clerk's address, care of Abnash Khanna, Clerk, Parliament Street Post Office, New Delhi.

The telegram: Jan 23, 1966

Beloved Baba

We are ready to surrender for the awakening of all, we exhort your Grace, we have come to You, should we come before you in Ahmednagar?

Mik and Uschi Hamilton

When I looked at what I had written I could not believe my

eyes. I had never used the word beloved before. I didn't know what it meant to surrender. Had I written that?

On January 24th we were invited to stay at the newly built, still incomplete bungalow of a local gentleman-farmer in Ghaziabad, a few miles East of Delhi on the Grand Trunk Road.

The bungalow just a concrete floor, and no doors or windows but it was free of cost, quiet and in the countryside. They grew mustard and the caretaker's hobby was grafting roses so there were dozens of rose bushes in bloom. In the meantime, we had run into Roger Yates in Delhi, so we invited him to stay with us in Ghaziabad. He was heavily into cocaine at the time. We, of course, told him the whole story.

We returned every day to the post office for the answer, but none came. On January 26th we were walking toward the post office and coming from the opposite direction was Kirk. Again! We told him where we were going and why. He said that we should not even bother, he had just come from Ahmednagar and there were huge signs by the roadside that said that Meher Baba was in seclusion and could not be disturbed.

We continued to the post office, Kirk joining us. There was an answer.

The telegram from Meher Baba: Jan 26, 1966

MIK AND USCHI HAMILTON CARE ABNASH KHANNA CLERK PARLIAMENT STREET POST OFFICE NEWDELHI 11

–

DON'T COME AHMEDNAGAR REMEMBER ME WHOLEHEARTEDLY AND YOU WILL FEEL MY PRESENCE WHEREVER YOU ARE MY LOVE BLESSINGS TO YOU STOP CONTACT MY LOVER WASEDO KAIN 16 PRESIDENT ESTATE NEWDELHI - MEHERBABA

I stood there in the post office reading the telegram with tears flowing down my cheeks. I had never felt so happy in my life. I didn't care if he said to come or not to come. The idea that he had thought about me for a single instant made that the happiest moment of my life.

We said goodbye to Kirk, got a rickshaw and went to 16 President Estate. It was an enclave for members of parliament. An older gentleman answered the door where he saw before him a young American, hair wild, eyes wild, dressed in Indian clothes clutching a copy of the Bhagavad-Gita in one hand and a telegram in the other and his long-haired wife dressed in pants and a shirt. I thrusted the telegram forward and he read it. "Come in, let's take tea." This is the Indian solution to any situation…and a good one I might add. When in doubt, take tea.

We had tea and he explained to me that, "Meher Baba is in very strict seclusion doing His Universal Work and no one, not even His closest lovers are allowed to see him, but I will try to intervene on your behalf. You should write him a letter and tell him everything and I will also write to him."

I noticed a part of the floor marked off with red ribbon in the next room. I asked Kain what it was. He told me that it was the center of the physical universe. He explained that when Baba came there he would lie on the floor and center his navel over that spot that Kain had marked off and said that it was the center of the physical universe. Wow, I had just witnessed the OM point. He marked it off to avoid that sacred spot being stepped on.

On leaving Kain's place, he handed me two small single Discourses by Meher Baba, one titled, "The Perfect Master" and the other titled, "The Avatar." This was the first I knew that there were any writings by Meher Baba besides what Steve Simon had told me. I took them back to the farm in Ghaziabad and devoured them. Roger read them and upon finishing stood up ran out of the house, flagged down the first car and got a ride into town where he took a taxi to the British High Commission and called his mother in England. He described the scene to me: He'd had a bad connection on the phone and was screaming at the top of his voice, "MEHER BABA IS GOD." The entire High Commission staff could hear him and, of course, thought him mad.

We wrote a letter to Baba and told him everything we could think of: "I'm American, she's German, we smoke hash, we are vegetarian, we plan on living the rest of our lives in India, we love you, we want to see you, please, please, please," etc., etc.

Baba wrote back saying that he appreciated the outpouring of our hearts in expressing our fine sentiments for him but that he could not be disturbed in his seclusion. We should not try to come to see him but should write back to him telling him of our plans and programs and when we plan to return to the West. Again, we wrote telling him that we planned to stay in India and begged to see him. Baba wrote back and told us that drugs are harmful physically, mentally and spiritually, that he wanted us to return to the U.S.A as soon as possible and not feel disappointed at not being able to see him. He said we should come to him with his other Western lovers when he gave the call, and that he would see that we both could make it along with his other Western lovers when the opportune time came.

These letters came by the hand of Adi K. Iran, Meher Baba's secretary. Meher Baba himself, not only maintained silence since 1925 but also did not write.

He instructed us to become introduced by Kain to his lovers in Delhi.

On February 13th we moved into town and stayed at the Madras hotel on Connaught Circle. At a nearby used bookstore, I found a copy of *God Speaks* by Meher Baba which explains how the creation began, how it functions, and its purpose. I took the book to the roof of the Madras hotel, read until I fell asleep, woke up in the morning and finished it. It was the most intellectually satisfying experience of my life. All the philosophy books I had ever read felt to me like someone's opinion of what was going on in life but when I read *God Speaks* I knew there was not a word of philosophy in it; that it was written with complete authority. Every explanation struck a chord within me and it felt like it was coming from inside my own self.

We explained to Baba that we could not return to Germany because we were wanted for drug smuggling and could not go to the U.S.A. because we had tried on two occasions, once in Germany and once in Japan to get a visa for Uschi and both times they had required a police clearance from Germany which we could not get. We begged to him to let us remain in India and to allow us to see him.

His reply was that if we loved him, we would follow his wish. We replied that we would follow his wish and start back immediately by road to Germany.

To this we got the following reply:

Feb. 15, 1966
Dear Mik,
Your letter of 10th to beloved Meher Baba was read to him.

Baba permits you both to visit Him only for five minutes at His abode "Meherazad," about 9 miles to the north of Ahmednagar, on 7th March at 9.30 in the morning. This is on condition that you leave immediately to go back to the U.S.A., for which purpose you must have with you sufficient funds.

Beloved Baba advises you, before coming here, to make all necessary preparations for leaving India, and keep ready your passage – tickets, visa and other travel documents. This will enable you to leave India according to His express wish, soon after seeing Him.

Please confirm this.
With kind regards,
Yours brotherly,
Adi K. Irani

P.S. When I receive your confirmation to this letter, I shall send you the train timings so that you can arrive in Ahmednagar on 7th March morning to see Baba and leave the same day.

I had a new happiest day in my life. I took the letter around the hotel, shouting for joy and shoving it in everyone's face. I could not believe my incredibly good fortune. I was going to see Krishna face to face. His name was Meher Baba.

We decided that we would hitchhike to Manmad and take the meter gauge train to Ahmednagar. We left five days ahead to be sure nothing could go wrong. The first night we stayed at a Tourist Bungalow in Agra, the next night in a truck on the way to Indore. The third night we stayed with a family in Indore. Indore looked like the moon. There had been a severe drought with no rains for three years. All vegetation was dead and blackened and women stood at wells for hours on end just to fill a pot with water to take home for drinking and cooking. We reached Manmad on March 5th and stayed at a Dak Bungalow.

I was getting nervous. The Dak Bungalow was beautiful. We were all alone there. It was a large clean bungalow with a shaded compound. We had stopped taking all drugs the day the letter arrived from Baba instructing us to stop. I was still smoking cigarettes like a chimney, though. We lounged for the extra day and waited for the train to leave. We boarded the train on the night of the sixth. It was a slow meter gauge train; it would take the whole night to go the seventy-five miles to Ahmednagar. I could not sleep a wink all night.

No sooner than I boarded the train and my mind started racing: What will I do when I see him? Should I throw myself at his feet, should I give him namaskar, should I surrender a coconut at his feet? Maybe I should take some bananas.

I thought: I did not come to India in search of my soul. I lived each day as an adventure with all its pain and joys. Where did it start, this journey that ends at His feet? Was it when the

Banarasi sadhu handed me the copy of the Gita? Was it on my first acid trip when I felt oneness? Was it when Steve told me about Meher Baba? Was it when I first became disgusted in Japan and longed to come back to India, when I read *Autobiography of a Yogi* and started keeping silence one day a week? I flashed back to the first time anybody ever said anything that made me ask what I was doing here. I remembered Pop Schedel, my high school teacher, asking me, "Have you ever heard of existentialism?" I thought, yes, that's where it all began: an old man asking me a question and refusing to answer it for me. No, I did not come to India in search of my soul but here I was hearing the wheels on the tracks taking me to see the living Christ in person. How could it be? How could it be?

I reflected on the past months and years that had brought me to this point. For the first time I saw the whole picture. It was a story. How could it be happening to me? I was a beatnik, road bum, freak, drug addict, smuggler, whose entire possessions were in a backpack that weighed five kilos, who had rebelled at every authority I had ever come into contact with since the fourth grade; from my teachers, to my superior officers and now, here I was on my way to surrender to the greatest authority in the universe. The search, first unconscious, now conscious was coming to an end. The search for the Beloved was nearing fruition. I felt blessed, bewildered, scared, nervous, and at peace, all at one and the same time.

The little meter gauge steam engine chugged its way slowly into Ahmednagar. We picked up our backpacks, threw it over our shoulders and got down on the platform. A fair-skinned, handsome, middle-aged Indian gentleman dressed in Indian made western clothes immediately approached us. He introduced himself as Adi K. Irani. Of course, I knew the name from the correspondence. He asked where our bags were, and we told him that this was it. He looked beyond us on the platform in disbelief, just to make sure. "Come with me," he said, and walked out of the station to a parked two-toned blue 1947 Chevy four-door sedan. "Now we are early so we will take tea before going to Meherazad."

As we negotiated the streets of Ahmednagar, Adi nonchalantly mentioned, "That's Baba's seat," gesturing to where I was sitting. I felt incredible awe. I looked down at the seat in disbelief that I could be seated in the same spot that the Avatar had sat in. Finally, we turned off the main road onto a side street and immediately into a compound. Inside the compound were several well-kept, single storied, stucco buildings. The compound was nicely shaded and potted plants were scattered around in bunches.

Adi's young Alsatian dog greeted us immediately. Adi ordered tea from the servants while greeting the dog. As we drank tea, he talked about breeding his dog, this, that and the other thing. Mainly, he told us how happy he was that we had come because now he also could see Baba. He explained that recently and for quite some time, Baba would not allow even his closest lovers to see him. He explained that previously he was with Baba day and night and that now Baba had pushed him away and made him stay in town doing secretarial work. He was sure that Baba was preparing him for something in this manner.

I was trying to hold up my end of the conversation but was preoccupied with thoughts of what was to come. Finally, Adi stood up abruptly and said it was time to go to Meherazad. "We must absolutely be on time. Once when Baba repeated to me several times to be on time for a meeting, and I delayed, having tea, and Baba made me hit a small child with the car on the road and the child was killed." I was shocked at his matter-of-fact attitude toward this. It was as if he was saying that the child had to be sacrificed in order to teach Adi to be on time when Baba ordered him to. I said nothing.

We got back in the Chevy and drove north out of town. My eyes were searching for something, anything that would give me a clue that we were nearing Meherazad. I knew from the correspondence that it was nine miles. Suddenly I saw a hill that stood out from the rest; somehow, I felt its vibration. "What's that hill, Adi?" "Ah, that is Seclusion Hill. Baba has spent long periods there in Seclusion." I knew what the word "seclusion" meant but thought to myself that I don't think I've ever heard it used in conversation. It was sort of like the first time K.K. Ramakrishnan casually dropped the words "Universal Work" on me. I knew both the words but never heard them used together before.

A few moments later we made a left turn into a tree covered lane. After a quarter mile we passed through a large green gate into a dirt compound. The car stopped and we all got out. Adi motioned that we should sit on a wooden bench and wait for him to return. He walked over to and opened a green door that was about five feet away from the bench, entered, and closed the door behind him. I remembered Nathdwara and the utter desperation I experienced there. I looked at the green door. I remembered that the man in the Jeep that took me to Nathdwara told me that "Nathdwara" means "Door of the Lord."

So, there it was; the full circle from the Nathdwara of Krishna to the Green Door of His present form. I knew he was behind that door; my heart pounded, and my mind raced. Again, I questioned myself: Should I throw myself at his feet, shall I give him Namaskar? My thoughts were interrupted when a tall Indian gentleman walked up to us, stopped and asked, "Amrika?" "Ji, Haan, Amrika," I replied. He disappeared into the surreal from which he emerged. Just then the door opened, and Adi emerged. He walked over to us and said, "Baba says you are not to touch his feet, you are not to give him Namaskar. He wants you to embrace him." He turned and led us to the door.

I followed Adi across the threshold and Uschi followed me. Adi immediately stood to the side. The room was deep and narrow with a dirt floor covered in carpets. As my eyes searched for which way to go, they passed over a group of people seated on the floor. I scanned so quickly to find Baba that I did not see how many were in the group, if they were male or female, what they looked like or anything else to distinguish them. My eyes fell on Baba, who was seated in an upholstered easy chair immediately to the right of the door in the near corner of the room. I started walking toward him. It was no more than a couple of steps but in that short distance I had time to fear that I would not get there. He seemed so near...but so far away. I approached him and bent over toward him. His arms went up and his hands softly touched the back of my shoulders and I felt him gently pull me to him and we hugged. I had his embrace and then stepped aside for Uschi. She had Baba's embrace and he motioned that we should be seated on the opposite side of the room, about eight feet away.

We sat on the floor next to the wall without leaning against it. Baba started gesturing with his hands. (Meher Baba had maintained silence since 1925 and communicated with a unique system of hand gestures) As he gestured, my eyes were locked on him and I heard a voice coming from my left, speaking out the gestures in English. I did not see the person speaking out the gestures, as I did not take my eyes from Baba. At the time I was only vaguely aware that Baba was gesturing and someone else was speaking. There was no delay and the communication seemed totally natural. It was completely direct from Baba to us and not as if through an interpreter.

"How did you sleep on the train last night?" Baba asked. "Fine Baba, I slept fine," I replied, completely forgetting that I had not slept a wink. It was not as if I didn't want to complain that I hadn't slept in his presence nor did I answer in the automatic sense as in: "How are you? I am fine." I just totally forgot in his presence.

"Mik, you look very thin. Are you keeping good health?" "Yes, Baba, this is my normal weight." "You must eat lots of chapattis," Baba said, holding his hands before him, first patting the bottom hand with the top hand and then turning them over and reversing the gesture, as if making chapattis.

Suddenly, Baba looked very serious. When his mood changed to serious, it felt as if the room shrunk. The ceiling came down to my head and the walls closed in on me. Baba leaned slightly forward and said, "Did you stop taking drugs?" I answered for both of us, "Yes Baba, as soon as your order came. We have not used any drugs since that time."

The room exploded. The ceiling flew off and the walls expanded to huge proportions. Baba beamed a radiance that made me feel that I had never seen anyone so happy in my entire life. It was like a loving father's proudest moment. The power of his presence was so overwhelming that it did not cross my mind to wonder *why* Baba was so happy but now I realize that it wasn't so much that we had merely stopped taking drugs, but rather because we had demonstrated our love and faith in him by obeying his order to stop taking drugs.

"You must not use drugs; they are harmful physically, mentally and spiritually."

"Have you read *God Speaks*?" I replied that I had and Uschi replied that she had not. Baba said, "You must read *God Speaks* and *Stay with God*. They are the most important books."

Baba looked serious again. He leaned slightly forward again and gestured, "What do you take me for? Who do you take me to be?"

I replied first, saying, "I take you to be Krishna; you are the Living Christ." Baba nodded understandingly. Then he looked at Uschi and a few seconds past before she replied, "I don't know." It was a perfect answer because it was totally honest. As soon as those words escaped her lips she began weeping. It was because (as she revealed to me later) as soon as she uttered those words, Baba revealed himself to her as the Avatar in His own presence. The moment after she uttered the words, "I don't know," she knew. She sobbed, wiping her nose on her shirt for the rest of the time we were there.

Baba answered: "I am God in human form. I know this through my constant experience of it. I never have to ask myself. Just as you never have to ask yourself if you are a man (looking at me) or if you are a woman (looking at Uschi), holding the tips of his thumb and forefinger together encircling his wrist and turning his wrist within the circle as if indicating a bangle); you know it through constant experience. Just as you know this...I know, through constant experience, that I am God in Human form.

"Do you love each other?" We both replied, "Yes."

"Do you want children?"

I replied, "No," and Uschi replied, "Maybe later." Baba nodded understandingly. He then asked, "Which of you am I to please?" I said, "Baba, you should please yourself." He replied that If I really loved Uschi, I should tell Him to please her and that if she really loved me, she should tell Him to please me.

"Is there anything you want to ask me?" Baba asked. Uschi sobbed and I said "No." Adi, who was standing beside Baba's chair at his right shoulder, urged me. "This is your chance to ask Baba anything you want. Are you sure there is nothing you want to ask him?" I thought to myself, "What can I possibly ask? How many Universes are there? Who was I in my last life?" At that moment in time, I had no questions. I was intellectually satisfied and emotionally content. I was just happy to be there in His presence. That's all I wanted. So...instead of asking a stupid question...I made a stupid statement: "Baba, perhaps I can't love you as you should be loved, but I can obey you one hundred percent." Baba made no comment.

"I love you both more that you can ever love yourselves and I will help you...inwardly." He let that soak in for a minute and then said, "Take the love that I have given you and give it as freely as I have. Come to me, kiss me and go."

I stood, walked over to Baba in his chair, bent forward, and embraced Him. We kissed on both cheeks followed by Uschi doing the same, and we backed out the door.

Adi, Uschi and I walked straight to the car. I felt like I had a whole new life ahead of me and my burning longing thirst had been quenched. Before getting into the car a woman, later known to us as Goher, walked up to Uschi and gave her a much-needed handkerchief. We got into the car and drove back the way we came, in silence.

After reaching the main road, Adi pulled out a packet of Char Minar cigarettes and offered me one. I asked, "Adi, Baba said we were not to use drugs; are cigarettes drugs?" He lit his Char Minar, took a long drag, exhaled the smoke and calmly said, "Don't run around at the base of the tree trying to pick up the oranges that have fallen off…just uproot the tree." I understood him to mean that I should not worry about eliminating individual desires but rather to just get rid of desire. I took a smoke and enjoyed it.

The train left in the early afternoon so that we had time to sit with Adi and talk and reflect upon our meeting with the God Man. At some point a bicyclist rode up and spoke to Adi. Adi came to us and said that the cyclist had been sent by Baba from Meherazad with instructions for Adi to ask us if we needed money. If we needed money, Adi was to give us 500 rupees.

I told Adi that we had enough money. In fact, I did have plenty of money but most of it was in the form of a $500 bill that my brother had sent me from New York as payment for a package of hash I had sent him and he had disposed of. I could not cash that until I got to the Russian moneychangers in Kabul. Outside of that I had very little money but felt strange accepting money when I, in fact had over $500 in my pocket.

At one point, I asked Adi why Baba had revealed to us the inner planes of consciousness by writing about them in God Speaks, giving us the opportunity to long for the experiences of the path rather than for the one real truth. Adi replied in a casual tone that these facts were purely for our "general information... and now you can forget them. If you are on your way to Delhi and along the way you see a bright orange light you may stop to observe it. You watch and watch and soon you become enchanted by it...before long you have forgotten that you are on your way to Delhi. It the same way, we must not dwell on the enchantments of the path but rather keep the goal in mind always."

Before we left for the train station, Adi, sitting across the desk from me, looked deep into my eyes and in a serious tone said, "I will tell you something that has taken me over forty years of being with Baba to learn. You will not understand what I am telling you at this moment but someday you will." I looked straight into his sparkling bright eyes and there was a long pause. He spoke again in a slow, deliberate, compassionate voice and said, "Just give God Realization to everyone else...let me serve Baba." I thought I understood exactly what he meant... and I did understand the words perfectly...but now I hear those words repeatedly and realize that I have not even begun to understand their significance.

Adi took us to the train station in the blue Chevy and we boarded the meter gauge train pulled by a small steam locomotive back to Manmad.

It was night when we arrived in Manmad and we had no place to sleep. I asked around and finally found a guy who rented charpois in a room. We went to inspect the room. (First and foremost, we always checked for bedbugs.) While looking at the dingy, poorly lit room full of about eight string beds for about two minutes, I looked down at my white pants and saw at least a hundred bedbugs on each leg. We bolted and when we got outside carefully removed the bedbugs. Finally, I found a gentleman who let us sleep in his car. It was cramped, hot and millions of mosquitoes buzzed us all night long as we imagined that half the village had malaria and the other half had elephantiasis.

Chapter Twenty-One

The Way Back

The hitch back to Delhi was uneventful, the landscape brutally hot and drought-devastated. We stopped for tea in Indore to witness the same drought-ravished deplorable existence as before. Women in hours-long water lines at the open wells wearing filthy faded cotton saris bearing gigantic brass water jugs on their heads. Their bare feet looked like reptiles' skin, so cracked, dried and splayed were they.

On arriving in Delhi, we checked into the Prabahat hotel on Connaught Circle. The next day we went to the U.S. Consulate to check mail. While there, I spoke to Mr. Chaudery, a consulate worker with whom I had become acquainted through our many visits. He was a short, wire-bespectacled man, middle aged, thin, well-groomed always wearing an Indian hand-made suit, white shirt and tie. He looked like a meticulous former clerk of the Raj.

As I sat across the desk from him, casually opening my mail, I wondered why he never gave the slightest hint of judgment about my appearance or purpose in being in India. He just seemed to accept me. I liked him and usually have samosas brought from the consulate canteen for us to have with the tea that he inevitably ordered to be brought when we arrived. During our conversation I told him that I needed an immigration visa for my wife, a German national. He said it would be no problem; fill out the form, leave the passport and pick it up in two- or three-day's time. When I confided to him that we had already attempted to get the visa in both Frankfurt and in Tokyo and had been turned down, he looked me in the eye through his round wire-rimmed glasses with a very compassionate look and merely said, "I shall arrange faar you. You just come back after three days' time and I shall have it faar you." I was thinking, "sure, sure." But, guess what? He did have it!

Two weeks after arriving back in Delhi we were heading north to the Pakistan border on a third-class train to Amritsar, visas in hand. We knew that the border was closed due to the recent India/Pakistan war but there was only one way back for us and that was across that border. So, without the slightest bit of apprehension we headed for the border. In Amritsar we met a Sikh gentleman, the owner of a trucking company, who told us that the Wagah border was, in fact, closed but that we may be able to cross at Ferozepore.

We went to the border crossing at Ferozepore and met the immigration officer in charge. He took us to the gate that crossed the road to Pakistan, and we looked over it. About a hundred yards down the road we could see seventy Pakistanis on the other side looking at us over a similar gate on the Pakistan side of the border. In the fields adjacent on the Pakistan side, we could see the ruins of several buildings. These were the immigration and customs buildings of the Pakistan government that had been recently bombed by India. There was nothing left standing.

The Indian immigration officer, a seven-foot tall Sikh in a stiff starched blue turban looked down at me and said, "Nothing is there, Sahib. We have informed Pindi (Rawalpindi, the then capital of Pakistan) that we shall open our borders on April 4th but we have had no response. Come back on that day. We will definitely open regardless of what they do." April 4th….hmmm, that was about ten days from now. What to do until then, because we had about two dollars to get us to Kabul where I could cash the $500 bill? We hitched back to Amritsar and went back to the trucking company, explaining that we had no money and would probably stay at the gurudwara at the Golden Temple and eat langar. The owner, a jolly and generous man told us that he had the perfect place for us to stay without cost to us and the accommodations were much better. He called for his assistant to bring the strong box and gave us money. He loaded us in his car and drove for some time out of town, turning off the main road at the Beas River, one of the five great rivers of the Punjab, to enter a small colony of buildings.

I was quite surprised to see dozens of westerners dressed in Indian clothing walking around the colony. As we walked toward the room where we were to sleep, I noticed that nearly all the people I saw were westerners, but not travelers. Straight people, middle aged mostly. As I passed them, they looked at me with a blissed-out glaze in their eyes and some surprise at my appearance. They joined their palms in front of their faces in the Indian manner of greeting and said something that I couldn't quite make out. It wasn't Namaste or Namaskar. We got to our room and closed the door and I asked Uschi, "What the hell is this place, anyway?"

I went out into a courtyard and sat on a bench, observing. They all used that same greeting and finally I made out what they were saying. Every time they passed someone, they put their palms together and said, "Radha Soami." Eventually I asked someone to explain to me where I was and what this place was all about. Someone, I don't remember who, explained to me that this was the Radha Soami Colony. Radha Soami was a deceased spiritual leader whose successor, Swaran Singh, or Charan Singh now led the group. Some of the followers told me that they thought that he, Charan Singh, was a Perfect Master (Sadguru). The place was immaculate. The kitchen was pure vegetarian and the food was the best we had had in a long time.

After dinner someone handed me a copy of the Master's Darshan/Speaking schedule. There were Punjabi discourses scheduled for this evening. We were asked if we would be attending. I politely declined on the excuse that we did not understand Punjabi. I was told that neither did they understand but they went anyway just for the opportunity to be in his presence. I thought, "Oh my God, what have I gotten myself into?" I just needed a place to crash and now I was in the colony of some spiritual group that wanted to convert me, fresh on the heels of having just met God in human form. I told them we would attend the English discourses the next morning. They were shocked and amazed but did not push the point, just drifted off on a cloud to somewhere else.

The next morning after breakfast we were summarily escorted to the living room of the "master" Swaran Singh, amid hundreds of "Rada Swami" greetings. He was a striking looking man; even beautiful I might say. He was quite tall even for a Sikh, probably over six feet. He wore spotless white Punjabi kurta and pajamas and the blue priest's turban of the Sikhs. His eyes were ocean blue with that sparkling transparency that one rarely sees even in the West. His beard was snow white although he did not look over fifty years old. Only some small smile lines at the edges of his eyes revealed that he was even that age. He sat in a wingback chair with his feet on a pillow. His wife stood at the side of the chair, slightly behind with one hand on his right shoulder. He discoursed for over an hour. I did not hear a word he said. All I could think about was that I must tell him immediately that the Avatar is here.

After he stopped talking, everyone in the room, including Uschi, backed reverently out the door so as not to turn their backs on him. I walked to his chair and sat cross-legged and bare footed in front of him on the floor. He looked down at me with a beautiful smile on his face and I asked him, "Who are you?" With compassion in his voice he answered, "Brother, I am a seeker, just like you." When I asked him if he knew that those people outside the hall thought that he was a Perfect Master, he said, "I allow them to think whatever they want to think." I replied to him that, that may be O.K. for them, but that he was probably walking on spiritual thin ice. He did not reply so I asked him if he had heard of Meher Baba. He said yes, he had and that they had all of Baba's books in their library. I asked him if he had read them and he said no. I recommended that he do so because Meher Baba was the Avatar of the age. He said he would. I stood and gave him Namaskar and backed out of the room.

As I emerged there was a huge throng to greet me. "What have you done? What did you say to him? You can't just approach the master whenever you want to!" I just smiled respectfully, went to my room and packed my backpack. We had been there three days and I believed the purpose had been fulfilled.

Our transport company owner/friend put us up in the Hotel Green until April 4th when we would again attempt to cross the border, meanwhile regaling us with the best Punjabi food I have ever tasted.

On April 4th, 1966, the day after my twenty-third birthday we went to the Ferozepore border and again spoke with our towering, giant, skinny Sikh border official. He seemed gaunter than I remembered. His cheeks were hollow, and he looked like he hadn't slept. Even though I knew it was not so, he looked like he was suffering from extreme malnutrition. In a very nervous and halting voice he spoke near perfect English and explained that India had opened its border unilaterally without hearing from Pindi. He explained that we would be allowed to leave India, but he had no idea how we would be greeted on the other side of the border. He informed us that if Pakistan did not allow us to enter, we should just return, and he would re-stamp our passports for reentry into India. I explained to him that my Indian visa expired today, and he said that I should not worry about that but under no circumstances should I make a scene at the other side of the border because it could spark an international incident. He stamped our exit stamp into our passports, wished us luck and then went to hide behind a tree to watch and see what happened.

As I approached the yellow line across the road, signifying the international border I saw two men on the left edge of the road. Each man was in military uniform with a Sten gun slung across his shoulder. The first man was a 6'5" heavy-set Sikh in an Indian army uniform. He held out his hand and said, "Passport." I handed him my passport and after examining my exit stamp said, "Hindustan theeke, Pakistan Jao. ("India OK...go now to Pakistan.") He then pointed down at the 5'6" green-eyed Pakistani soldier, his mortal enemy, standing at his left shoulder. He never once looked at him. I handed my passport to the obviously Pathan soldier and glanced over my right shoulder to see all the border buildings still in ruins. He handed my passport back after looking at it and said, "Pakistan nishta."

I knew just enough Pashto to understand that to mean that Pakistan is "not available." I spoke in English and said, "I want to speak to an officer," glancing back over my left shoulder to see the Indian officers peeking out from behind trees. He repeated, "Pakistan nishta." "I want to speak to an officer." We each repeated these two sentences back and forth about four times, until I gave up and returned to the Indian immigration building, a small adobe hut with a tile roof. As promised, we received an "entry" stamp and were sent on our way.

The next day every major newspaper in India carried the story on its front page. The headlines read: PAKISTAN FAILS TO KEEP THE SPIRIT OF THE TASHKENT AGREEMENT by failing to allow western travelers to cross its international border.

Our friendly transport company owner was so shocked that he immediately purchased two tickets for us to fly to Kabul by way of Ariana Royal Afghan Airlines. We later dubbed it "Inshalla Airlines." (God-Willing Airlines).

We arrived at the Amritsar airport, went through immigration and got another exit stamp in our passports without mention that my visa had expired. We boarded the 1935 model C 145

"Gooneybird" on the tarmac, taxied to the end of the runway, taxied back to the terminal and disembarked. We were told that the mountains in the Hindu Kush over which we had to fly were 12,500 feet and this airplane would not fly over 10,000 feet. As a result, we would have to fly through the passes to cross over into Afghanistan and since the weather was bad we could not fly in the passes so the flight was cancelled for today. "Come back tomorrow please." We were given another India entry stamp in our passport and put up in the Ritz Hotel in Amritsar at the expense of Inshalla Airlines.

On arriving at the hotel, I was deliriously happy. It was the first hot water shower I had seen for, my God, how long had it been? Cold-water bucket baths, drainage ditches, rivers, and open wells were my only bathing places for probably over a year. I could not remember the last hot shower I had taken. It was heaven. I showered several times that day, then we went to the Golden Temple just for the love of it. It is unique and one of the few places in the world that I can say really moved me and touched my heart.

The next day we went to the airport, got our exit stamps, the weather was checked, we were told that again the weather was bad, we got our re-entry stamps, were instructed to return the following day and were transported back to the Ritz Hotel. Hot showers and good food for another day!

The following day we got our exit stamp as usual, taxied the runway and took off. Yeah! The airplane was full of Afghans, their goats and chickens. The seats were wired to the floor where they had broken and some of the windows were loose and cracked. As we flew over the Hindu Kush range I went to the cockpit and chatted with the pilot and co-pilot. The pilot was a young Afghan who had taken flight training in the U.S.A. and spoke English. I had a panoramic view of the Hindu Kush Range. It was breathtaking.

As we began to fly through a pass, the peaks on each side

were about 500 yards off to the right and left of our wingtips. They met below us about 1000 feet from our belly. All of a sudden, the sky turned black and the plane hit an air pocket and we dropped instantly what seemed a couple of hundred feet. The pilot quickly told me to go back and be seated. I turned and entered the passenger area to find everyone scrambling to find a place in the aisle to pray, amidst shouts of "BISMILLAH NIRACHMAN NIRAHEEM," chickens flying all over the place, scattering feathers everywhere and goats bleating as if there was a wolf on board.

After some very lucky and good maneuvering and a few hair-raising minutes, the pilot emerged from the cockpit looking white as a ghost and said, "There is bad weather. We are turning around. We will land in Amritsar in two and a half hours."

New entry stamps, transport to the Ritz, hot showers and good food again…worth it. I was in no hurry. I was enjoying this to the fullest.

The next day, April 17th, 1966, now almost two weeks since the border incident, we got our seventh and last exit visa from India and flew safely to Kabul where I changed money and checked into the Maiwand Hotel. We stayed here for two days. It seemed weird to pass all the places we used to smoke hash without stopping in, but I had no craving. It seemed as if Meher Baba had just removed the desire and we were still intoxicated with the knowledge and remembrance of having met him.

The next day we hitchhiked to Kandahar where we stayed in another cheap hotel, the Hotel Shahi. Early the next morning right after tea, yogurt, honey and bread we had a ride to Herat, in western Afghanistan near the Iran border. Amazingly, considering everything else in Afghanistan seemed from a past age, the roads were fantastic. They had been built in sections from Herat to Kandahar, Kandahar to Kabul and Kabul to Landi Kotal through the Khyber Pass, by the Germans, Russians and Americans, respectively. The terrain was mountainous desert, a terrain in which I was not used to seeing good roads. As we approached Herat, the road passed through a tree-lined section, about a mile long, of flowering trees with a scent like Jasmine. It was like being in a tunnel of jasmine as the trees from each side of the road met above us.

Herat was a beautiful ancient place with a walled old city, entirely made of mud adobe. It is situated at an altitude of about 3,000 feet, just south of the Paropamisus Range on the Harirud River. The area is one of the most densely populated areas of Afghanistan because of its fertility and irrigation from the Harirud. Herat has a very rich history as several ancient cities have stood near here. Some of the greatest conquerors of all time have ruled from here, including Alexander the Great and Timur (Tamerlane). Herat was later disputed between the Persians and Afghans and changed hands many times until the mid-19th century when it became a permanent part of Afghanistan.

We stayed in a cheap hotel in Herat and left the next morning for Mashhad. Unfortunately, one must cross the Iran border, which gave me malignant diarrhea. Although I was not smuggling anything, I was so used to crossing borders with either drugs or stuff to sell, that it was a conditioned response. Plus, I realized that although I had no drugs in my possession, I still had a small leather pouch that I had carried hash powder in for years and its inside was infused with hash. As soon as you opened it, the scent of hash would instantly fill the room. I should have thrown it away but it was a keepsake from my mother-in-law, so I kept it.

They had the death sentence on drugs in Iran at the time. We were traveling with a busload of Pakistani Hajis on their way to Mashhad on a pilgrimage to the tomb of Ali ar-Rida, the eighth imam of the Twelver Shiite sect of Islam. I had long hair and beard just like they did, and I also was still wearing Punjabi dress so it was "salaam a laikum Haji, and malaikum salaam" all around at the border. They border officials all called me

"Haji" because they thought I was one of the Pakistani pilgrims. That is, until I pulled out my blue passport! Fortunately, we had broken the ice enough with the friendly greetings that they passed us through routinely.

As soon as we crossed the border the roads changed from paved to washboard desert earth. We hitched a ride in a truck going to Mashhad and slept fitfully in the truck that night. The next day we arrived in Mashhad and decided to splurge on a hotel. (I had changed the $500 bill in Kabul and had what to me, was a fortune in cash.) At the hotel I was again greeted as "Haji" and told that I could have a beautiful room with a view of the mosque. That was, until I pulled out my blue passport. Suddenly the hotel was booked full as was every other hotel in town.

It was blatant discrimination. We finally said, screw this and went to the railway station and slept on a bench all night. You might think that sleeping on a bench at the railway station would be uncomfortable but compared to the brutal constant pounding over dirt washboard in the truck the night before, it was bliss. And it was with this thought in mind that we decided to splurge and take the train to Teheran.

Teheran felt different this time. Maybe it was because it seemed more familiar; maybe it was because we were used to negotiating our way around Asian bazaars in foreign languages. In any case Teheran looked beautiful. We hadn't seen the luxuries of a city since Delhi. That seemed like a long time ago. We taxied along the beautiful boulevards in the perfect night air, had lunch, tea and hookah at fashionable sidewalk cafes. We went to the rug bazaar and visited Hassan, Ebrahim's cousin-brother where we were treated like long lost family members. we even bought a small rug to take back to Mutti (my mother-in-law) as a gift. It was our first and only purchase of merchandise not meant for immediate use or sale on our entire journey so far.

We only stayed three days and two nights in Teheran then

hitchhiked to Tabriz, spent the night in a hotel and the next night we were in Ezerum, in Eastern Turkey. We were pretty beat up by this time so, remembering the dangerous roads through the mountains of Eastern Turkey and, having enough money to afford the luxury, we decided to take the train to Istanbul.

The scene in Istanbul was different. We spent three days and two nights there. There seemed to be a lot more people on the road. And not just European gammler and junkies, though we did see a couple of old acquaintances at the "pudding shop" near the Aga Sofia. I couldn't quite figure it out. They had long hair and smoked dope, but they were different; a new wave of adventurers, especially a lot of Americans, younger than we were by several years. They were the hippies. Many of them recognized us as experienced on the road. I had not shaved or cut my hair for a long time by now and was still wearing Indian garb. My backpack was well worn. They had a million questions about what lay to the east. Most of them thought it quite strange, with our appearance, that we did not smoke dope. We told them about Meher Baba, the Avatar of the Age. Only he knew the fate of those who heard his name at that time.

We decided to travel back to Germany by the southern route through Northern Greece, so we rapidly hitchhiked our way back staying one night at a time in Alexandropolis, Thesaloniki, Mitrovica, Lyubliana, and Munich in five successive days, arriving back home in Frankfurt on the sixth day. I remember the last ride into Frankfurt very well because the truck driver questioned us thoroughly, not believing a word we said about who we were and where we had been. My German was about as good as his, so he didn't believe I was an American. He had been a merchant seaman years ago and had visited Viet Nam, so he asked us testing questions like, "How long did it take to sail from the mouth of the Mekong River to Saigon?" Finally, we answered all his questions to his satisfaction so he believed us.

We spent a month in Frankfurt from May 6th, 1966 to June 8th.

The price of an airline ticket from Luxembourg to New York on Icelandic Airlines was still $167 U.S but the $500 I started from Kabul with was dwindling fast. We did not have enough money for the tickets.

Spring was beautiful in Frankfurt. It seemed great to be back in the West, especially at home in the Friedrichstrasse in Frankfurt's Westend. The temperature this time of year was in the low 70s. The skies were blue and clear. We were high on God.

We had come full circle after two years. I didn't realize it at the time, but I was in a little bit of an identity crisis. I was really a changed person. I had left Frankfurt with the aim of avoiding work, staying high and having an adventure. Now I was still a freak, but I didn't smoke dope. I didn't really fit in. I had not cut my hair or shaved my face for over two and a half years. I was still wearing all white Punjabi clothes and sandals. I weighed about 113 pounds. I stood out like a sore thumb. Germans would talk about me in public loud enough for me to hear them. "Ai, kuk amal da, es ist doch Jesus," ("Look, there goes Jesus.") or, regarding my hair, "Kuk doch amal was Zoettel." ("Look at those filthy pigtails." I would just laugh it off or make some comment back in Frankfurter slang, like "Gell, da klotz de, aber." ("Makes you stare like an idiot, huh?") I was heckled on the streets. None of our friends from before were in town.

Mutti and the Baron made no judgment about us. They just were glad to see us and happy we were back safe and sound. I was sure that Ushi's sister Otti met us with ambivalence to say the least.

We savored Mutti's home cooking and enjoyed the sanitary conditions of the West. We still hung out at the Jazz Keller and Jazz Haus in the Kleinebockenheimergasse. One night, while entering the alley to the Jazz Keller, I spotted a nerdy looking American Jew handing a small packet to an American soldier and taking money from him with the other hand, blatantly making a deal right in the open. I approached him after the soldier left and asked him if he was out of his mind to be so obvious. I explained that the Frankfurt KRIPO (Kriminal Polizei) knew that a lot of people who came to listen to jazz smoked dope, and they watched this area.

We struck up a conversation and he invited us to his apartment in the Ostend, near the zoo. He was a New Yorker named David who had gone to Israel to work on a Kibbutz. He was traveling with his Israeli wife whose name was Sabra and she was an actual Sabra (native born Israeli). They did not use drugs, but he had a kilo of hash that he had bought in Lebanon as an investment. He heard you could make a ton of money selling hash in Europe, so he was trying it. I told him I knew the whole scene and he should be more careful. He told me that someone told him that evening that he had just sold to an undercover cop and he was totally freaked out that they would be banging his door down any second. He asked me if I would take the kilo of hash for a few days for safekeeping. I had already told him that we had stopped using so he felt safe that we would not smoke it up. The next day we heard he was busted. We sold his hash and bought airline tickets on Icelandic Airlines from Luxembourg to New York City and got the hell out of there.

I have no memory of how we got from Frankfurt to Luxembourg. We would have either hitchhiked or taken the train. The Icelandic airlines plane lands at Keflavik, where the airport of Reykjavik, capital of Iceland is located, on the flight to New York. We landed in a blizzard. The plane stays on the tarmac and you must walk to the terminal. It's only about fifty meters but it was snowing heavily, below zero temperature and winds of over fifty miles per hour. They had extended a thick rope from the terminal to the airplane to hold onto so that we would not get blown away into the blizzard. Still, even while holding the rope, you had to lean forward into the wind at a thirty-degree angle to keep from being blown over.

Landing in New York I got the "border jitters." I wasn't carrying anything illegal but having lived as a smuggler for the past couple of years, it was a conditioned response. Also, this time it wasn't just a matter of customs. Uschi had a German passport with an immigration visa issued in New Delhi. Then of course there was that little matter of having previously been on the Interpol list for kidnapping minors. I had no idea what the status of that was. Also, I had long hair and a beard and was wearing a white, thin, cotton, flowing Lucknow kurta and white cotton Punjabi tight-legged "pajamas."

Luckily, before we knew it, we were sitting in Bobby Brown's girlfriend Elaine's pad on West 10th street. She had a cool apartment on the corner of 8th Avenue that overlooked the Women's House of Detention. Elaine had always liked me but only tolerated some of my bad habits, especially drugs. She totally adored Bobby even though she knew that their relationship would always be platonic because he was gay. Uschi had had a lifelong dream (and intuition) that she would live in the United States. She told her mother as a little girl, "Someday I will spend only dollars." Well, there we were in New York City, one of the greatest cities in the world. But its face had changed since I was last here. We saw our first hippies. We had seen a few here and there on the road, pothead flower children, but now we were seeing them everywhere.

Baba had instructed us to contact Fred and Ella Winterfeld, two of his "lovers," when we get to New York. We phoned them and they told us that all the New York "Baba Lovers" met on Monday nights at a room at Carnegie Hall. Although we had attended the Birthday Celebration in New Delhi where there were lots of Meher Baba's followers, I believe this was the first time I heard the term "Baba Lover." I did not know that he had followers in the U.S. beyond the names he gave me to contact, Fred and Ella Winterfeld, and Robert Dreyfuss. They insisted that I must attend the meeting the following evening because they were longing to hear any word of Baba, since Baba was in strict seclusion, no one could see him, or write to him. They received only the barest of "official" communications from his secretary, Adi K. Irani. We agreed to attend the meeting.

Our taxi dropped us off at Carnegie Hall and we went inside. Besides the infamous main hall, there are many meeting rooms on the upper floors and the New York Baba group rented one of these rooms for their Monday night meetings. As I approached the door, a man blocked the entry. He asked who we were and what we knew about Meher Baba. "Not just anyone can come in here," he said. I replied, "We've just come from Meherazad." His entire personality changed. "Oh, my dears! Come right in."

A somewhat older crowd of very straight people, solid citizen types, greeted us profusely with warm enthusiasm and big hugs. This was when I found out that Baba Lovers hug each other when meeting. I flashed back to Baba's all-encompassing embrace. Accepting and giving "Baba hugs" all around, we were the center of attention, surrounded by the crowd, pelted with question after question. "You must tell us the whole story, everything that happened from beginning to end."

I was seated at the front of the hall facing the crowd of Baba Lovers. Some of them became life-long acquaintances. I told the whole story to a hushed, sometimes sobbing, sometimes laughing, on the edge of their seats, group of people who hung on every word I said just to get a tiny whiff of fragrance from Baba. Afterwards we were swarmed with affection and a group of us who stayed later went across the street to a restaurant where Uschi and I were regaled with food and love, pelted with question after question for any morsel of His presence. I always claimed thereafter that I had once performed at Carnegie Hall!

I had told the Winterfelds that Baba had also instructed me to meet Robert Dreyfuss while there. They said that he would not be there for the meeting but that he was coming from Boston the next day. As I remember, we met Robert in a pizza parlor. Finally, a Baba Lover that was my age. It was like meeting a long-lost brother and that feeling has never waned since that day. We told Robert that we were going to Santa Barbara to stay with an old Army buddy of mine, Chris West and would contact him when we were settled there. He gave us his contact information and said he may be heading out to see us when we get there. We all rejoiced in our mutual love for the Beloved, ate pizza and parted with eager anticipation of meeting again soon in Santa Barbara.

The next day, I received a phone call from Fred Winterfeld informing me that he had received a phone call from another New York Baba Lover named Dr. Harry Kenmore informing him that he, Harry, had received a telegram from Baba that he should meet us while we were in New York. Fred gave me the address and I called to arrange a time to meet with Dr. Kenmore. We set a time to go to his office and upon arrival there, I immediately realized that he was totally blind. He said that he was a Doctor of Chiropractic. I had no idea what that was but as he led us through his offices, I saw several very large, beautiful, framed photos of Baba adorning the walls. He had a booming, arrogant, obnoxious voice. "See these pictures? They're beautiful, aren't they? I can't see a damned thing, I'm blind as a bat," he shouted. We sat in his office, he behind his desk and the two of us opposite. "What do you look like?" he boomed. "I look like a man." I answered, somewhat evasively. I had the idea that he didn't like young people with long hair, and I was pretty freaky looking for his conservativeness. "I can't see a damned thing. I palpated Baba's face," he continued. I had never heard the word "palpated" before but figured from the context that it meant to feel in place of sight. I felt like every sentence he uttered was in capital letters and punctuated by a huge exclamation point at the end!

Finally, we left, and on the elevator down I said, "What the hell was that all about? Why was he supposed to meet us?" Little did I know that the seed of my eventually becoming a chiropractor was probably planted by Baba, through Harry Kenmore, at that meeting. He told me that Baba had had him adjust his neck for forty days in a row and that Baba had told him that chiropractic was "the healing art of The New Humanity." I figured that Baba wasn't just taking forty days off from his Universal Work to get his neck worked on, so there must be something beyond this that I just didn't understand. I forgot about it until a long time later.

We moved to my brother Tom's pad on East 13th Street for one night, and then on June 15, 1966 caught a Greyhound bus to Chicago.

We went to the address that I had for Harry Hamilton, the stepfather who raised me from the time I was four and whom I had not seen since high school. He was somebody about whose love I was certain all my life.

He wasn't home when we got there so we just walked in and made ourselves at home. He didn't know we were coming. I turned on the TV and saw color TV for the first time in my life. I thought it was totally psychedelic, so I made everybody purple and watched it for a while. When my dad got home, he freaked out. He could not believe my appearance. He was at a total loss. "How can I take you out to a restaurant? How can I introduce you to my friends?" he asked in desperation. I was astounded at his reaction. He had been such a huge influence in my life and taught me so much. I didn't understand his reaction at the time but now I can see how very foreign it must have seemed to him. We stayed one uncomfortable night with him in Chicago and the next day went to Racine, Wisconsin, my birthplace, to see my mom.

My mom had remarried since I last saw her, to an artist named Rodney Bussler. He was a good but unknown painter working mostly in watercolors. He worked as a commercial artist for an advertising agency to make a living. I had the feeling that Rodney didn't like me. My mom, on the other hand, didn't care if I had demons growing out of my head. I was her son and she loved me and totally accepted me. We spent two days there then hitchhiked to Bloomington, Illinois, my hometown from age five, where my grandmother, "Sammie" and grandfather lived.

Sammie and Granddad didn't care what I looked like either. We stayed there for about three weeks. I bought a '57 Chevy for fifty bucks that looked good but didn't run. I worked on it and got it running and in mid-July we headed for California on good ole Route 66. Bloomington is on Route 66 and I always thought that maybe my wandering urge was the result of growing up on that famous highway. So here we were, off to our new life in California and the world of hippies, drug free, high on God, and as usual, no idea what fate awaited us, or how we were going to survive. We had a '57 Chevy, our backpacks, about three hundred dollars and a shoebox full of genuine Phoenician trade beads that I had bought from an African guy for one hundred dollar the night before we left Frankfurt. I also had a two-thousand-year-old stone Buddha carving that I had stolen from a museum in Peshawar and shipped to Sammie's address. I was sure would bring a fortune.

At the time that I took the piece from the museum, I felt like I was liberating it. It was an entire museum dedicated to Gandharan art from the time of Alexander the Great: most of it was stone statuary made of schist. The museum was empty of people. No one cared about this stuff. It was a forbidden graven image of a foreign god to them. Some of it was displayed but there were piles of stuff in corners everywhere. From one of these piles I "liberated" my Buddha. It was about eighteen inches tall and twelve inches wide. I planned on selling it in Los Angeles to a museum or antique art dealer. One other significant thing happened in Bloomington: We got a dog.

One day, my birth father, Fern Welch, drove down to Bloomington from Racine, Wisconsin to visit his mother who lived in the small town of Danvers, a few miles away. Uschi and I went to visit my grandparents while my dad was there. He had just bought a brand new white Toranado. It was beautiful. I saw a sign at a local store that some farmers had Irish setter mix puppies and were looking for good homes. I asked my dad to drive us to the farmhouse and he agreed. Unfortunately, the county had just oiled the gravel roads and the car was covered up to the middle of the doors with tar when we returned from picking out our puppy. We spent the entire rest of the day, in hundred-degree heat and 99 percent humidity, cleaning the tar off his new car. It was brutal. I had to constantly remind myself that we must have some work karma to work out together for this to have happened. We named our puppy Sita. Sita was the consort of Rama in the Hindu epic Ramayana. She was the cutest little thing. She looked just like an Irish Setter, perhaps a little smaller, with dark chestnut brown hair.

Our goal was to drive to Santa Barbara where my old army buddy Chris West lived. We left on July 12th, 1966 and spent the first night in our car in Oklahoma, the next night in Texas, then two nights in Espanola, N.M. with a friend. Then we drove up through the four corners area, Shiprock, Tuba City, Grand Canyon, and the Mojave Desert to Santa Barbara. Since I had been in contact with Chris, he had married a woman named Cynthia. She was recently divorced from her first husband and they lived in her house in Montecito, just south of Santa Barbara in a beautiful, huge Spanish house with a gigantic orchard. They told us that they had just bought some land outside of Taos, N.M. and were planning on moving there very soon.

In the first week that we were there Chris told me he had to go tow a jeep that he had turned over into a ravine in Gaviota. Chris and Cynthia had recently been run off some land in Gaviota, just north of Santa Barbara where they had established a hippie commune. The owners knew of the commune but the time was running out on the squatter's rights law, so they forced them off the land. I went along to help him.

As we drove to the foot of State Street to Pacific Coast Highway, I saw dozens of hippies hitchhiking. If I thought I had seen hippies before, it was just a primer for what I saw in Santa Barbara. There were thousands of them. One of the hitchhikers caught my eye. He was tall and thin and looked more like Chris' and my age, unlike the other hippies who were in their teens. He had long black matted hair and a long black matted beard. He looked like he had been on the road for a few years. He had a majestic look to him like an ancient Hassidic or a Hindu Sadhu.

After we pulled the Jeep out of the ravine, we towed it over to the gas station at Gaviota Beach. As I looked down the beach, I saw the same Sadhu-looking guy that I had seen hitchhiking in Santa Barbara walking along the beach. I watched him as he walked seemingly aimlessly down the beach. Then I spotted another guy standing next to a station wagon. He looked like a hippie too but was also older, possibly even older than I. He was standing next to a station wagon. As I approached, I saw him looking inside his car shaking his head. As I got closer, I saw that the car had been on fire and burned out the insides including all his belongings. The back of the car was charred but the rest of it looked pretty good. I asked him what he planned to do with it and he said he didn't know. I offered him twenty-five bucks for it and he sold it to me.

Chris and Cynthia packed up and left and said we could help ourselves to the orchard until the house sold. That was great for us because we were vegetarian at the time and the orchard had, plums, peaches, avocados, nectarines and other fruits that I can't remember. We literally lived off this orchard. We rented a two-bedroom house in a mixed neighborhood between the freeway and the Mesa for seventy-five dollars a month. I spent several days cleaning up the burnt-out car and repairing it with a few cheap parts that were needed and sold it a week later for $250 to a hippie who wanted to buy it and sleep in it.

In the meantime, we were starting to meet some people. One night we were invited to a party. At the party, I saw the guy I bought the car from (Ron Ormerod) and the Sadhu-looking guy from Gaviota. His name was George. He was making flutes from bamboo that he cut himself and was selling them to eke out a living. He gave me one as a gift. It was at this party where I found out that people like me, who had been on the road for a while and especially in India were looked up to with near adoration by the teenage hippies. They seemed to flock around asking questions about the road and about India. The subject would eventually get around to drugs and that led to me having to tell them what Meher Baba said about drugs.

Our house was constantly full of people wanting to hear about India, especially about Meher Baba and his message of love and truth to humanity. I had learned how to make Indian chai (milk tea), strong and sweet, from watching the Chai Walla make it in the tea stands of the Indian road and had become very fond of it. I would make pot after pot of chai for our visitors and sit cross-legged on the floor, long hair and beard flowing, dressed in Indian shirt and pajama pants for hours on end answering questions about Meher Baba.

One day I made a trip to L.A. to try to sell the Buddha. I went to place after place, but no one wanted to pay more than a couple of hundred dollars, so I held out. But in the meantime, every time I looked at it sitting on my dresser, I remembered that I had stolen it. I realized that I had a bit of a guilty conscience about it so I packed it in a box, placed a copy of Meher Baba's Universal Message inside with it and shipped it back to the museum with a note stating that I had stolen it a few years ago and was returning it. They probably just threw it back onto the pile where I found it.

One day there was a knock on the door and Uschi opened it to see Sadhu George' another guy whose name was Jerry Paulson and Ron Ormerod, the guy I bought the burned-out car from. They said that they had heard that I never eat and wanted to talk to me about it. They started talking about becoming "breatharians," who live only on the air that they breathe. They were all on macrobiotic diets at the time and lived almost exclusively on brown rice. I told them that in fact, I did eat, even though it might look like I didn't. Someone probably heard Uschi say, "Oh, he never eats," and thought that she was being literal. In any case, that was the pretext upon which they entered my life. The real reason was so that they could hear about the Avatar of the Age, Meher Baba. Jerry (later to be known as Mark Paulson) became a lifelong friend and brother as did Ron Ormerod.

So life went on, day after day, week after week, a really magical time in Santa Barbara, living off the orchard, talking to people all day long, making jewelry from the trade beads to sell so that we could get the necessities.

The day Robert Dreyfuss showed up from the East Coast was a day that changed everything. Suddenly the conversation drifted to how much we missed India, being on the road and the entire road lifestyle. We discussed how Baba had told us to return to the West and not to come back to India until he called us for his Darshan along with his other Western Lovers. Baba had indicated that it would be next year. Suddenly we were hatching up a plan to ask Baba if it was alright if we started on the way now if we did not enter into India. That would allow us to spread his message about drugs to the people with whom we felt the greatest affinity, the road bums. We drew up the letter to ask Baba and sent it, then took a short trip to San Francisco together.

If I thought Santa Barbara was full of hippies, it was only getting me ready for San Francisco. We crashed with some hippies we met in the Haight and wandered around the city taking a little side trip to Berkeley. I had never even heard of Berkeley at that time. It was only a couple of days, but we had a great time.

Robert left for the East Coast and we returned to Santa Barbara to await Baba's reply to our request. Unbelievably, he consented. We were shocked; we never thought he would consent to such a plan. Now we were faced with a lot of problems: Where would we get the money to make the trip, how would we get visas, how would we sell everything off, how would we arrange for our dog, Sita?

The dog part was easy; she was coming with. We sold all the household goods and drove the '57 Chevy to New York, stopping for a couple of days in Bloomington to visit Sammie and a couple of days in Racine to visit my mom.

THE SECOND ROAD TRIP TO THE EAST

FRANKFURT

In New York we sold the Chevy that I had bought several months earlier and bought two tickets to Luxembourg on Icelandic Airlines. It was still $167 one way. In Germany we stayed in the Friedrichstraße family flat and for $250 bought an old VW van that we outfitted with a mattress platform in the back.

We arrived in Frankfurt on November 17th, 1966 and by December 4 we were ready to hit the road. Within a few days Robert showed up as well as my brother Tom from New York. After a few days of construction and maintenance on the VW, getting visas, and a little shopping, we were ready to go. I was short on money because my brother had surprised us by showing up in a taxi he'd taken from the Luxembourg airport to Frankfurt without money to pay for it. It was a fortune. He had never traveled outside of the States and had no concept of distances or foreign currency. By this time he was a total crystal meth freak with a needle habit.

Robert was driving on the night of the 5th when we reached Poetchen Pass in Austria. We were all (I, Uschi, Tom and Sita) sleeping in the back. Robert got tired and pulled over to sleep. When we awoke in the morning we were halfway buried in snow. He had no idea where he was or that he had pulled over at the top of the pass.

The next day we drove through Yugoslavia and on the following day reached the Bulgarian border. The immigration officials told us that we were not allowed to enter Bulgaria because our hair was too long. A lengthy discussion took place (without the mention of a bribe, which, based on my past experience crossing that same border with Abrahim, would have worked easily.) I told them that we would not be stopping in Bulgaria; we were driving straight through to Turkey. They said no. They said, "We have things here that we don't want you to see." We knew that what they really meant was, "We have people here that we don't want to see *you*."

Towards the end of the conversation, they told me that this was a communist country and they did not allow long hair on men. I pointed to the picture of Karl Marx on the wall and mentioned that his hair was as long as mine. Nope. We couldn't come in unless we agreed to let them cut our hair. I pulled out the map, glanced at it to make sure my memory served me right, then looked up at my fellow travelers and asked, "You guys interested in seeing Northern Greece?"

Within minutes we were traveling south towards Greece. In the middle of the night as we drove eastwards through Northern Greece, we encountered a monsoon-like rainstorm. Rain came down in sheets. You could only see a couple of feet in front of you. Suddenly there was a big tree down in the road. We turned right into a driveway and, as luck would have it, we were in the parking lot of a taverna, a Greek roadside inn.

We went inside and the place was full of local village inhabitants all warm and happily feasting. The music stopped immediately, and all eyes were on us as we stood there, long-haired, wet and bedraggled. The main man of the group walked up to me, smiled, and hugged me, drawing me closer to the fire and handing me a glass of wine. He nodded to the musicians, the music resumed, and we were all seated amongst the people, eating, drinking and laughing. Before long everyone was on their feet, dancing, drinking and throwing empty glasses into the fireplace with loud shouts of "Opa!" resounding throughout the inn. It was like we had just happened into a scene that had been going on for hundreds of years: The same food, the same wine, the same music, the same dance, the same people, just a different generation. It was magical.

ISTANBUL

The next day we drove along the north coast of the Aegean Sea, the Dardanelles, and the Sea of Marmara to Istanbul where we stayed at the Palace Hotel for two days, then in the van for about ten days outside the Sultanahmet police station across from the Aga Sofia. It was cold in Istanbul and the city was full of junkies. Australian John was there. My brother Tom and he became instant buddies, of course, both being needle freaks. I had a good supply of antibiotics and a sterile syringe on hand and they came in really handy because a lot of the junkies had infections. I treated them all. I boiled water on my primus stove in the back of the van to sterilize, not that they gave a damn; they shared dirty needles without a thought.

All the junkies used pacifiers with eye droppers and needles attached, cooked in a bent spoon, drew it up through a cotton ball and tied up with a belt. God, I prayed that Australian John would get off the junk. Hermes was there and a couple of other gammler that we knew from the road. This was our first test: being with drug users all day long and not using. Plus, we had to tell them that we had met the Avatar and he'd told us to tell them that they should not use drugs! It was quite easy, as it turned out. We told them and they ignored us as if we hadn't even spoken.

It felt good to be back in Istanbul. We were on the road again and that felt natural and invigorating. We rarely left the Sultanahmet district, hanging out for days in the infamous pudding shop and tea shop drinking tea and smoking nargile, the Turkish hookah, with brief trips to the incredible Kapali Karsi, Istanbul's amazing covered bazaar.

The crowd was a bit different this time. There were the usual road freaks that we knew from before, the beats, vagabonds and gammler, but unlike the fall of 1964, just over two years earlier, the place was full of hippies. The hippies were scoffed at by the old time road freaks as posers.

It was cold in Istanbul, very cold. It was time to move south so after two weeks in Istanbul we started driving towards Syria and made it to Konya the first night all sleeping in the van at a crossroad. Having left Tom in Istanbul in Australian John's dubious care, it was just Uschi and I, Robert and the dog Sita. We picked up a couple of hitchhikers, an American named Larry, and his gorgeous long-haired blond girlfriend, Susie. By the next night we were on the Syrian border where we again slept in the VW van. In Homs the engine started making horrendous noises. Fortunately it was right in front of a garage that had a big sign that the owner was a German-trained VW mechanic. We limped in and he told us to go have lunch and come back.

We walked down the road and found a restaurant with a pool table so we ate and shot pool for a couple of hours before returning to the garage. When we got back the mechanic was sitting on a low stool staring at our engine, which he had taken out of the van and placed on the floor. He looked up at me, shrugged, and shook his head as he wiped the sweat from his brow with a greasy rag as if to say, "I have no idea what is wrong." I walked over to the engine and squatted next to it. I reached down and flipped the retainer over that held the rocker arm cover onto the engine block and let the cover fall to the floor.

I looked inside the cover and saw a one-inch piece of the lifter rod lying in the cover. I pointed to it and looked at the mechanic. He lit up as if he had just discovered gold and said, "No problem, I fix."

I asked if he had a part and he said, "No problem, I fix." He took the rest of the lifter out, went over to his welding equipment and started welding the two pieces together. After an hour, the engine was back in and we were humming along on the road to Damascus.

In Damascus we attempted to get visas for Jordan but the consulate told us that we had to cut our hair to get a visa. When we ask them how short our hair had to be they said, "Like the ordinary Arab on the street." We went to the Damascus bazaar and bought keffiyeh, the traditional head dress, or scarf, of Arab men, made of a square of cloth, usually cotton, folded and wrapped in various styles around the head. It is commonly found in arid climate areas to provide protection from direct sun exposure, as well as for protecting the mouth and eyes from blown dust and sand. It is held in place by a rope circlet called an "agal." In Jordan and Syria they are usually either black and white or red and white.

We started out again with our heads and faces covered like this for the Syria/Jordan border. When we arrived at the border, I said, "Ah-Salaam-Alaikum" to the border officials as we drove up. They replied "Ma Alaikum Salaam" and waved us through. By evening we were in Jerusalem. We obtained permission to park our van from the officials of the Church of Saint Peter of Gallicantu, the place where Jesus was arrested and led off and where Peter denied him three times before the cock crowed, just as Jesus had told him he would.

The church is directly on the Jordan/Israeli border. (Or, what *was* the border at that time.) Armed Jordanian army personnel stood around the concertina wire that marked the border. They were quite friendly and we smoked and chatted with them in whatever language we could find in common. We parked and slept there for the next week while hanging out in Jerusalem.

JERUSALEM

We entered the Old City through the Damascus gate. Not far inside we spotted a tea shop and entered. A large Muslim man, the owner walked straight up to me and put his arms around me and lifted me all the way up off my feet and hugged me. When he set me back down I looked at him and he said, "Welcome, Brother." He had one of the biggest moustaches I have ever seen and was known far and wide as "Uncle Moustache."

The café had several books filled with notes from previous travelers that were fun to browse through. One interesting thing about them was that anyone who had written in them referred to "Disneyland" quite frequently. I didn't get it at first so I asked Uncle Moustache about it. He said that the name of the country across the border (Israel) could not be mentioned as it did not exist. Thereafter when speaking of Israel we only used the word "Disneyland." Everyone knew what you were talking about. We found out that the Mandelbaum gate opened once a year, on Christmas day, to let people make a one-way trip to and from Jordan and Israel. We did not plan on going to Israel despite wanting to because we did not want an Israeli stamp in our passport while traveling through the Arab countries. If any official saw an Israeli stamp it could mean long interrogations, arrest and possible jail time.

The next day was Christmas Eve so we decided to go to Bethlehem. After finding a safe place to park the van we walked towards the Church of the Nativity. There were loudspeakers in the trees playing "Jingle Bells." We laughed at the very thought of this. We walked up to the Door of Humility to pass through it but it was closed and locked, another disquieting fact. We wanted to see the spot where Jesus had supposedly been born.

It was in the basement of the church marked in the floor by a fourteen-point star. The line was long and people grabbed our asses in line. We were planning on this being a spiritual event but with "Jingle Bells," the Door of Humility locked, and Arabs grabbing our asses in line to see the spot where Jesus was born, most of the sanctity was blemished for me. But we did see the spot and headed back to Jerusalem.

On New Year's Eve we drove to the Dead Sea and found a series of freshwater pools near Qumran that emptied into the Sea. We camped overnight and bathed and washed our clothes in the fresh water. There were Arabs with prostitutes parked in their vans nearby. On January 1st, 1967 we drove back to Jerusalem and stayed one day and night getting our stuff in order and headed the next day to Amman and Baghdad. The drive from Amman to Baghdad was surreal. The Syrian Black Desert was beautiful: sand covered with huge black boulders. When we crossed the border station at al Rutbah, somewhat inside Iraq, it was raining heavily and we missed stopping at the border station to get our passports stamped.

We spent the next day in Baghdad checking out the bazaar, having tea and smoking hookah. We headed the next day to Basrah. We were going to Kuwait to sell blood. Arabs don't donate blood and they were paying 10 English pounds per pint, about $28 at the time. We figured with the three of us we could get an extra $84 which, as frugal as we were could last quite a while and help out a lot. When we tried to cross the border at Basra they checked our passports and saw that we did not have an entry stamp into Iraq and wanted to know how we got there. We explained that we'd driven from Amman and must have missed the border station in al Rutbah. This was not good. Luckily, instead of putting us directly in jail they said that we would have to drive back to al Rutbah and get an entry stamp into Iraq. We told them that that was three days' drive each way and we had to get to Kuwait today. After a whole afternoon of haggling, they finally agreed to let us pass without paying a bribe.

On the drive to Kuwait City you could see tents in the desert with Cadillacs parked outside them. The oil money had just started to flow in and though some still lived in tents, they had Cadillacs.

Kuwait City was nice. We gravitated towards the Pakistani restaurants where we had delicious food but only in the evening. Ramadan had started and restrictions were strictly imposed. We were accosted by police for smoking during the day on the streets, even though there was supposed to be an exemption for travelers.

We went to sell blood but they would not take mine because I have type A-B, the universal receiver, but we did, in fact, get ten pounds each for Robert and Uschi's blood. We spent about five days there and headed for the Iran border, east of Basra.

In Abadan I studied the map to see the best way to get to Shiraz and noticed that the road just inside Iran went north quite some distance to Ahvaz, then turned directly south again, making a big whole-day's-drive loop before heading east again for Shiraz. I noticed that there was a pipeline that headed directly east across the desert which cut out that whole loop and reasoned that they must have gotten that pipeline in there somehow so we could probably just follow the pipeline and meet the main road at the other end. It could not have been much worse than the road itself. It worked; we drove out across the desert and got to a town the town of Kazar. We met a man who invited us to stay in his home and during the course of the evening he offered to trade his sixteen-year-old daughter for Uschi. I feared that he would be insulted so took some time deliberating, inspecting his beautiful teen daughter's, hair, teeth, feet, etc. before declining.

By the next evening we were in Shiraz. We checked into a hotel and went to visit the tomb of Hafiz, Meher Baba's favorite poet, and the tomb of Saadi. Shiraz is absolutely beautiful. It is known as the City of Gardens and the home of the white marble tomb of the 14th century poet/perfect master, Hafiz. It is a place one must see and I don't say that about many places.

We headed for Kerman the next day. We were in the middle of the Dashe Kevir, the Great Salt Desert. The roads were washboard and there was nothing but barren desolation. If you drove too slowly you were pounded to death. You had to drive just fast enough to "float" over the washboard but then you had almost no friction contact between the tires and the desert floor, making it like surfing the desert with the van swaying from side to side.

We stopped in a small village where there was nothing. We were hungry. I asked a villager to kill one of his chickens and cook it for us. He agreed but the price was unbelievably high. When I told him that the price was too high, he pointed in all four directions briefly stopping at each direction to say Sahara, Sahara, Sahara, Sahara. In other words, there is nothing but desert here so you either pay what I want or you don't get any chicken. I paid his price and we ate.

That afternoon we stopped in the middle of nowhere to pour gas from a Gerry can into the gas tank before continuing. After a couple of hours I noticed that Sita was not sitting next to me on the seat. I called to the back of the van and asked if she was back there and they said no. I realized that we had left her at the spot where we filled the gas tank.

We stopped and luckily, a truck was coming from the other direction, only one of four or five that we had seen all day. We waved the truck down and with arms and legs and "woof woofs" tried to explain what had happened. I remembered that there was a group of three trees about half a kilometer off into the desert at the spot where we fueled and off went Robert and Uschi to find the dog! Several hours later they reappeared having caught a ride in another truck coming our direction with the dog. She was sitting at the side of the road exactly where we had left her. We had a big reunion and rejoicing and started out again. The road was so pounding that we had seventeen flat tires that day. The last one happened after it was dark and as I got out of the van to look at the flat right rear tire, I saw a single light heading towards us in the desert. A motorcycle pulled up with an Army man on it and he repaired our flat for us then pointed in the direction we were traveling and said something in Farsi, the only part of which I understood was "do kilometer." (Two kilometers.)

Within about a hundred feet the tire went flat again but I kept driving, thinking whatever it is was two kilometers away, and that's where I'm going. We limped into the place and lo and behold, it was the same Army camp, converted Caravanserai , that we had been to in 1964 when we passed through here, called Shams (Sun). We entered one of the main rooms and noticed that they had made some really big improvements, blankets and primus lamps marked "U.S. Govt," modern bunk beds, and clean floors. As I was standing there a man walked in and looked directly into my eyes. It was the sergeant that had taken us to his hovel across the road and given us gruel and opium. I looked at him and using my few words of Farsi, pointed over my shoulder to indicate the past and said, "teen saal?" meaning "three years?" He turned on his heel and left. Two minutes later he reappeared, reached into his pocket pulled something out, held it up, and I heard a "click." It was the lighter I had given him burning brightly in his hand. He beamed at me and brought food. After the food he offered us opium and could not understand why we refused. I didn't think he would understand that the Avatar of the Age had forbidden us to use drugs, so offered no explanation. He smoked anyway.

The next morning he flagged down a bus and Robert left with the wheel for Rafsanjan, the next town, to get a new tire. Rafsanjan happens to have the world's best pistachios and was known in Iran as the "Pistachio Capital of the World."

He returned with the new tire which we mounted and

headed on out towards Kerman passing through Bam on the way. We stopped at the hut at the edge of town and looked at the messages on the walls and found our writings from three years' previous.

We spent the night in Kerman and drove the next day to Zahedan where we stayed for two days before heading out into the desert of Baluchistan for Quetta, passing again through Mirjaveh and Taftan. In Quetta we stayed at the house of a man who invited us and the next day headed out for the two day drive to Karachi.

In Karachi we got permission to park our van outside the Y.M.C.A. and slept there for two days, enjoying being in a port by the sea again after two months in the desert. We visited all our favorite bazaars and restaurants then went looking for a Baba lover that we had heard of by the name of Minoo Kharas. We found his house in the Lily Road, behind the Frere Hall post office and were greeted graciously by him and his family who invited us to stay in their home, where we stayed for about ten days.

This would turn out to be a monumental, fortuitous meeting that inspires me to this day. Minoo Kharas became a giant mentor to me, teaching me things that I will never forget.

When Minoo was a young man he was already in search of God. He had pictures of Zoroaster, Ram, Krishna, Buddha, Jesus and a symbol for Mohammed on his wall and had left a blank space for the One he was in search of. He and three friends set out in four directions with an agreement to meet in one year to see if any of them had found the Avatar of the age, which he was convinced they would.

He returned after one year and his friends were not there so he took a pistol and left for a secluded place where he would previously frequent to shoot himself for having failed. Just as he was about to perform the deed, he heard a voice calling, "Minoo Kharas, Minoo Kharas." He stopped and waited and said to himself, "If he finds me, OK, but if not I will kill myself."

His friend was told that Minoo had gone out so he went to the place that he knew Minoo used to go to be alone. His friend found him and told him about a man that said he knew where the living Avatar is. Minoo found this man who told him about Meher Baba. When Minoo saw Baba for the first time he knew immediately that He was the One and surrendered his life to him. Minoo attended the police academy in Nasik near the place Meher Baba stayed. He would do anything to come into Baba's presence and became known as a "madman" for Baba. He would literally make a fool of himself in any way just to be in Baba's presence, thus earning him Baba's nickname, "Double Donkey." Khar is Gujerati for donkey (their common mother tongue) and ass is another word for donkey in English, thus Khar-as: Double donkey.

I was myself a Baba Lover but only knew the western Baba Lovers I'd met in the States. Minoo told me personal stories about his times with Baba that moved me deeply. I would like to tell a couple of them.

Once, when Baba was in Delhi, Minoo met him there and told him about a man that explained reincarnation to him from the Buddhist standpoint. He asked Baba about it and Baba said to him, "Minoo, I have told you that for my 120 (Baba's circle) there is no rebirth…and you are one." I knew from that point on that Minoo was in Baba's Circle of 120.

Minoo told me that he used to perform certain "things." He would allow someone to blindfold him and then stick a pin in the wall and take it back out and hand the pin to Minoo. He would walk to the hole, blindfolded, and stick the pin in the same hole. People would come to him with snakebites and he would pass his hand over the wound and heal them. He told Baba about this and asked Him whether he should continue to perform such acts, given that Baba spoke out about the spiritual uselessness of such things. Baba told him, "Read, read, read."

Minoo read every word that had been taken down up to that point, then went to Baba and said, "No more." Baba embraced him and said, "You have learned."

Minoo told me an amazing story regarding Mahatma Gandhi, and while pulling pile after pile of papers from his chest with the correspondence to document the story, related the following:

Baba was in Karachi when it was announced that Gandhi would attend the Round Table Conference in London regarding independence of India. He would travel aboard the *Rajputana.* Baba said that he must be on that ship. At the time there was an airline strike in Karachi so no commercial flights were available. The Mayor of Karachi arranged for Baba to get to Bombay by a private flight and he and a few Mandali were on the *Rajputana,* sailing for London. This same mayor wired Gandhi and told him of Meher Baba's presence on the ship. Gandhi sought Baba out and Baba allowed an interview.

Apparently there was one question that Gandhi posed to anyone whom he thought was spiritually advanced, the nature of which I do not know, but no one had answered his question thus far. When he posed the question to Baba, Baba reached into the pile of manuscripts he had with him, "The Book" that Baba had written with his own hand and which up to this point no one had read. Baba had told some of His Mandali that if they read even one word, they would be reduced to dust, it was so powerful.

He handed one or two pages to Gandhi, who read them, handed them back and said, "My question is answered," and asked Baba for God Realization. Baba told him that he was destined for it and by His hand alone. He also told him not to accept partition of India at the Round Table conference. When the ship arrived in England, Gandhi walked down the gangplank in his dhoti with his goat and the press clamored for him. "Mahatma, Mahatma," they cried. Gandhi said, "Don't call me Mahatma.

Behind me is someone to whom I am not equal to the dirt under His fingernail." Many of the press sought to find out who he was talking about but by this time Baba and his Mandali were gone.

When Baba and his Mandali returned to India later, Baba announced that he had important work in Lahore. He and some of his men traveled to Delhi and a few people joined there. They took the train to Lahore and at a point between Amritsar and Lahore Baba got out of the train and paced back and forth, after which he declared that his work was done and they returned. That is the exact spot where the international border was established at Wagah between India and Pakistan. So even though Baba told Gandhi not to accept partition of India, he created the border Himself.

When Gandhi returned to India, he was in Delhi planning for Independence. On his way from Bombay to Delhi he reputedly stopped in the village of Sakori in Maharashtra and had the darshan of Upasni Maharaj, one of Baba's spiritual masters. In spite of the fact that Baba had told Gandhi that he would get God realization through His hand alone, Gandhi asked Upasni Maharaj for God realization. Upasni told him he would certainly give it to him but he would have to wait half an hour. Upasni, who wore only a sack cloth to cover his body, reportedly then defecated in front of Gandhi, at which point Gandhi said that he was a madman and left. Upasni was said to have told his Mandali that he would have given it to him if he had waited.

Baba had also told Gandhi to come to Him before going to Delhi when he returned to India. Gandhi did not follow Baba's instructions but wrote letter after letter asking Baba for God realization. Baba's Mandali would question Baba, "Oh, Baba, if ever there was anyone deserving, it must be Gandhi. Baba said, "Oh you think so? Let's see. I need two volunteers to deliver a message to Gandhi in Delhi but before you volunteer I must warn you that if you do not follow my instructions one hundred percent it will mean your death."

Two men volunteered. Baba told them that they should go to Gandhi and tell him that Baba says that you are to come with us right now to Him. If he gave any objection whatsoever they were not to ask again or give any explanation but to return immediately. The men went to Delhi and Gandhi was in a conference when they arrived and they were not allowed to see him. They gave a "chit" and asked that it be delivered to him. Gandhi immediately came to them and they told Gandhi what Baba had said. Gandhi said he could not come now because important meetings regarding the independence of India were taking place but that he would come in two weeks' time. The men turned and left for the train station.

Gandhi apparently realized his mistake and sent some men to get the Mandali from the train station but they went to the New Delhi station and the Mandali went to the Old Delhi train station. The next day Gandhi was shot dead. The correspondence that I saw was between Gandhi's followers and Baba's Mandali. They apparently did not like the idea that Gandhi was pursuing Baba and were trying to turn it around so that Baba was pursuing Gandhi.

Once, after Partition, which took place in 1947, Minoo visited Baba at a time when Baba was very involved with working with the masts. (God intoxicated.) Some of the masts that were brought to Baba turned out to be mad. Only Baba could tell the difference. Baba established a "Mad Ashram" in Rahuri. When it came time for Minoo to leave back for Karachi, he sneaked into Baba's hall and hid some small pictures of himself in various places including under the cushion of Baba's chair with the idea that when Baba would find them, He would think of Minoo.

On the morning he was supposed to leave, the photos kept popping up. Baba squirmed on his chair as if sitting on a saddle burr and pulled out yet another photo of Minoo. Baba called Minoo to the hall and questioned him about the photos. Minoo pulled his own "double donkey" ears and confessed that he had hidden them there. Baba said, "This man is mad; take him to Rahuri!" Minoo rejoiced because this meant he did not have to return home.

On the crowded bus to Rahuri at one of the stops a sadhu (Indian holy man) got on. After the bus started again, he began shouting at the driver, "Stop the bus, stop the bus. You fool, don't you realize who you have on this bus?" The driver stopped the bus and the sadhu went through the entire bus, bowing down to all the ones that had come from Baba, passing by the others. He exited the bus and the trip to Rahuri continued.

At Rahuri Minoo was locked inside the Mad Ashram, a big building with very tall iron gates. In the morning Minoo went to the front gate and lay in the dirt facing the road. When asked what he was doing he said that he was waiting for Baba to arrive. He was told that he was an idiot and that Baba was not coming to Rahuri. After some time, a cloud of dust was seen in the distance, on the road approaching the ashram. Baba was making a surprise unannounced visit. When Minoo told Baba what happened on the bus, Baba just looked at him compassionately and said, "Minoo, I have told you over and over, you have no idea who you are."

Years after Baba's last trip to Karachi, the waiting room at the airport where he had been seated was converted to a toilet. Minoo could be seen regularly bowing down to the toilet on the spot where Baba's chair had previously been.

One day while we were staying with Minoo, he picked up a young Muslim man and brought him home and showed him pictures of Baba and told him that he was the Avatar. (Rasool or Sahib-e-Zaman) The man objected and held out his Koran. Minoo said, "If I put the Koran here and the Prophet here, which one do you want?" He explained that the accidental spill of just one small drop of ink in writing down the words in the Koran can change a meaning completely.

Minoo told me over and over, "Never forget Baba. Remember

him constantly." Once when we were sitting around laughing and joking and having a good time, I saw him look at me with his darting eagle eyes and raise his brow. I knew he was saying, "Even now, when you are laughing and joking, don't forget Him."

Minoo's wife Freny was wary of me at that time. I can't blame her. I looked weird. I had long hair and a beard and dressed like an Indian. She warmed to me over the years. I totally adored their son, Meherji, and daughter Goher, two of the most beautiful children I have ever seen in my life.

Minoo took me under his wing and I felt an affinity for him that can only be explained through lifetimes of past connections. He could read my mind and I could almost always tell what he was thinking. I named my first son for him and I was crushed when Minoo died.

On February second 1967 we boarded the van and started our way up the Indus towards Lahore. Again, I was floored by the beauty of the Indus Valley. An amusing event happened in Sukkur. We were in the main street and could not figure out how to get to the Sukkur Barrage where the road north to Lahore was. Robert was driving. He stopped in the middle of the teeming masses, stuck his head out the window and asked the first person whose attention he could get, "Lahore, Lahore?" It would be like stopping in Times Square and asking someone, "San Francisco?" We never let him forget it.

Our mission at this point was to take the van to Kabul and sell it. We slept in the van in Lahore one night and the next night stayed with our old Quetta friend, the Botanist, Hafiz Ullah in his home in Sheikupura, a town on the Grand Trunk Road (G.T. Road) about 35 kilometers northwest of Lahore on the way to Rawalpindi.

We had stopped at the scientific store in Lahore to visit our friends the Chauderys that we knew from 1964 and they called Hafiz and told him we were coming. He now had a position as a botany professor at the Government College at Sheikhapura. It was a surprise for him to see us and of course we had an incredible story to tell about what had happened to us in the meantime. He seemed a bit dubious regarding Baba's spiritual status, but listened with attentiveness and respect. He was convinced that Baba was a "saint" and after hearing that we were in correspondence with Baba, asked that we write to tell Baba of his family problems and ask Baba to pray for him. I wrote to Baba and told him about Hafiz.

Baba's reply which came later (written and signed by Adi K. Irani) said that if Hafiz "has seen a photo of Baba or has one and remembers him devoutly...that he would be benefited." Adi went on to say that "You see, faith works wonders and here we have our faith for one who is the Lord of Creation and everything everywhere. Beloved Baba these days is repeating that the sole remedy for all human ills is His loving remembrance. So if Mr. Ullah can do it, it would be to his advantage."

Hafiz seemed to have aged past the three years since we last met. He seemed much more troubled and world-weary; not the happy man that I knew before. He spoke openly, frankly and sincerely about his problems, in some way hoping that I had an answer for him.

The next day we stopped in Rawalpindi for lunch and slept that night on the side of the road somewhere between Pindi and Peshawar. As we found a wide spot to the side of the G.T. Road, we all got out including Sita and stretched our legs. Suddenly we heard a man shouting at us..."KUTA, KUTA...NEINGH... MASJID...MASJID." We could not figure out what he was talking about until we looked around and saw a few stones marking the perimeter of what he was calling a masjid, mosque. He was trying to tell us that our DOG WAS IN THE MOSQUE! We quickly put Sita in the van and bowed deeply with folded hands, lest he call others to have us lynched for allowing a dog in the mosque. Dogs are considered unclean in the Muslim faith and if a Muslim even touches a dog, he must wash five times before he can pray. The dogs of Pakistan are filthy, mangy mongrels that are apparently there only for kicking.

The following day we passed through the Khyber Pass into Afghanistan. I was amazed how much faster travel is when you have your own transportation; we were in Kabul by evening. We checked into our old haunt, the dollar-a-night Maiwand Hotel which I have described earlier with its shaft-of-shit toilet. The next day we found a better hotel for the same price so moved to the Banazer Hotel. We wandered through the Kabul bazaar which is really an ugly bazaar by the standards of other major Asian cities. Amazing but filthy lanes, muddy nearly to the ankles when it rains. We went to the Russian money changers and changed money then went to the Kabul Hotel on Pushtunistan Square right on the Kabul River to check for other travelers and see if anyone was in town we might know. It was a whole different scene than last we were there; none of the interesting characters like I described previously.

We sold the van without difficulty and, as it was cold as hell, headed back to Pakistan the following day, hitching a ride to Peshawar where we took the train to Lahore. So we had left Lahore on February 4th and were back by February 20th. Only a little over two weeks to travel all the way to Kabul, sell the van, and return.

In Lahore we checked into the Y.M.C.A., on the Mall Road, next to Anarkali Bazaar, having lost our sleeping quarters with the sale of the van. We were under strict orders from Baba NOT TO ENTER INDIA until he called us but in two and a half months we had gotten about as close to the Indian border as you can get. We decided to try to rent a place to stay for a while until Baba allowed us to enter India. I met a woman who worked in a travel agency on the Mall Road and asked her if she knew of any places. She told me that her brother, Mickey (an odd name for a Pakistani Muslim) had a place in the Ichra Mohulla, on Ferozepur Rd for rent that was in the same lane as their home. We rented it immediately and moved in the following day. Little did we know that this was to be our home for the next few months. Looking back, it seemed like we lived there for a year or more.

Mohulla means neighborhood. Ferozepur Road is a major road leading to the City of Ferozepur which was now the site of the Indian border, Wagah border between Lahore and Amritsar having been closed since the last war. Ichra Mohulla is a warren of small dirt lanes (or mud, depending on the season) leading from the main road into the neighborhood. The lanes are lined with ten-foot mud walls with doors that lead to individual smaller lanes that have their own walls with doors leading to individual courtyard homes, usually two on each side of the lane, making four nearly identical living spaces. Ours was the second one on the left directly across from Mickey, his sister and family. Our entire area was about thirty feet square. The entire back walls were lined with individual rooms with a veranda all the way around.

At one end of the veranda was the kitchen which was nothing more than a mud stove where you could burn wood to cook. As you enter the door to our "compound" you saw a courtyard with a single pomegranate tree. Immediately to the right was a small six-by-six concrete slab which drained through a hole in the wall to the gully in the lane. There was a water spigot on top of a four foot tall pipe; that was the bathing room. There were no walls around it so baths had to be taken in the open by filling a bucket with cold water and pouring it over yourself with a small pail.

Immediately to the left as you entered the courtyard was a four-by-four structure with walls, (two of which were the lane walls themselves), one window approximately twelve inches square and six feet up one of the inner walls, and a door. This was the toilet. As you opened the door to the toilet you saw nothing but a concrete floor with two concrete block steps to squat on. You squatted on the blocks and did your business on the floor. The sweeper came with a bucket once a day (twice in the hot season) and swept the mess into a bucket, washed down the floor, and carried the mess away. Lest you think this was quite sanitary, he didn't carry it that far away; only out into the main lane where it was dumped onto a giant pile of shit that had accumulated for God only knows now long.

Across Ferozepur Road on the opposite side was an ugly, dirty little bazaar, the Ichra Bazaar; really just a dirt road with shops on either side of the road. Most of the shops you did not enter, but stood on the road and purchased from the owner who sat or squatted in his little "shop." The butcher shop was just a counter with carcasses hanging from hooks, out in the open. Flies covered the carcasses in a buzzing hum. Next to that was a guy on the street who sold sugar cane, equally covered with flies. He squatted on the ground with a round, two-feet diameter pan with cut pieces of sugar cane perfectly arrayed in round rows. At first I couldn't even tell what he was selling; it just looked like a dark brown layer of moving something. As I approached he shooed the flies away with a woven fan to show his wares under the pile of undulating flies.

At the beginning of the lane on our side right on Ferozepur Road was a chai walla who also cooked food. It was like a mini dhaba. He had a tandoor so we could go to him for chai, beef curry and tandoori rotis. The chai was 25 paisa; the beef curry one rupee and the rotis 25 paisa. (One Rupee was about 10 cents American if you changed your money on the black market.) The curry was fiery hot, but for about 20 cents you could have a curry, two breads and a cup of chai.

It was still relatively cool in Lahore so we were quite comfortable in our little "house." The word spread fast about Mik & Uschi's place on the Ferozepur Road and pretty soon we were having regular crashers: road bums looking for a free place to stay. One guy said he thought "Miknuschi" was one Japanese person. He had heard about our place all the way back in Paris.

Most of the people on the road had diarrhea from bad water and food so the state of their stool was always a topic of discussion. "Did you have loose motions this morning?" "No semblance of solidity," was the usual answer. "My stool was grand! Long, firm and tapering on both ends." Those were usually the new people on the road. Some took opium just to harden their stool. The bathroom floor was a gigantic mess by 9am and as the day heated up it stunk like the shit hole that it was. As the season advanced and the temperatures climbed more flies were present; you had to do your morning bowel movement as early as possible so that there would be fewer flies. People with diarrhea, however, have to go frequently. By the time summer came, if you opened the door of the toilet in the afternoon there was a wall of flies buzzing in front you so thick you couldn't even enter. The solution to that was to stick the D.D.T. can in the window and pump the poisonous spray and wait five minutes until all the flies dropped to the floor. Then when you opened the door there was no wall of flies in the air but the floor was about an inch thick with dead ones. You had to take at least one step to get up onto the blocks so there was always the crunch of flies under your feet and you knew that there was a layer of human excrement under that. After the sweeper left in the afternoon there was a rush to the toilet. The flies and shit were swept up and the floor disinfected with God knows what chemical.

There were always people around and all of them did drugs, mostly hash, but for some reason we were seeing a lot of junkies also. One American, Jeff, who only smoked hash, was traveling with a seventeen-year-old Swedish kid who was hooked. He shot heroin about fifteen times a day. His name was Christian and he was beautiful. He had a hairless face with light flawless skin. His hair was long, straight and blond. It broke my heart when I would walk in and see him with a belt around his arm, one end between his teeth pulling it tight, while he tapped his vein to make it big enough to stick a needle in. He was gentle and quiet and when he shot up he would just lay his head back and roll his eyes back into his head. He asked me to fix him all the time and I just loved him so I did, all the time telling him about Baba's message that drugs are harmful physically, mentally and spiritually.

The American that was traveling with him, Frank, was a little more aggressive than most people you meet on the road. They stayed with us for a few weeks but I had to throw them out and make a spectacle of it for the neighbors after an incident in the bazaar. Mickey came to me one day and said that one of the people staying with us had been harassing some of the women in the bazaar by clapping his hands together inches in front of their faces (which were covered in burqas) in the bazaar. Word travels like wildfire in these small mohullas so everyone knew of our presence there and, in this case, also knew what Frank had done in the bazaar.

This was a terrible offence in a country where even looking at another man's wife can mean death. I had to call them out in front of Mickey, on whom the entire mohulla was relying to solve this grave problem. I'm not being facetious, either. This was a major, major event that could have resulted in a lynching. I confronted Frank on what was reported and he said he was just "kidding around." I told him to get his stuff and be out of there in three minutes, not just for my own face-keeping and safety but for his own safety. He and Christian left with the entire lane lined with people watching me scream at him to get out. Mickey said that I responded responsibly and correctly and there would therefore be no further ramifications.

At the beginning of the lane was a large bungalow right on Ferozepur Road. The inhabitants were a well-to-do well-educated family that spoke perfect, but of course heavily accented, English. They invited us to tea one day and told us that the entire mohulla suspected us of being C.I.A. agents. When ask why they explained that everyone reasoned, "Who else would have all these foreign visitors coming and going from India across the Ferozepur border?" It was only two years previous that Pakistan and India fought a major war between April and September of 1965 which resulted in thousands of casualties. It was fought mostly along the India/Pakistan border in Kashmir but the Wagah border was completely demolished as you may remember from my explanation of trying to cross that border in March/April of 1965 and thus the Ferozepur border became the main international border, somewhat to the south of Wagah at Attari.

Another visitor was Mike McAllister, a skinny blonde-haired junkie from Devon who was obsessed with his stool. He spoke in a West Country brogue, an accent that is long and broad and drawn out. "Fruit…that's the main thing," he would drawl when referring to how to improve his stool. I think he had amoebic dysentery. He shat about thirty times a day.

We made nearly daily trips to Mall Road and Anarkali bazaar.

It's easy to draw a crowd in Pakistan. First of all, there are a lot of people; secondly, at that time only one in ten males worked so they had a lot of idle time to fill. Anything remotely different or interesting was fair game for the long-staring session. Unfortunately that also included Westerners, especially road bums. You had to keep moving or a crowd would gather just to gawk and stare. And they would stay there as long as you did, sometimes asking such questions as, "Gentlemen, how do you function?" or "I believe you must be coming from the U.K. is it?" or "Are you traveling at the expense of your government?" These questions all boil down to this: "Where do you get the money to travel around like this and why are you here?"

We would spend day after day in Lahore walking through Anarkali, enjoying the hustle-bustle, smelling the scents of incense, fresh fruit, samosas, kebabs, wood and dung fires, human body odor, and the general stench of various and sundry detritus.

It was in a shop off the main drag of Anarkali that I met the "Mirror Walla." He had a small shop, one that you could actually walk into, up a few steps from the dirt lane. I don't remember his name, though we became business partners later; I always just called him "The Mirror Walla." He was a happy-go-lucky, short, stocky, roundish middle-aged man with eyes that bugged out. He was always cheerful and never failed to order someone to run to the nearby chai walla to bring country tea for us. We would sit in his shop for hours and hours watching the scene go by like a movie.

The Mirror Walla was from Quetta where he owned a cottage industry making mirror embroidered textiles. He made pillow cases and tapestries, the usual mirror embroidered items, but in addition he made clothing; pants, frontispieces for dresses, and vests. The first thing I noticed was that the quality of his products was far superior to any mirror embroidery that I had ever seen before. The mirrors were of good clear quality, not the usual thin splotchy type that is usual. He explained that the reason for this is that he imported his mirrors from Belgium. The second thing was that each mirror (they were round and about a half-inch in diameter) was very neatly and securely stitched. He explained that he used only the finest quality thread and that each mirror had seventy stitches around it, about twice the usual. He had been to London where he had the clothing items designed. I thought that they were of a high enough quality that they could be sold in the States for big bucks. We started negotiating and he made me the sole importer of his products. I thought the hippies would go crazy for this brightly colored flashy stuff; it was psychedelic.

Uschi and I would hang out in his shop all day drinking chai and watching the Anarkali crowds go by, making plans to make a killing on mirror embroidery. The one problem for the Mirror Walla was: When is this all going to happen? We didn't seem like we were in any hurry to go back to the States and start placing orders. Such was our life at the time. We were just waiting for Baba to say we could cross the border. He was right, we had no immediate plans that would bring about his dream. (He later did come to the States and we met in San Francisco and finalized the deal and I actually did become the sole importer.)

Sometimes I would hitchhike or take a bus down to Ferozepur and walk to the border and just put my nose on the other side of the fence and smell India, then return to Lahore satisfied.

One day I was alone in the house. This was very unusual for anyone to be alone in the house; there were always people there. It was made especially more odd because, even if there we not guests there, Uschi and I were seldom apart. I don't remember where she went. Robert was also not there. I saw a chunk of hash lying on the table. I picked it up and smelled it. Just the pungent scent of Landi Kotal Charce was intoxicating. I don't know what got into me but I made a charce joint and smoked it. When they returned in the afternoon I told them what happened, that I had disobeyed Baba's order and smoked some charce. They were shocked. Not because I had smoked hash but because while they were out they had separately and independently done the same. None of us had done any drugs whatsoever since receiving Baba's order not to. We then disobeyed Baba further by smoking hash together. With a fair amount of guilt attached, I might add. We actually wept for each other for our transgression. We continued smoking for some time; I don't remember how long, but weeks, I would estimate.

On one occasion, a well-known Baba Lover was visiting Lahore from Dacca, then East Pakistan, where he had been temporarily transferred by his employer and was living. He paid an unexpected visit to us in Ichra. While serving him tea we were trying our best to be hospitable, polite and coherent but were stoned out of our minds. After he left, we all looked at each other and nearly simultaneously said, "This has got to stop." We stopped using drugs immediately and some weeks later wrote to Baba to confess our lapse.

(Baba's response to our confession (dictated to Eruch Jessawalla) and received by us in Frankfurt after our return there was as follows:

"July 9, 1967

Baba has forgiven you both for having taken the drugs and for having continued to take for quite some time. Baba wants you both NOT to feel worried or anxious over your having disobeyed Him, because He has forgiven you both. Once again Baba sends His ORDER to you both Not to take DRUGS for the sake of just taking them when you get a whim or craving to do so. Baba does NOT want you both to take any DRUGS except, of course, medicines when prescribed by medical practitioners."

When I got this letter I sobbed tears of joy that Baba had forgiven me but even more so because I was awed at his unconditional compassion.

It started to get hot in Lahore; summer was in full force by the end of April. In fact I have never been anywhere in my life where it was this hot. At the same time I was getting very sick. Uschi and I had gotten hepatitis from the water and received a letter from Robert who had left several weeks earlier to return to Europe and the States, saying that he was in a hospital in Istanbul looking out through yellow eyes at the Bosporus. It was between 115 and 120 degrees F. every day, day after day. I can't really express how hot this is but just let me say that just the difference between 110 and 120 seemed like it was logarithmic. Horses were dropping dead on the streets from the heat.

Our lease was up at Ichra so on May 1st, 1967 we stayed with a couple that we had met in Lahore proper by the name of Joan and Holbrook Teeter. They were with the Quaker group, American Friends. Joan was related to J. Robert Oppenheimer, the American theoretical physicist who headed the Manhattan Project and was known as the Father of the Atomic Bomb.

We rented a room in the Mayo Road Hotel for about ten days and just lay around trying to keep cool, getting sicker and sicker. We then met someone who had an empty room and rented that for another week. The room had no fan so I had someone bring a fan on the back of a bicycle and install it on the ceiling and rented it for a week. The whole fee for delivery, installation and rental was about $1.25.

I went to the mission hospital and was admitted and treated (wrongly) for malaria. I was wasting away to nothing. I could not eat, the heat was oppressive and I was losing weight at an alarming rate, until at one point I was down to eighty-seven pounds. At this point Uschi wheeled me out of the hospital, took me to the airport and flew us to Karachi where we stayed with Minoo Kharas and family on Lily Road again for ten days. As soon as I got to Karachi I started feeling better. It was much cooler, my appetite returned and by the second day I was eating voraciously. I shaved and cut my hair for the first time in years and regained my health. The very unfortunate and sad part of this hasty retreat from Lahore was that we had to leave our dog, Sita. The good part was that we left her with Joan and Holbrook where we knew she would have a good home. It broke my heart to leave her. I had been through a lot with her and really loved her and was very much attached to her. But in order to save my life we had to leave her behind.

Ten days later we were on a plane to Istanbul, landing there on June 9th, 1967. The following day we boarded the Orient Express for Munich and two days later we were in Frankfurt. Otty, Uschi's sister, did not want to accommodate us in the family flat so we rented a room from a neighbor across the street for four or five days, while we decided what we would do next. Since we could not stay in the family flat we thought maybe we would go to Stockholm and try to get jobs and earn a little money. We were flat broke by now.

We crashed here and there in Copenhagen and Stockholm trying to find some work that could pay us something and ended up taking night jobs at a newspaper stuffing advertisements inside the paper. That lasted about a week and we said, "Nah...this is not for us," and hitchhiked back to Frankfurt. We crashed with some friends for a week or so, here and there, then rented an apartment for DM 100 per month (about $20) where we lived for the next four months while earning enough money to return to the States.

Uschi applied for a job operating a "wasserhäuschen" in the northern Frankfurt suburb of Rödelheim. A wasserhäuschen is a little kiosk or shack usually on a sidewalk or corner of the street where you can buy bottled water, tobacco, beer, schnapps, newspapers, magazines, chocolate and various other sundry items. Wasserhäuschen means Little Water House. It was a small hut with windows around the corner and halfway along two sides. There was a counter on the outside of the windows and ran along the two windowed sides of the shack. Customers walked up to the window and ordered through the open part and you passed their order to them through the window.

If someone was having a beer or soft drink, they would often stand at the counter and drink it and chat. Before I had this job my German was fluent but after four months of this, it was much better, even adding some Rödelheimer dialect. We had our regulars who always ordered the same thing day in and day out; some just a pack of cigarettes every morning on the way to work, others who hung out most of the day, drinking beer and talking trash.

Armin, a gammler that we had known for years and who was a junkie was around at this time and hanging around our pad and work place. He was like a brother to me. It killed me to help him shoot up.

At some point during this time I got really agitated that I had left my dog in Pakistan and it even got to the point where I would envision her and call out her name on the street. I decided I would go get her. I calculated that, alone, I could go and come in about three months by hitchhiking. I don't know what Uschi really thought about this but she did not object. I just said it's something that I have to do.

I got my visas in order in about two weeks, packed my backpack and was ready to leave the next morning. When I went to Rödelheim to help Uschi close up the night before I left, I got the shock of my life. Lying on the sidewalk outside the wasserhäuschen was Sita! I could not believe it. She looked beautiful, her coat was shiny and she had obviously been well fed. Uschi and Armin just stood by watching and laughing as I had my reunion with my beloved Sita. A few minutes later I found out from them that they had known for a week but kept it a surprise that Joan and Holbrook Teeter had contacted her and told her that they were flying Sita to Frankfurt. While I was picking up my passport from the Iranian embassy, they were going to the airport to pick up the dog.

After a couple of months at this, we had saved a little money for our tickets from Luxembourg to New York. Icelandic Airlines was still the cheapest ticket. There was elderly gentleman that came to our kiosk regularly by the name of Alexander Müller. He explained that he was an expert at roulette and that he had made and spent fortunes at various casinos around the world but now was banned from most because they all knew he had a near foolproof system to win. His system was simple and effective but very difficult to accomplish because of the memorization involved. It worked like this. Ordinarily you have a 35-to-1 advantage over the house; you have 35 numbers and they have one. Of course, if you bet 35 numbers you break even. If you watch the numbers (or the odd/even, red/black, etc. sequences) for seven spins, then bet against that same pattern repeating itself you increased your odds to something over 5,700 to one. The only caveat is that you have to double the bet every time so you have to have enough to double the bet seven times in a row. He took me to his room where he had a small wheel and showed me how it worked and it worked every time. I still was not convinced so he got a list of the actual numbers that had come up on wheel number one at the Wiesbaden Casino. (The wheels are regulated and balanced everywhere in the world, except Las Vegas and each number has to come up the same number of times.) They are also required to publish the actual numbers that come up every month. When we played the actual numbers, given the stake I had, we made thousands of dollars.

But here again, Alexander was banned from the Wiesbaden Casino. But...there was a smaller casino on the side that only locals who lived within a fifty-kilometer radius could play in and he was not banned from that. The next problem was that they didn't have a full wheel. They had what they called "Little Roulette." It had thirteen numbers, a zero, and a double zero. That gave the house another half number. That is what killed me and I lost our entire savings in half an hour.

The apartment building we were living in was being torn down and we had been given several notices to vacate. On the night that they moved the wrecking ball outside of the building we went through from floor to floor and crashed and smashed as much stuff as we possibly could, just for the fun of it. They were wrecking the place the next day anyway.

We rented another apartment in a building in the Robert Mayer Strasse where we lived from November 1967 to March 1968, near the University. There were a lot of Spaniards in the building and there was always the smell of fried fish in the common kitchen. On the corner under our window was a popular hooker hangout. Prostitution was legal in Germany but the girls had to get a health checkup on a regular basis. When they went for their checkup they would present their prostitute identification card and the officials would make a slash-mark (Strich, in German) on it to show that they had complied. Therefore when you wanted to say that a girl was a prostitute, the Frankfurt slang was, "Sie geht auf dem Strich." Literally, "She's on the slash." I got to know a lot of these girls but never did business with them.

Around this time Uschi got another job for a research institute doing accounting, so it was a long winter for me traveling by open street car to Rödelheim every morning, half an hour in the freezing German winter. I ran the kiosk by myself for some months. Strictly speaking, the company that owned this kiosk (and a lot of others) didn't even know I existed. It was all in Uschi's name. I didn't even have a work permit. We only earned a commission on what we sold. It was a lot of work for the meager amount we made.

By spring I got wind that the KRIPO (Kriminal Polizei) had been asking around about us. I was still wanted in Germany for the pot smuggling thing and they had heard that we were back. We knew we had to get the hell out of there. I wrote to my buddy Chris West and he sent us money for the tickets to fly to New York. (He was in New Mexico still.) We made a getaway in what I remember as being the nick of time and arrived in New York on April 2nd 1968, the day before my birthday without incident, outside of the fact that when we landed in Reykjavik they were gale-force winds and sub-zero temperatures. The plane stopped on the tarmac and you had to walk about fifty meters to the terminal. They had a rope to hold on to so that you would not blow away. I remember having to walk at a forty-five-degree angle to fight my way through the icy wind, reminiscent of my previous experience there.

My brother Tom had not made it far into India. I think he got to Delhi and couldn't cope so he had himself repatriated. He had an apartment on E. 13th Street between B. and C. in the Lower East Side. We goofed around in New York, visiting friends for a couple of weeks and then got a drive-away from New Jersey to Oregon to get back to California. Robert was living in Berkeley so we figured we may as well go there. We stopped in Wisconsin for two days to visit my mother and two days in Bloomington, Illinois to visit Sammie, my grandmother, then drove straight through to Oregon to drop off the car and hitched down to Berkeley, arriving there on April 25, 1968. Robert was moving out of a studio in a back house on Channing way to a larger apartment in the front house so we took his studio for seventy-five dollars a month.

We started doing freelance gardening to make ends meet and then I got a job parking cars at the Claremont Hotel in the Berkeley Hills. Life was great. I could work Saturday and Sunday nights and make about $40-50 a night which meant I could work two evenings a week and survive.

Chapter Twenty-Two

Berkeley 1968-1969

Meher Baba had been in "strict seclusion" doing his "Universal Work" and no one could see him. He opened the door briefly for a few people of my generation and, as far as I know, there were only about six or eight of us, four of us were in Berkeley at this time and became fast friends.

The Haight Ashbury scene was still going strong but disintegrating into harder drugs and more desperate people, unlike the previous year's "summer of love" hippie scene.

I didn't know it until I got here that, besides the New York City "group," there was a group in San Francisco under the aegis of "Sufism Reoriented." After the death of Inayat Khan and the resulting schism in Sufism, there was a succession of Murshids with the eventual succession of Murshida Ivy Duce. The duty of the Murshid is to guide her mureeds (students) until the Avatar returns to Earth (every 700 to 1,400 years). Murshida Duce, recognized Meher Baba as the Avatar of the age and turned the Sufi charter over to him to re-orient. Upon completion of this, the American sufi order, under Murshida Duce became Sufism Reoriented.

Uschi and I went to visit their headquarters located on Van Ness Avenue in San Francisco. Murshida Duce expressed that she was dumbfounded as to what to do with all the "long haired" hippies besieging her to find out more about Meher Baba. She asked me to come back and speak to her group about my meeting with Meher Baba, which I did to a spellbound, rapt audience of her mureeds, about a hundred people.

Murshida Duce had also had one of her mureeds start holding weekly presentations in a rented room at the student union of U.C. Berkeley which had a usual attendance of about 10-25 people or so. I also spoke there on many occasions. Around the same time, a group of Southern California Baba Lovers started a group in a store front in Pasadena.

The studio I lived in was in the small backhouse of a property with a larger house in front and a large courtyard/driveway between the two. Both houses were now full of Baba Lovers and the house next door had four or five Baba Lovers, most of whom became life-long friends, and a bunch of political radicals (all of whom I knew from Germany). I had nothing to do with politics. I didn't know what "right" or "left" even meant. I had never even voted. This was the time of huge antiwar protests against the Viet Nam war. When riots broke out in Berkeley, and the national guard was called in, we did not participate in any demonstrations. There were injuries and the protests were taking place two blocks away. A first aid station was set up in the front yard of the next-door house by the radicals.

My studio was becoming so jammed with people every day, that we could not accommodate any longer. One day, while crossing the courtyard between the big front-house and the small back-house, I noticed a small door hidden behind the exterior staircase of the big house. I looked inside and saw a small three-room space. It was like a little hobbit home. For some reason it only had a six-foot ceiling. After asking the owner, I found out that it did not meet code and could not be rented out for a living space. I told him I would give him ten dollars per month to let me use the space, to which he agreed. We wrote to Baba and asked his permission to start a Baba Center in this place. He gave his blessing and gave the name Mehersthan.

The concept was not to have something formal but just a place for people to meet and talk about Baba, like the Persian "tavern of love" celebrated in the ghazals of Hafiz and other Sufi poets. There were four or five main people involved in this project, but it fell on me to be the leader for a few reasons. First, it was my idea to begin with and I was in communication with Baba about it. I had the energy and enthusiasm to carry it forward. Also, the place had to be rebuilt and I and two others were the only ones with building skills, skills I had learned from my grandfather as a result of being his helper from the age of nine. The others had plenty of input, however, and it became a beautiful collaboration. We had to dig out the floor a foot deeper and construct forms under the dangling walls and pour concrete foundations under them and then pour a concrete floor. All of the materials were scavenged, from wood and nails for the forms and paint for the walls to fabric for making curtains. We did have to pay for the concrete. Someone made a hand-carved, painted small wooden sign the said MEHERSTHAN, the name which Baba himself gave.

In a short time, Mehersthan was flooded with visitors. It was like a Meher Baba honeymoon, every day. I can't even estimate how many people heard about Meher Baba at Mehersthan. Even decades later, people still talk about having first heard about Meher Baba at Mehersthan.

Everyone was still waiting for news from India that Baba would be giving Darshan to his lovers. The news finally came that there would be a mass darshan in Poona at Guru Prasad in April to June of 1969. Guru Prasad is the palace in Poona that I had originally gone to in order to find Meher Baba. In the meantime I found out that this palace is owned by the Maharani of Baroda who donated it for Baba's use during the summer months when he and his mandali would escape the torrid heat of Ahmednagar (Meherabad/Meherazad) to come to the slightly cooler climate of Poona. The darshan would be in three groups: The East Coast group, the Southern California group, and the Northern California group, aka the Sufi Group. Each group would stay for several days (four or five days, if I remember correctly), leave, and the next group would arrive. Sufism Reoriented chartered a plane to fly our group to Bombay where busses were arranged to drive us to Poona, about ninety miles away over the Western Ghats to the Deccan Plateau of Maharashtra State.

Everyone started scrambling to find jobs to get money for the ticket and other expenses for the visit. I got a job at the Education Testing Service (ETS), counting test pamphlets that were returned after completion of the test.

Then the world shook. On January 31st, 1969, I received a phone call to inform me that Meher Baba had "left his body." Meher Baba died on January 31st, 1969.

I don't remember how it was decided that I should break the news to the community at the Student Union meeting place on campus, but there I was standing in front of hundreds of people who were waiting to hear what would be revealed.

I was standing on a small podium about a foot off the floor. The room was packed with people oozing out the door and streaming down the hallway; both eager lovers longing for someone to tell them that what they had heard was not true and curiosity seekers trying to get a glimpse of just how it would be revealed that the man who claimed to be the Avatar of the Age had died the day before.

Although I had spent the past day and a half in tears, I mustered the fortitude to be strong and factual: "Avatar Meher Baba has dropped his physical body." For a minute, there was a hush in the room that seemed to go on forever. Then a general buzz hovered over the atmosphere like a swarm of bees as some talked animatedly in astonishment while others mumbled into their shirts in a stupor of disbelief.

I waited for a few minutes to let the clamor die, then read the official announcement composed by Meher Baba's Mandali and signed by his mandali/secretary Adi K. Irani

AVATAR MEHER BABA DROPPED HIS PHYSICAL BODY

TODAY FRIDAY 31ST JANUARY AT NOON AT MEHERAZAD TO LIVE ETERNALLY IN THE HEARTS OF ALL HIS LOVERS EVERYWHERE STOP BELOVED BABAS BODY WILL BE INTERRED AT MEHERABAD ARANGAON ON 1ST FEBRUARY AT 10 O'CLOCK MORNING IN THE TOMB HE HAD ORDERED TO BE BUILT FOR IT LONG AGO - ADI K. IRANI

The unthinkable had happened. Not unthinkable in the sense that no one thought it was possible but, in the sense, that no one had even thought about the possibility.

Immediately, people started cancelling their reservations for the flight to India. We received a telegram from Adi K. Irani dated February 9, 1969:

DESPITE BABA'S PHYSICAL ABSENCE THOSE LOVERS WHO DESIRE TO VISIT GURUPRASAD POONA TO HONOR BABA'S INVITATION FOR DARSHAN UP TO TENTH JUNE CAN STILL COME ABIDING STRICTLY TO THE SCHEDULED DATES AND CONDITIONS AS PER FAMLY LETTER DATED FIRST NOVERMBER. JOURNEY WILL NOW INCLUDE HALF DAY VISIT TO MEHERABAD TO PAY HOMEAGE AT BABA'S TOMB.

AFTER TENTH JUNE ANYONE CAN MAKE PILGRIMAGE TO POONA AND BABA'S TOMB INDIVIDUALLY OR COLLECTIVELY UNDERSTANDING THAT ALL ARRANGEMENTS MUST BE MADE ON ONES OWN. All CONCERNED YOUR AREA. JAI BABA ADI K. IRANI.

At least half the people canceled. It was no-brainer for us. We had waited years for Baba to call us back to India and there was not even a faint thought of canceling. Most of our close friends felt the same way. By the time we left for India, we were a group of about fifty.

After a brief stop-over for refueling in Anchorage where I anguished in the airport gift shop whether to buy a fossilized walrus dick or not (I did not), we flew to Tokyo for a sleepover and then on the Bombay. When the plane landed in Bombay, we boarded the busses directly on the tarmac for the trip to Poona. Before we left, however, an Indian official came on the bus and paged me, telling me that there was some bum asking to see me. I got off the bus to see who it was, and it was an old friend from Frankfurt, Karl-Heinz Kraemer, who had somehow figured out when we were arriving and hitchhiked to India to meet us.

Suddenly India started flooding my senses. You can only understand this if you have ever landed at an airport in India. The smells, the sounds and the sights are overpowering: people jostling impatiently for position to get through customs and immigration, men with scarves wrapped around their heads trying to guide you to taxis or hotels so they can get commissions, the scent of burning fires of wood and dung hanging in the air, a cacophony of noises from voices shouting, loudspeakers blaring and horns honking.

The drive to Poona over the Western Ghats was uneventful and beautiful. No one else on the bus had ever been to India and since Uschi and I were the only ones who had, and had also met Baba, we were the target for information. Some were clinging to us.

We had been assigned hotels and the bus drove from hotel to hotel dropping each group off accordingly. The problem for us was that they were the most expensive hotels in town. We were not used to these prices in India and had not planned for it, so we did not check in and went to a cheap hotel near the train station, the Green Hotel. When word got back to the mandali, they sent someone to fetch us and said that they did not want us to stay in such a seedy place. We told them we could not afford to stay at the hotel they selected for us. They said it would be no problem. We could stay at a room they had at the Poona Club.

The first day we all arrived at Guru Prasad, Uschi and I were met by Baba's mandali. The first was Eruch, who threw his arms around me and said, "Welcome home, Brother." I had corresponded with Eruch and he was the man who interpreted Baba's gestures and spoke them out in English to us when we were in Baba's presence, but I had never laid eyes on him or spoken to him before. The same was true with the rest of the mandali, men and women alike. Because we had met Baba, we were family.

Those days at Guruprasad were heady and filled with the undeniable presence of Meher Baba. Everyone felt it, to a person. He may have not been there physically but there was not a shadow of a doubt in anyone's mind that his presence was there. It was palpable. Tears flowed and hearts melted. Nothing existed outside that place. The rest of the world disappeared in the beauty and glory of his being. Each person who was there had a story to tell, each more incredible and moving than the last.

Arriving back in Berkeley, my life changed in a pretty shocking way. One fine day Uschi told me out of the blue that she was in love with a friend of ours and wanted a divorce. Also, she said, she did not think I would ever be able to offer her the stability in life that she wanted.

I was shaken to the core. I had never felt so betrayed or hurt in my entire life. It was the most painful thing I had ever experienced. I told her that I did not approve of a divorce but would not stand in her way; she would have to do everything without my participation. The reason for this attitude was that Baba had given us certain orders that I thought should have been accomplished by us together. I have never spoken to anyone about these orders because they are extremely personal and because they are the opposite of what he has written for the general public. Uschi did not interpret this order the same way I did.

I moved out of our studio and rented a one-bedroom apartment that was zoned commercial and opened Berkeley Massage Studio. It was the first massage studio in Berkeley and still exists today, having gone through owner after owner. I started making good money.

I met another massage therapist by accident on campus, a stunningly beautiful blonde who was also a concert harpist. She took one look at me and took me home. We became passionate lovers for a few months. I cannot remember how it ended but it was amicable and after a half dozen one-night stands, I met another girl, a Baba Lover from New York and we were together for several months until I left Berkeley.

While working as a massage therapist, I studied with the world-famous astrologer/healer Francis Sequoian. We focused on magnetic healing, directing healing energy through the hands to the ill. I got to the point where I could feel and see the energy.

After some time, I began to feel numbness in both hands and could not feel the energy any longer. Coincidentally, a client told me that she had a chiropractor in Walnut Creek that she attended and had told him about me. She said that he wanted to meet me so that we could refer patients back and forth. I went to visit him, and he asked me if I had ever had an adjustment. I said I had no idea what an adjustment was. He took some X-rays of my spine, drew some lines on the X-rays, made some measurements and put his hands on my neck and adjusted my spine for the first time. Within five seconds, I felt the life force rush down my arms to my hands. I was completely normal. I asked him what had happened and he explained that because of the spine's relationship to the nervous system, if there is a misalignment of the bones, called a subluxation, it can interfere with the transmission of nerve impulses to parts of the body. The symptoms depend on the type of nerves involved. He said, "I just turned the power back on." This was the master Gonstead practitioner Frank Young.

I was in a state of shock. Here I was lending out my energy to a few people a day trying to help them, and he was seeing a hundred people a day and turning on the power from within.

Three weeks later I was enrolled at Palmer College of

Chiropractic, Davenport, Iowa. I sold my truck, and Melanie, the blonde masseuse, bought my business. I bought a cherry 1956 Buick Roadmaster with just a couple thousand miles on it for $250, loaded all my possessions in it and headed for Davenport, Iowa.

A friend in Berkeley told me about a friend of his who was attending Palmer and arranged for me to stay with him when I arrived there in the fall of 1969.

I applied for the G.I. bill and got enough money to pay my tuition and rent for the whole period of my attendance at Palmer. I rented a three-bedroom duplex for a hundred dollars per month and moved there.

On January 15th, 1970 I was visiting this same friend and his wife's sister asked me if I could give her a ride to her classmate's apartment so that they could study together, both being enrolled in the Chiropractic Assistant's Program at Palmer College of Chiropractic. It was a cold and snowy night. I gave her a ride but when we arrived, I had to walk her to the second-floor door of her friend because she was blind and could not make it on her own. We knocked on the door and I stood to her left. When her friend opened the door there were two girls standing there, her friend and her friend's sister, standing to her right. My eyes locked on her friend's sister's eyes and for about three seconds we were both stunned. I saw her lean to her left and whisper into her sister's ear. (I later that night learned that she whispered, "Invite him in.") At the same time, I leaned to my right and whispered, "I'm coming in." That is how I met Mary Callahan.

A few months later we were married and one year later our first son was born. I finished the four-year chiropractic curriculum in three years, and we moved back to Berkeley where, while waiting to take the state examinations for my license to practice, our second son was born. In 1975 I opened my practice and was immediately flooded with patients needing care. Within a couple of years, I was a millionaire, owned properties, had fine cars, designer clothes, enjoyed the best things in life and was able to send my sons to the best schools.

Even though I had everything, I was not attached to my possessions. Money was never the focus of my career. Nor was it humanitarian. The humanitarian serves the many in the one; the mystic serves the One in the many. Meher Baba told me that what I was looking for I would find in society, among people, by trying to be of service to them. Humanity is suffering; physically, mentally and spiritually. I am not spiritually advanced so I cannot help them spiritually. Maybe some have been helped "through me" as many have told me they were, but I had nothing to do with it. I also cannot help them mentally because it is not in my training, but many have been helped mentally (at least they have said they were) but that also was not conscious on my part. But I can help their physical suffering and chiropractic was the path given to me to fulfill that and simultaneously allow me to fulfill my secret goal of Mastery in Servitude. Chiropractic was not my goal in life. It was a tool that I used to fulfill my higher goal of service to humanity.

So many times, in my life I looked at myself and asked, "How did I get here?" We think we have free choice and the choices we made and decisions we made got us here, but many times I felt more like a rock that someone higher had picked up and flung me here. And so, here I landed. I harken back to that day in New York City when I got the phone call from Fred Winterfeld saying that Meher Baba had sent a telegram to Harry Kenmore (the blind chiropractor) that said that he, Harry, should met us while we were there. I remember thinking what an obnoxious man he was and wondered why the hell Baba would say he should meet us rather than we meet him. I now realize that this is where the seed of my future career was planted. Harry Kenmore was the agent of that. Kenmore had also said that Baba told him that chiropractic was the healing art of the New Humanity. It makes perfect sense. It takes nothing from the body and adds nothing to it and relies on the inherent recuperative powers from within to heal the body when it is sick and keep it healthy when it is not sick. The power that made the body heals the body.

The other events of my life have all dimmed in memory with time, regardless of how exalted or sorrowful they felt at the moment. No matter how honorable or debased the event was, its meaning lessens with the passing of time. Meeting Meher Baba is the one experience of my life that gains more meaning as time passes. In fact, my current feeling is that I don't think I have even begun to understand the significance of it.

I recently retired from 45 years of private practice. Both my sons are healthy, successful and have children. I am still married to the same woman that whispered, "Invite him in."

Danish Suzy and Dal
Globe Cafe Katmandu

Mik Kota Bharu 1965

Roger Yates, Englishman, Mik, Sikh Temple, Singapore

Armin 11.17.70

Mik on his first acid trip Singapore 1965

Queen Street Sikh Temple Singapore

Baba's Chevy

Chan the Trishaw Driver
Singapore 1965

Uschi with Roger and Boomer at the Chai Walla outside the Sikh Temple

Kirk

'69 Darshan, Guru Prasad, Poona, India. Mik Front Center

Meherazad Gates -Credit Naozer Dadachanji

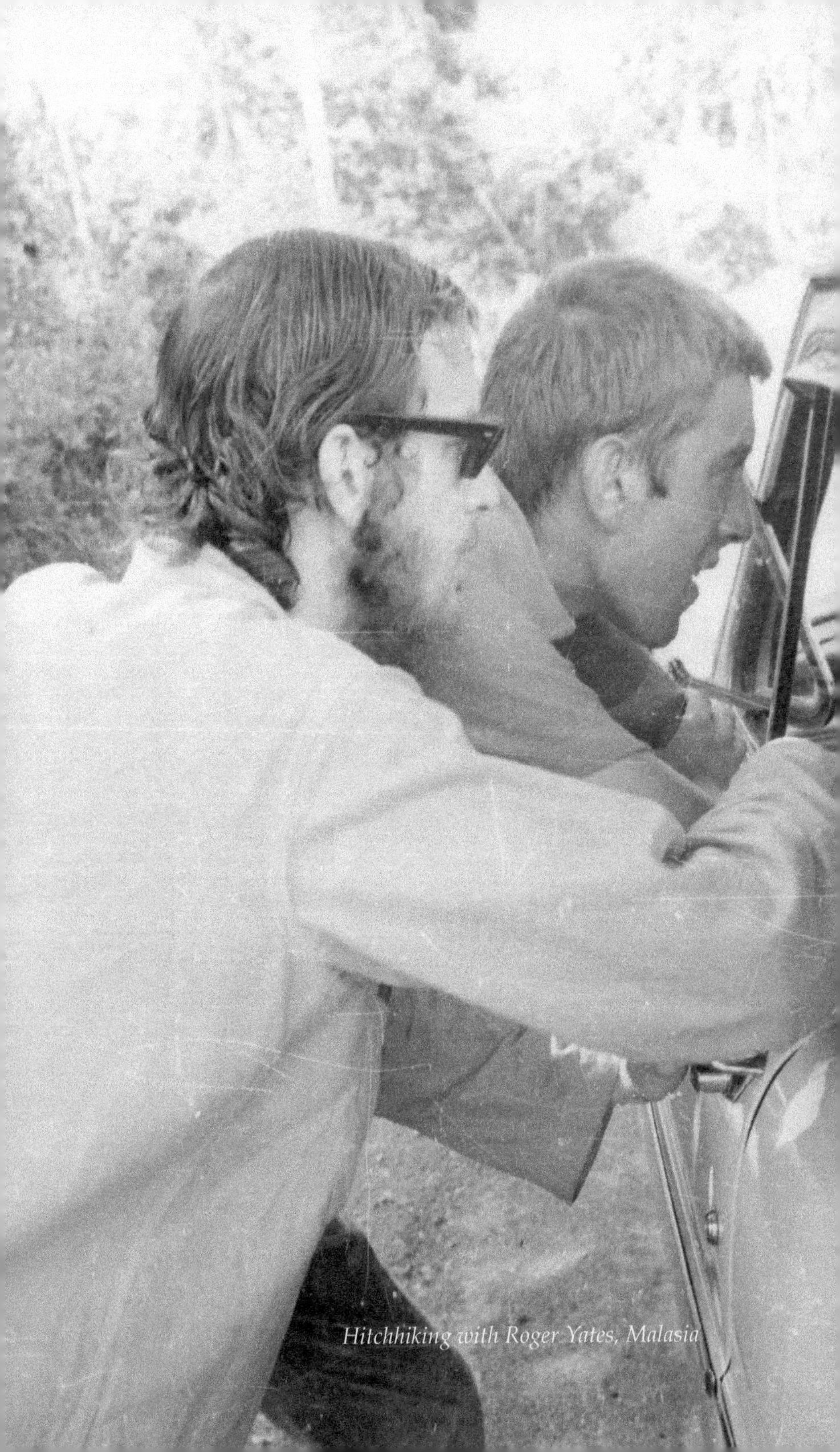

Hitchhiking with Roger Yates, Malasia

Katmandu 1965
Eight Finger Eddie, Danish Susie,
Dal, Uschi, Mik, Unknown American

Mik and Uschi with Schieke in Angkor Wat 1965

Mik Thailand with Buettner

Mixing a batch on the Gulf of Siam

Makin' a batch in the Park Singapore

Smoking a Chilum by the roadside

Mik 1965

Snake Charmer Singapore with Roger,
Englishman, and Uschi

Queen Street Sikh Temple Singapore

Saigon October 1965

Hindu Firewalk at Mariamman Temple, Singapore 1965

Chinese street festival, Singapore

Uschi at the American Embassy, Saigon, 1965

Singapore Trishaw driver napping in the mid-day sun

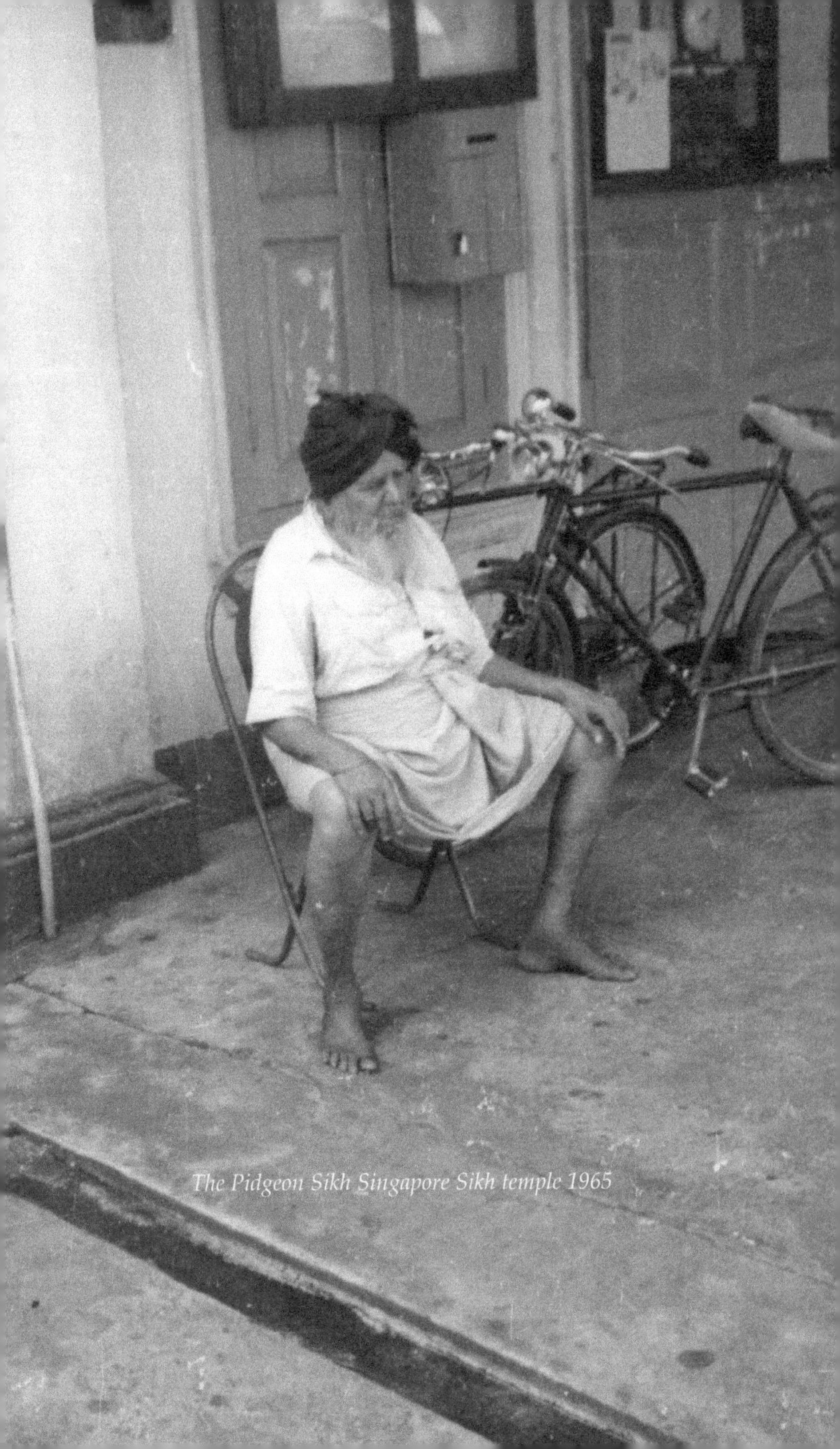

The Pidgeon Sikh Singapore Sikh temple 1965

Steve Simon
Colombo 1965

Uschi with Steve Simon Colombo Ceylon December 1965

Uschi with Boomer the gibbon aboard the S.S. Viet Nam

Uschi and Mik Berkeley 1968

Uschi with Englilsh Roger & Ray Ordas at Chai Walla in Singapore

ABOOKS

ALIVE Book Publishing and ALIVE Publishing Group
are imprints of Advanced Publishing LLC,
3200 A Danville Blvd., Suite 204, Alamo, California 94507

Telephone: 925.837.7303
alivebookpublishing.com

Milton Keynes UK
Ingram Content Group UK Ltd.
UKHW021633010524
442054UK00009BA/11